LA BOHÈME

LA BOHÈME

SCÉNES DE LA VIE DE BOHÈME

by

HENRI MURGER

Translated by

ELIZABETH WARD HUGUS

With the original introduction by

D . B . WYNDHAM LEWIS

And a new introduction by

HERBERT JOSEPHS

Illustrations selected by Henry Russell Hitchcock, Jr.,
for the 1930 edition

PEREGRINE SMITH BOOKS
Salt Lake City

Reprinted from *Latin Quarter: Scénes de la vie de Bohème* by Henri Murger,
published by Dodd, Mead & Company, New York, 1930.
Copyright © 1930 by Edwin Valentine Mitchell.

Cover design by Smith and Clarkson

Cover illustration from an original oil painting by Randall Lake entitled
Musetta Entering the Cafe Momus.

Printed in the United States of America

LIBRARY OF CONGRESS CATALOGING-IN-PUBLICATION DATA

Murger, Henri, 1822-1861.
  [Scénes de la vie de bohème. English]
  La bohème / Henri Murger ; translated by Elizabeth Ward Hugus ; with the original
introduction by D. B. Wyndham Lewis ; and a new introduction by Herbert Josephs.
      p.   cm.
  Translation of : Scénes de la vie de bohème.
  ISBN 0-87905-335-6 (pbk.)
  I. Lewis, D. B. Wyndham (Dominic Bevan Wyndham), 1894-1969.
II. Title.
PQ2367.M94S42 1988
843'.8 — dc19

CONTENTS

INTRODUCTION

MURGER'S PARISIAN SCENES
AND PUCCINI'S *LA BOHÈME*

Giacomo Puccini's *La Bohème* (1896) is perhaps the most universally beloved opera in the entire repertory of the lyric stage. It has been sung by the most celebrated operatic voices throughout the world and it continues, with each new staging, to create an aura of emotional magic that elicits in its devoted public a special warmth and affection. It is to a large degree from Puccini's musical portrait of the artist's life in the Latin Quarter of Paris in the 1840s that subsequent generations have derived their poetic image of the joys and sorrows, the carefree idealism and the harsh realities of the artist's existence. If Puccini's musical tale of the ephemeral loves of Mimi and Rodolfo, of a seamstress and a poet, has proved to be a drama of timeless appeal, it is because the Italian composer had succeeded in finding a voice for the simplest of human experiences, one that tells of youth and dreams, of the passing of youth and dreams, and of the heart-rending loss of love. And the literary inspiration for Puccini's poignant story of love and death was a French novel of the mid-nineteenth century, Henry Murger's *Scènes de la vie de Bohème* (1851).

Originally a series of prose sketches and anecdotes relating to Bohemian life that were written beginning in 1845 for a periodical called *Le Corsaire*, then collected in a book entitled *Scènes de la Bohème*, and later adapted for the stage in collaboration with Theodore Barrière (1849), Murger's book captures the charm of Bohemian life in the materially oriented society of Paris during the reign of Louis-Philippe. Less a novel than a collection of unrelated episodes, Murger's text owes its permanent place in literary history to the author's significant achievement of having fixed permanently in the spirit of its reader an image of the Bohemian life style.

Just one year after the world première of Puccini's *La Bohème* in Turin, another opera (*La Bohème*, 1897), also based on Murger's sketches, by Ruggiero Leoncavallo, composer of *I Pagliacci*, had its first performance in Venice. But it is Puccini's that has remained the treasured possession of the opera public for almost one hundred years. Luigi Illica and Guiseppe

Giacosa, the same librettists who were to provide the words for both *Tosca* (1900) and *Madama Butterfly* (1904), combined and reshaped the varied episodes and characters that fill the pages of Murger's book. With no special dramatic focus, the sketches merely juxtapose the cruel realities of a day-to-day existence structured only by unrelieved material need with fantasies of wealth, comfort and delightful suppers in the Latin Quarter. Many of the details that form the substance of the novel reappear in Puccini's opera, transformed and assimilated by the exigencies of theatrical and musical convention: Marcello's painting of the Red Sea crossing that hangs as a sign above the tavern in the third act; Rodolfo's (Rudolph in this translation) play, sacrificed to the fire act by act; Colline's overcoat, its pockets stuffed with thirty books and continually borrowed by his fellow Bohemians, which becomes in the opera the inspiration for the philosopher's moving death-scene aria; the episode of the extinguished candle, and the lost key, incorporated with slight alteration into the first-act meeting of Rodolfo and Mimi; Schaunard's account of his poisoning of a parrot by playing the violin, the details of which are obscured in their lyric form for even the most attentive adepts of the opera.

Yet, it was really the spirit and not the letter of Murger's stories which ultimately shaped the glamorous image of the artist's life that Puccini's opera has preserved for subsequent generations. Murger's impressions were read as a celebration of the artistic temperament that spawns images of poetry and love. As the details and specific circumstances of the literary text are dissolved by the activity of memory and the imagination, what remains is a sense of the hardships and pleasures, of the illusions and the stark awakenings that made up the way of life in the Latin Quarter, once capital of the artistic Bohemia. "Charming yet terrible lives, which have their conquerors and their martyrs," was Murger's summary characterization of the Bohemian milieu in his preface, a phrase that Puccini selected as an epigraph which he affixed to his score to introduce the entire opera. First there was the city of Paris itself, emblematic for so many of love, of beauty, of a *joie de vivre* offered by no other city. The images of Paris, its cafés, a snowy winter night at the city's gates, merging with the world of fantasy inhabited by the indigent artists, the gaiety, the melancholy, the passionate existence of the Bohemian group — all these evocations of a student life that he himself had known in Milan possessed a dramatic potential that fired the creative imagination of the Italian composer. Murger's text provided Puccini with the substance for his most enduring expression of a dream of love that haunted him until his death and that occupies the center of most of his other great operatic creations: *Manon Lescaut, Tosca, Madama Butterfly, La Rondine,* and finally, *Turandot.*

It is of the nature of the operatic medium, where a musical phrase replaces long prose passages, that it must sacrifice the subtleties of psychological realism and the nuances of moral conflict which constitute the richness of the novel. In contrast, the lyric drama is able to endow with a force of expansion and profundity the life of the emotions, of the imagination, and the unconscious. Despite the absence of a dramatic center to bind the various adventures of the Bohemian clan, Murger's work offered to Puccini a canvas on which he could chart with his characteristic lyrical brilliance his personal vision of the ephemeral beauty of a pure and absolute love. From Murger's group of Bohemians, Rodolfo and Mimi emerged to occupy the limelight of Puccini's stage, the poet-dreamer and the frail, tubercular dreamer, whose tendencies to embellish and idealize reality made of them the proper vehicles for the portrayal of the quest for the beautiful and the infinite. Abetted by his astute librettists, Puccini concentrated a touching love story into a few scenes of indelible lyric beauty, selecting only the strong dramatic situations, the moments of emotional richness that beckon to the genius of opera. The text and the score of *La Bohème* succeed in endowing with poetic dimensions the banal stuff of daily existence and the perennial struggle to transform reality into something beautiful. Opera-goers live again and again the chance meeting of the seamstress and the writer, the instantaneous harmony of their simple dreams, the perfect merging of the poet with poetic inspiration, the evanescence of their innocent love, the hardships of cold, hunger and sickness, the painful separation feared and postponed, the consolation of an idyllic past recollected with tenderness and, finally, the peaceful death of the beloved Mimi.

The decor that provides the backdrop for Puccini's sentimental drama was created from reminiscences, some joyous, some melancholy, of Murger's diversified portrait of the Parisian milieu. The spirited conversations at the Café Momus captured by the French writer were translated by Puccini into opera's conventions to achieve the remarkable second act that takes place outside the café on Christmas eve. The Momus scene provides nineteen minutes of festive atmosphere and of an infectious joy complete with marching band, vendors, and cries of children, the pranks and the celebrated waltz of the extravagant, outrageous Musetta, as well as the first delights of innocent love. The opera weaves into a single, complex tableau the alternating strands of reality and idealism, the difficulties of paying rent and the artists' pursuit of a life lived as poetry. (Both the libretto and the score are resonant with poetic and musical figures that are carefully balanced and blended into a rigorously coherent operatic structure. The opera's affective force is transmitted through images of flowers and spring, hope and dreams, snow and winter, solitude and death. Mimi's cold hands become the simple poetic detail that provides the dramatic focus for the encounter of the lovers and again for the powerful emotional climax in Mimi's death-bed scene.)

It is impossible to locate the original model for the memorable image of fragility and tenderness identified with the opera's Mimi in the character of Murger's book who bears her name. The Parisian world evoked in the novel provided Puccini and his librettists with a series of forms for a certain "type" known as the *grisette*, a young woman of the lower classes who, shaped by economic motives, was usually known to be coquettish and seductive. These women share, in Murger's work, a happy if impoverished existence with students and artists in garret apartments, spending a night or two struggling against cold, hunger and frequently against death. Murger's figure of Mimi is represented as possessing a disagreeable temperament, as faithless, insensitive, even shrewish and cruel, given to dreams of elegance and fortune. Puccini's Mimi, on the other hand, is really a poetic fusion of several of the women who appear intermittently in Murger's book; more loyal, more tender, she becomes the first of the delicate, suffering heroines that the composer so adored.

The precise source for the operatic loves of Rodolfo and Mimi is provided by an isolated episode near the end of the novel which introduces Jacques, a sculptor and friend of the narrator, and Francine, his working-class lover of but a single season. The much discussed details of the lost key and the groping in the dark of the lovers' first meeting are contained in these pages. It is Murger's Francine who possesses the qualities of fragility, tenderness and simplicity for which the operatic Mimi has become emblematic. The scene of Mimi's death, however, with the overflowing of generous sentiment and nostalgic emotion—profoundly moving no matter how often one relives it imaginatively—is entirely an invention of the operatic spirit. The characters of Marcel and Musette, on the other hand, recede in dramatic importance when they are repositioned in

Puccini's tightly composed musical argument to provide, especially in the memorable quartet that concludes the third act, a stormy and virulent counterpoint to the romantic pathos of Mimi and Rodolfo's pure but transient love.

At the conclusion of the novel, the youthful fervor of the Bohemians has waned and their dedication to ideals of beauty has yielded to a sense of practical realities. For the twenty-five-year-old Rodolfo and Marcel, for Schaunard the musician and Colline the philosopher, success and ambition dispel dream, stability chases adventure, and the passionate intensity of their more youthful days takes on the aura of yesterday's illusions. Even in the opera's heart-warming second act, in a voice already filled with regret, Marcello sings Murger's more lucid, unspirited vision:

> O bella età d'inganni e d'utopie! (O beautiful age of deceits and utopias,)
> Si crede, spera, e tutto bello appare! (One believes, hopes and all
> seems beautiful.)

There is a season for each stage of life, the now "mature" bourgeois author of the *Scènes* reminds us; the heart's most cherished dream gives way in Murger's final chapter to the compromises that guarantee respectability. But Puccini's lyrical translation of Murger's novel preserves the joys of falling in love while it sings of the heart-rending loss of hope and dreams. Murger's series of impressions had provided Puccini with the impulse to celebrate in his most inspired melodic voice the delicate beauty of simple love, and, above all, our nostalgia for poetic emotion.

Herbert Josephs
Professor, Department of Romance and Classical Languages
Michigan State University

INTRODUCTION

"C'est ma Jeunesse qui s'en va;
Adieu! la très gente compagne . . ."
—Hilaire Belloc: MSS. *in the Library of the
Abbey of Theleme.*

On a wet April night in Paris years and years ago, with the
scent of the dripping chestnut-trees in the air, mixed with flying
aromatic whiffs from the roast-chestnut stall round the corner;
amid the noise of traffic, with the clustered lamps beginning
to twinkle in the violet dusk of the Boulevard, and over all the
exquisite, indefinable, heart-stirring rustle of a Parisian springtime, I first read this little classic, at a café table opposite the
church of St. Germain-des-Prés. For every book worth reading
there is the one perfect time and place. Where would you ex-
tract the fullest flavour of *A Christmas Carol* but by a London
fireside in a brown December fog? Or the final essence of
Rabelais, save in his own Touraine in vintage-time? I thought
then, I still think, that I was fortunate in my introduction to
Murger.

This book is a classic. There is an obvious reason for its per-
petual freshness and that vitality which, in Dr. Johnson's phrase,
preserves it from putrefaction. It is woven out of the gossamer
stuff of Youth, careless, happy, defiant Youth, so precious and
so fleeting. There are pedants who say that Murger drew a
Bohemia which never was on land or sea. They lie in their
dusty throats. Rodolphe and Marcel, Colline and Schaunard
stretch out their hands back to the Middle Ages and clasp the
hands of Villon and his troop of *escholiers*, as laughing, as des-
perate, as hungry, as in love with love and life as they; and
then reach forward to our own time, linking with that Bohemian
company of whom M. Francis Carco has recently written a
memoir—Utrillo, in the van of modern painters, and Guillaume
Apollinaire, the poet of *Alcools*, Picasso, Max Jacob, Dorgelès,

Marie Laurencin, all the joyous band of the tavern of the once
glorious Agile Rabbit in Montmartre. These too have starved, and
slept under the stars, and rioted, and laughed, and loved, and suffered. It is the mode today among certain Parisian men of letters
to be half-seriously and slightly snobbishly morbid over the death
of such academies of gaiety and intelligence as the Lapin Agile
(more properly the *Lapin à Gill*), the Chat Noir of the nineties,
and the Closerie des Lilas in Montparnasse, where up to the eve of
the late European war Paul Fort held his nightly court of roaring
poets, where also a student with sallow Kalmuck features named
Lenin could be seen, with associates of his type, discussing that
movement which ultimately landed him on the throne of the
Tsars. In such moods of gently maudlin retrospect the mourner
is apt—forgetting that Bohemia is a state of the mind rather than
an area situate between the Fifth and Sixth Arrondissements—
to imagine the pale ghosts of Murger's characters hovering disconsolate and aghast over Montparnasse, their dear ancient terri-
tory, the present stronghold of the British and American middle-
classes, over its huge gaudy cafés, in which the jazz-band and the
Arts Décoratifs together wage war on ear and eye, and over the
cynical commerce of Montmartre, paradise of the *métèque* and
the holidaying Puritan. Actually, I think, the Rodolphes and
Mimis of 1840 would after a shrug or two shake down comfortably enough into a louder, swifter, costlier, more blatant
and cosmopolitan Paris. Their successors of 1930 seem to carry
on without too much difficulty. The mediævals and the moderns
alike are blood-brothers to Murger's Bohemians, and it is with
something more than the French instinct for a graceful gesture
that Murger's bust in the Luxembourg Gardens is covered with
roses once every year by the youth of the Quarter. This whole
book is vibrating with youth. Not even the pink sugar of Puccini's music has been able to candy the essential lustiness of it.
In only one modern book—and how different!—that I know of
is there to be found this same authentic note; and that is Max
Beerbohm's *Zuleika Dobson*. Compare the verve of *Vie de
Bohême* with Alfred de Musset's variations on a similar theme in
Mimi Pinson, and observe the difference between the chocolate-
box prettiness of

"Mimi Pinson est une blonde,
Une blonde que l'on connait;
Elle n'a qu'une robe au monde,
Landerirette!"

and Murger's etching. I think I am correct in saying that de Musset was never hungry in his life.

It was a pleasant, intimate Paris to be young and poor in, the Paris of Louis-Philippe, the Paris of the 1840's, when Henry Murger the tailor's son was living in his garret in the Quarter. The ruthless Haussmann had not yet appeared to drive his wide, straight avenues, fields of direct fire, through the old Paris of the barricades. A tangle of antique dark streets, as grimy and delightful as Wych Street and Holywell Street off the Strand before Progress got them, preserved to the Latin Quarter a great deal of its mediæval aspect. Montmartre was still a village, with windmills turning and gardens blooming. The rhythm of the town was leisurely; one could lounge on the boulevards, one could linger to watch the marionettes and the strolling musicians under the trees. On the Boulevard du Temple there were acrobats, dancers, and the Funambules. Beyond the Boulevard Montmartre, where the pomaded, tight-waisted dandies ended their promenade, stretched the Boulevard du Crime, with its popular theatres, the Porte St. Martin and the Ambigu. There was dancing for light hearts and slim purses at the Bal Mabille and the Chaumière. And everywhere in odd nooks and corners of the town one came on old quiet gardens full of lilac and birds, the last remains of vanished convents and town-houses. Omnibuses ran to Chantilly, and for a franc one could take the railway train to the forest of St. Germain, a journey lasting, as it did till lately, a little over half an hour. What is the present value of the 1840 franc? For forty sous Rodolphe and Marcel make their Christmas Eve supper of bread, pork, and wine, with tobacco, candle and firewood included. Supper for four, festal, with wine, costs 25 fr. 75. Schaunard does not quail at the prospect of squandering eighteen francs to dress his Phémie. What do these figures represent now? One has rarely got it, whatever it is; but what does it matter when one is young? Kisses and laughter are cheap enough.

I would once more observe, to the confusion of those arid imbeciles who pretend Murger's atmosphere is false, that this authentic note of defiant gaiety pervades M. Léon Daudet's recent recollections of his student days and M. Carco's memoirs of the Bohemia of just before the world-war. Stomachs are empty, and the wind blows icy cold, and the odour of roast chestnuts is a torment, and shivering Genius tramps the town all night and, if lucky, is able to make off with a milk-bottle at dawn from an unguarded staircase; but there is always plenty of verse to recite to hearten one, and this night, or the next, there will be a tribal gathering at the café of the moment, and there will be songs, and criticism, and shouting, and the girls, and argument, and a bottle, and a scrap of something to eat. And here one may be permitted to underline the essential difference between the Bohemia of the Gauls and that of some Anglo-Saxons. The Bohemians of Murger think of the Bohemian life as something transient, something which accompanies youth and must pass inevitably; riot and folly and living from hand to mouth are very well when one is in the twenties, but it is necessary *se ranger;* one has one's future to think about; the native, sound, square, practical common-sense of the French begins to stir. "We've had our youth," says Marcel to Rodolphe on that melancholy Christmas Eve spent with the ghosts of the past. "We've had our fun and our paradoxes. It's all very pretty, and would make a good romance; but this comedy of wild loves, this wasting of our days with as much prodigality as if we had Eternity at our disposal—all this must have an ending." And the comedy ends, a little too rosily in Murger's last chapter, with artistic success and fortune for all four Bohemians. A likelier dénouement is suggested by MM. Robert de Flers and Francis de Croisset in a recent charming operatta in which Murger's Rodolphe himself appears, middle-aged, a little melancholy, occupying an assured position as a minor official at the Central Markets of Paris. "And where are your comrades?" asks a breathless girl of him. "My child," says Rodolphe sadly, "in France there are only two careers possible: one is either a lover or a functionary. That's where we are now—Schaunard, Marcel, Colline, Rodolphe, all four. We're all *dans l'administra-*

tion." And without doubt many a prodigal son of the Muses, slippers on feet and pipe in mouth by his own fireside, or soberly clicking the nightly dominoes at the corner café with the notary, may glance at his paunch and heave a light sigh for the days when meals and money did not come round so regularly. It is melancholy thus to remember one's youth; but what is one to say of the conscientious Nordic, not an uncommon type in London, who continues stubbornly to eat out of sardine-tins off the floor until well into middle age?

Murger's book, then, for all its light-heartedness, is ruggedly sound *au fond*. His Bohemians do not pose, beyond the natural posings of youth. Their friendships are stout and enduring, and their loves, if fleeting, are intense enough to hurt. Neither are they idle: recollect what work Marcel, grinding his teeth, puts into his *Passage of the Red Sea* before the Jew Medicis buys it for a shop-sign. Their separate personalities are vivid and distinct, and I confess they throw their lady friends well into the shadow. (Mimi and Musette—their originals existed, like those of the male characters, and Murger drew on them fairly steadfastly. Mimi was Lucile Louvet, a florist and his own mistress. Musette was an artist's model named Mariette—are the stock *grisettes* of the period, dainty, capricious, industrious, frugal, generous, eupeptic yet fastidious in love, disdaining to sell their favours unless driven to it by want. Mimi in addition is the stock consumptive of the period, the diaphanous young *poitrinaire*, dying to slow music which even in the 40's must have resembled Puccini's. But she is authentic. Lucile's end was Mimi's, even to the macabre error at the hospital; all that Murger has added is her lover's cry at the graveside: *"O ma jeunesse, c'est vous qu'on enterre!"*) The men are not guttersnipes but men of education, ex-students, like Villon, of the University of Paris, and in Marcel's case the Beaux-Arts. Their ironic gaiety in difficulties is true to type. Murger knew what he was writing about. The evenings at the Café Momus in the Rue des Prêtres-St.-Germain-l'Auxerrois (Momus is long vanished; on its site stand the offices of the *Journal des Débats*) were something else beyond mere noise and babble; and when wine was added to reckless high spirits the resultant effervescence could take the form of that fantastic imbecility which is the relaxation of the intelligent. When M. Blancheron, the rich client, recites to Schaunard the composer, after an excellent dinner, his pamphlet on the Sugar Industry, Schaunard accompanies him on the pianoforte. This is at 8 p. m. At 10 p. m. the two are dancing. At eleven—without doubt at Schaunard's suggestion—they are drawing up their wills and bequeathing each other reciprocally their entire fortunes; and at midnight they are crying on each other's shoulder. Of all the four Bohemians, Schaunard the musician is to me personally the most sympathetic figure. He hovers about the stage like Harlequin, he has no serious love-troubles like Rodolphe and Marcel, he has little or no conscience in the matter of food and wine, and he has a genuinely kind heart. He is, moreover, the most imaginative, artistically speaking, of the band, and a direct forerunner, with his *Symphony On the Influence of Blue On the Arts*, of Mr. George Gershwin. On the very real art of this apparently useless, effortless book one need hardly insist. There are a hundred instances scattered through its pages of keen and delicate fancy. For example:

Some time afterwards—it was during the fine season—Rodolphe lodged in the Avenue de Saint-Cloud, the third tree on the left as you leave the Bois de Boulogne, and the fifth branch.

M. Benoît (the landlord) exhaled a pestilent odour of bad brandy and unpaid rent.

He was the Asmodeus of the arts. He would sell you cigars for the scenario of a short story, slippers for a sonnet, fresh fish for paradoxes.

"I am certain" (said Mimi) "my poet's heart is broken." "Possibly," said Marcel, going away; "nevertheless, if I am not mistaken, the fragments are still serviceable."

Try as he would Rodolphe, after four days of separation, was utterly unable to recall the features of the mistress who had very nearly shattered his existence between her delicate hands.

It is not sufficient to wear a summer overcoat in December to prove talent; one can be a real poet or artist with warm feet and three meals a day.

But over and above the charm of style, the comic ingenuity of incident and the patent authenticity underlying it, the tender melancholy, and the whole decorative atmosphere of the 40's, it is, as I have said, the spirit of youth in this book, filling its pages like the wind in the trees, which secures its place in one's affection. For the years fly on and youth, alas! slips away; as it is sung in Mr. Belloc's sad little chaunt:

". . . Oncques ne suis moins gai pour ça,
(C'est ma Jeunesse qui s'en va)
Et lon-lon-laire, et lon-lon-là————
Peut-être perds; peut-être gagne;
C'est ma Jeunesse qui s'en va."

To catch at the skirts of the iridescent, heartless, airy creature as he flies, to retain enough of his shimmering vesture for the contemplation to give a man a stab at the heart and the half-forgotten taste of his own departed youth—this is surely within the power only of an artist above the common. Henry Murger was such an artist.

D. B. WYNDHAM LEWIS

Paris, 1930

NOTE
ON THE ILLUSTRATIONS

NOTE ON THE ILLUSTRATIONS

The nineteenth century was one of the great ages of book illustration. The woodcut vignette, which could be set up with the type, provided a medium peculiarly suited to illustration since it permitted a more or less continuous graphic commentary on the text. It was, moreover, inexpensive and could be used generally in regular editions whereas engraving in the previous century, like the more sumptuous processes of our own day, was of economic necessity restricted to small and special editions.

The present volume is illustrated in the fashion of a century ago with woodcuts taken chiefly from *Le Diable à Paris* which is exactly contemporaneous with the *Scénes de la Vie de Bohême*. They do not, of course, directly illustrate the events of Murger's story, but they provide a continuous visual background to the text with scenes of the Paris of the Romantics, human types such as appear in the story and anecdotal episodes paralleling those which Murger develops at greater length.

Gavarni, to whom these woodcuts are due, stands in the history of Romantic art in a position more or less equivalent to that of Murger in Romantic literature. Both represent the transition from High Romanticism—such as that of Victor Hugo or Delacroix—to Realism which came with Flaubert and Courbet. Both draw their subject matter from the Paris of Louis Philippe in which they satirize gently the dominant bourgeois world and contrast it unfavourably to the freer artistic air in which they themselves live. Neither of them is bitter, although both may on occasion be sharp, and their interest lies primarily in the picturesque rather than the political aspect of social contacts and conflicts.

Illustration is anything but a pure art in the sense of the criticism of the last two decades. It is literary or it is nothing. For that reason there is little advantage in attempting a serious visual compositional relation between text and picture. The pictures are from a visual point of view definitely extraneous decoration, exactly in the same fashion as the Black Letter casually introduced in standard thin serif Romantic typography. Romantic book making is not to be judged by severe Classical standards. But in presenting an archaistic imitation of it, it should be pointed out that it is psychologically functional—different sorts of type permit great freedom, particularly on title pages, of providing different sorts of emphasis, and casual asymmetrical placing of vignettes offers opportunity for relating naturally and with the least friction parallel ideas in literary and graphic form. Thus for all its archaism, Neo-Romantic book design comes closer to the book design of clear and functional character the most advanced modern typographers are seeking to evolve than does the formal and generally Neo-Classic book design which is almost universal today.

In addition to the Gavarni woodcuts from *Le Diable à Paris*, a very few by other Romantic designers taken from Nodier and Lurine's *Les Environs de Paris* have been used.

HENRY RUSSELL HITCHCOCK, JR.

THE ORIGIN OF THE BOHEMIAN CLUB

THIS is the way chance, which sceptics call God's Manager, one day brought together the persons whose brotherly association was later to be the basis of the Club established from that portion of Bohemia which the author of this book has attempted to introduce to the public.

One morning, it was April 8th, Alexander Schaunard, who pursued the two liberal arts of painting and music, was abruptly awakened by the chimes which a neighbouring cock rang for him, thereby serving as his alarm clock.

"Oh, bother," groaned Schaunard, "my feather clock is fast. Today can't have come so soon."

So saying, he jumped quickly from a piece of furniture of his own ingenious contrivance which, playing the role of bed by night—I oughtn't to say so, but it played it badly—assumed during the day the role of all the other pieces of furniture which had been sacrificed to the severe cold which had marked the preceding winter—a Jack of all trades in furniture as one can see.

To protect himself from the blasts of a morning wind, Schaunard hastily put on a petticoat of rose satin embroidered with spangled stars, which he used as a dressing gown. One night of a masquerade, this faded finery had been forgotten at the artist's studio by a follies girl who had been foolish enough to be taken in by Schaunard's promises—who, disguised as the Marquis of Mondor, rattled enticingly in his pockets a dozen crowns— money of the imagination, to be sure, cut by a machine plate, and borrowed from the theatre property box.

When he had made his toilet for indoors, the artist opened his window and shutter. A ray of sun, sharp as a flash of lightning, shot suddenly into the room and forced him to shield his eyes, still veiled by the mist of sleep; just then a clock in the neighbourhood struck five.

"It is Daybreak herself," mumbled Schaunard, "how amazing! But," he added, having consulted a calendar hanging on the wall, "there is not the slightest error. The declarations of science affirm that at this time of the year the sun must only rise at five-thirty; it is just five o'clock and there it is risen already. Over-anxious enthusiasm—this planet is in the wrong. I will complain to the bureau of longitudes. Meanwhile," he added, "I must busy myself a bit; today is certainly next day to yesterday and yesterday was the seventh; unless Saturn moves the wrong way, today must be the eighth of April; and if I understand the purport of this document," said Schaunard re-reading an order to leave from the sheriff, fixed to the wall, "today at noon exact I must have emptied these rooms and have put into the hands of Monsieur Bernard, my proprietor, a sum of seventy-five francs for three quarters rent, which he demands from me in very bad handwriting. I had, as ever, hoped that chance would take it upon herself to settle this business—but it would seem that she has not had enough time. Oh well—I have yet six hours before me; if I use them well, perhaps something—come, come, to work," added Schaunard.

He was about to put on an overcoat, the material of which, originally of long fur, had become extremely bald, when suddenly—as if he had been bitten by a tarantula—he commenced right there in his bedroom to execute a dance of his own origination, which in public dance halls had often won for him the attentions of the police.

"Wait a minute—wait," he said to himself, "it is amazing how the morning air gives ideas, it seems to me that I am close on the trail of my melody. Let me see."

And Schaunard, half naked, sat down at his piano. Having awakened the sleeping instrument by a tempestuous barrage of chords—he commenced, all the while carrying on a monologue, to pick out the melody which he had been searching for so long.

"*Do, sol, mi, do, la, si, do, ré,*—boom, boom. *Fa, ré, mi, ré.* Oh dear, oh dear. It is false as Judas, that ré," Schaunard complained while beating violently upon the note with the false tone. "Let me try the minor key—it must show plainly the irritation of a young lady who is pulling the petals of a white daisy and throwing them in a blue lake. Behold an idea which is not in its infancy.—Then, since it is the fashion, and an editor could not be found who would dare publish a romance which didn't have a blue lake, it is necessary to conform—*do, sol, mi, do, la, si, do, ré*—I am not unpleased with this, it gives the idea of an Easter daisy well enough, especially to all those who are long on botany. *La, si, do, ré*—Blackguard of a *ré*, leave! Now in order to understand properly the blue lake, there ought to be a certain amount of moisture, of blueness and of moonlight for the moon is there too—stop, but it will come—I must not forget the swan, *fa, mi, la, sol,*" continued Schaunard, making the crystal notes of the base octave resound. "Now all that remains is the adieu of the young girl who has decided to throw herself in the blue lake—to rejoin her lover buried under the snow; this climax is not clear," murmured Schaunard, "but it is interesting. I must have a little tenderness, some melancholy,—it's coming, it is indeed. Here are a dozen measures which weep like Magdalenes,—that break the heart!—Brr, Brr," Schaunard shivered in his skirt embroidered in stars, "if they could break wood: that rafter in my alcove bothers me terribly when people come for dinner; I could make a bit of fire with . . . *la, la . . . . . . ré, mi*—for I feel that inspiration is coming to me when I have a cold in the head. Ah, bah! so much the worse! Let us continue to drown my young girl."

And while his fingers tormented the throbbing piano, Schaunard, his eye sparkling, his ear extended, continued his melody which, like an elusive sylph, fluttered about in the midst of the heavy fog, which the vibrations of the piano seemed to send forth into the room.

"Let me see now," Schaunard resumed, "how my music blends with the words of my poet."—And he hummed in his unpleasant voice this fragment of poetry used especially for light operas and stories for reed pipes:

> Casting off her cloak
> The maiden young and fair
> Does starry skies invoke
> With glances soft and rare.
> And in the azure depths
> Of the lake with silver waves—

"What's this, what's this?" objected Schaunard, carried away by a righteous anger. "The azured depths of a lake of silver, I have never perceived that— It is too romantic at the end. The poet is an idiot. He has never seen silver or a lake— His ballad is stupid, moreover, the division of the verses cramps the style of my music;—in the future I will compose my own poems myself; and right now as I feel in the mood, I shall make some couplets as models for my melody."

And Schaunard, putting his head between his hands, assumed the serious pose of a mortal who would have intercourse with the gods. After some minutes of this holy union he had conceived one of those deformities which the makers of opera call, and rightly too, monsters, and which they can make up easily enough to serve as a rough draft as a guide for the composer.

Only Schaunard's monster had common sense and showed quite clearly the agitation aroused in his mind by the brutal arrival of this date—April 8. Here is the verse:

> Eight and eight, sixteen I add—
> Put down six and carry one
> I'd be feeling very glad
> If I could find someone,
> A poor and honest guy
> Who'd lend me right away
> Eight hundred francs to satisfy
> My debts on some far day.

And when was struck the final hour,
A quarter to twelve—I'd pay
My quarter's rent to M. Bernard,
An honest man that day.

"The devil," said Schaunard, re-reading his work, "hour and Bernard—that is not a million-dollar rhyme but I have not time to enrich that. Let me see how the notes mingle with the syllables."

And with that frightful nasal tone which was peculiar to him alone, he resumed the performance of his song. Completely satisfied with the result which he had just achieved, Schaunard congratulated himself by a joyful smirk which like a circumflex accent sat astride his nose each time that he was pleased with himself. But this proud pleasure did not last long.

Eleven o'clock was chimed from a neighboring belfry; each stroke entered into the room and was lost in jeering sounds, which seemed to say to the unhappy Schaunard: "Are you ready?"

The artist jumped from his chair. "Time runs like a deer," he said . . . "only three quarters of an hour remains to me to find seventy-five francs and my new lodging. I shall never succeed—if I did, it would savour of magic.—Let me see, I shall give myself five minutes to ponder," and burying his head between his two knees, he fell into deep meditation.

The five minutes passed and Schaunard raised his head without having found anything that resembled seventy-five francs.

"I have decided only the role I must play when I leave here, that is to leave very naturally; it is beautiful weather, perhaps my friend Lady Luck is taking a walk in the sunshine. She must befriend me until I find the opportunity to pay my debt to Monsieur Bernard."

Schaunard, having packed the pockets of his great coat with everything they could hold (they were deep as cellars), then folded in a silk handerchief some pieces of linen and left the room, not without touching words of adieu to his home.

As he crossed the court the janitor of the house, who evidently was lying in wait for him, stopped him suddenly.

"Say, Monsieur Schaunard," barring the advance of the artist, "can it be that it has occurred to you? Today is the eighth."

Eight and eight, sixteen I add—
Put down six and carry one

hummed Schaunard, "That's all I think about."

"You are a bit late in breaking up your housekeeping," said the janitor, "it is eleven-thirty and the new incumbent to whom your room has been rented may arrive any minute. You see that you must hurry."

"Then," responded Schaunard, "let me go, I am going to find a carriage to move my things."

"No doubt, but before moving out there is a slight formality to go through. I am ordered not to permit you to carry away one single hair until you pay the three terms rent due. No doubt you are ready to?"

"My God," said Schaunard, taking a step forward.

"Then if you will go into my room," the janitor resumed, "I will give you your permission to leave."

"I will take it when I return."

"But why not at once?" the janitor insisted.

"I am going to the money changer. I have no money."

"Uh, huh," the other one responded worried, "you are going to look for the money? Then to oblige you I will keep this little package you have under your arm, which might bother you."

"My dear janitor," Schanuard spoke with great dignity, "by any chance do you lack confidence in me? Do you think perhaps that I am bearing away my furniture in my handkerchief?"

"Pardon me, sir," replied the janitor in a slightly softer tone, "it is my order. Monsieur Bernard has particularly said to me not to permit you to remove a hair before you have paid."

"Now look," said Schaunard opening his package—"these are not hairs, they are shirts which I am taking to the laundress who lives next door to the money changer, just twenty steps from here."

"That is different," remarked the janitor after he had examined the contents of the package. "If it is not too bold, Monsieur Schaunard, may I ask your new address?"

"I live on the rue de Rivoli," the artist replied coldly as he put his foot on to the street and got away as quickly as possible.

"Rue de Rivoli," murmured the janitor rubbing his fingers meditatively over his nose—"it is indeed strange that someone has rented him a place on the Rue de Rivoli without even coming here for information or recommendations—it is very strange. At least he will never carry away his furniture without paying; provided the other tenant does not happen to move in at the same time Schaunard is moving out. That would cause a commotion in my hallway. Everything is all right,"—so saying he suddenly put his head out the casement window, "there he is this minute, the new tenant."

Followed by a porter who didn't appear to be sunk under the weight of his burden, a young man wearing a white hat of the fashion of Louis XIII had just entered the vestibule.

"Sir—is my apartment empty?" he asked the porter who went out to meet him.

"Not yet, sir—but it will be. The lodger who lives there has just gone to fetch a carriage to take away his effects. However, while you wait you could have your furnishings placed in the courtyard."

"I am afraid it will rain," responded the young man quietly chewing a bunch of violets which he was holding between his teeth; "my furniture might be spoiled. Porter," he added, to the man who had remained in back of him, bearing a hook filled with objects whose precise nature the janitor was unable to discover, "drop that in the vestibule and go back to my old lodging and collect what remains yet of precious belongings and art objects." The porter placed along the wall several screens from six to seven feet high, whose panels bending at the moment, one on top of the other, seemed to be able to unfold themselves at will.

"Stop," said the young man to the porter as he half-way opened one of the shutters and pointed out a tear which he found on the canvas, "that is unfortunate, you have torn my great Venetian glass—try to take care on your second trip,—above all, take care of my library."

"What does he mean, his Venetian glass?" muttered the janitor as he wandered uneasily around the frames placed against the wall. "I don't see any glass, no doubt it is a joke. I only see a screen—at least I can examine what they bring on the second trip."

"Will your tenant not go soon in order to leave the place free for me? It is twelve-thirty and I would like to move in," the young man said.

"I don't think he will be long now," the janitor answered; "furthermore, it is not so bad since your furniture has not come," he emphasized the words as he uttered them. The young man was about to answer when a dragoon in the capacity of orderly came into the court.

"Monsieur Bernard," he asked for, taking a letter from a great leather brief case which bumped against his leg.

"He is here," responded the janitor.

"Here is a letter for him," said the messenger, "give me a receipt for it," and he handed the janitor a dispatch bulletin which the latter signed.

"Pardon me if I leave you alone," said the janitor to the young man, who was impatiently striding up and down in the court—"but I have here a letter from the administration for Monsieur Bernard, my proprietor, and I must take it to him." At the moment when the janitor entered his apartment, Monsieur Bernard was in the act of shaving.

"What do you want, Durand?"

"Monsieur," answered the janitor, removing his cap, "a messenger has just brought you this—it comes from the administration," and he extended to Bernard the letter which was stamped with the seal of the War Department.

"My God!" Monsieur Bernard was so agitated that he just escaped giving himself a gash with his razor—"from the War Department. I am sure that it is my election to the rank of Knight of the Legion of Honour, which I have been seeking for ever so long; at last they render homage to my good deportment. Here, Durand," fumbling in the pocket of his vest, "here are one hundred sous to drink to my health. There, I haven't my purse with me. I will give them to you in a moment, wait."

The janitor was so amazed by this overwhelming generosity to which his proprietor was not accustomed, that he put his cap back on his head. But Monsieur Bernard, who at other times would have very harshly complained of this infraction of the laws of the social scale, did not seem to notice it. He put on his spectacles, took the envelope with the awe of a vizier who receives a firman from the sultan and began to read the message. After the first lines a horrible grimace made crimson creases in the fat of his monkish cheeks, and his little eyes darted forth sparks which just failed to light the locks of his wig. In fact all his features were so distorted that one might say that his face had just undergone an earthquake.

Here are the contents of the letter written on the letter head paper of the War Department, brought at full speed by a dragoon, and for which Monsieur Durand had given a receipt to the government.

"MR. PROPRIETOR:

Politeness, which if one believes mythology is the grandmother of good manners, forces me to let you know that I find myself in the cruel position of not being able to adhere to the custom of paying my rent—above all when I owe it. Up to this morning I had clung to the hope of celebrating this lovely day by paying the three terms of rent I owe—chimera, illusion, vain ideal. While I slept upon the pillow of security— bad luck—'ananke' in Greek—bad luck scattered my hopes. The receipts upon which I counted—God, but business is bad— have not materialized—and of the large sums which I was to have, I have just received three francs, which have been loaned to me. I do not offer them to you. Some good days will come for our beautiful France and for me, do not doubt it, Monsieur. As soon as they come, I will fly to tell you of it and to take out of your building the precious things which I have left there, and which I put under your protection and that of the law, which forbids their sale before a year, in the case that you would like to try to realize from them the sums for which you are credited upon the books of my faith. I recommend to you particularly my piano, and the large frame in which is found sixty knots of hair whose colours run all the gamut of capillary nuances and which have been taken from the foreheads of the graces by the scalpel of Cupid.

"You may then, Mr. Proprietor, dispose of the ceiling under which I lived. I grant you my permission herewith, sealed with my blood.

ALEXANDER SCHAUNARD."

When he had finished this letter which the artist had written in the office of one of his friends employed in the War Department, Monsieur Bernard crumpled it in his wrath; and as his glance fell upon Durand waiting the promised favor he abruptly asked what he was doing there.

"I am waiting, Monsieur!"

"What?"

"Why the gift that Monsieur . . . because of the good news!" blurted forth the janitor.

"Get out. What, scoundrel! you dare stand before me with your hat on?"

"But, Monsieur. . . ."

"Get out, don't talk back, leave, or no rather, wait for me. . . . We will go up to the room of that crook of an artist, who left without paying me."

"What," said the janitor, "Monsieur Schaunard . . . !"

"Yes," continued the proprietor, whose rage was directing itself to Nicolet. "And if he has taken away the least article I will fire you, do you understand,—I will fiiiiiiire you."

"But it isn't possible," muttered the poor janitor. "Monsieur Schaunard has not left. He went to seek money with which to pay my lord and to order a carriage to carry away his goods."

"To carry away his goods!" ejaculated Bernard; "we must hasten, I am sure that he's now in the very act of doing so; he has decoyed you away from your place to make his attempt, fool that you are!"

"Ah, my God, fool that I am!" sobbed old man Durand, trembling all over before the colossal wrath of his employer, who led him to the stairway.

As they came into the court the janitor was addressed by the young man with the white hat: "Ah, there you are, janitor," he cried, "am I soon to be put in possession of my domicile? Is to-day the eighth of April? Isn't this the place where I have rented my room, and have I not already given you the earnest money, answer me, have I, or have I not?"

"Pardon, my dear sir, pardon," said the proprietor, "I will take your place Durand," he added turning to the janitor, "I shall respond myself to the gentleman. You go upstairs, this scoundrel of a Schaunard has without any doubt entered to gather up his things; you lock him in if you surprise him and come down to find a policeman."

Father Durand disappeared up the stairway.

"I beg your pardon, my dear sir," so saying the proprietor bowed to the young man who was the only one present, "to whom have I the pleasure of speaking?"

"Monsieur, I am your new tenant, I have rented a room in this house on the sixth floor and I am beginning to be impatient because this lodging is not vacant."

"You find me in despair, Monsieur," replied Monsieur Bernard. "A quarrel has arisen between me and one of my tenants, him whom you replace."

"Sir, sir," shouted Durand from a window of the highest story of the house; "Monsieur Schaunard is not here . . . but his room is . . . fool that I am, I mean that he has taken nothing away, not even a hair, Monsieur."

"That's good, come down," shouted back Bernard.

"Just a little patience, I beg you," he resumed his conversation with the young man. "My janitor will carry down to the cellar the things which furnish the room of my insolvent tenant and in an half hour you may have possession—moreover, your belongings have not yet arrived."

"I beg your pardon, sir," quietly responded the young man.

Monsieur Bernard looked around him and could see only the great screens which had recently upset his janitor.

"What, I beg pardon, what," he stuttered, "but I see nothing."

"There they are," the young man replied in turning the leaves of the frame thereby giving the now agitated proprietor a view of a magnificent interior of a palace with jasper columns, bas-reliefs and pictures by the great masters.

"But your furniture?" demanded Bernard.

"There it is," the young man answered pointing to the elaborate painted interior in the palace which he had just bought from the Bullion gallery where he had taken part in the sale of the decorations of a theatrical society.

"Sir," resumed the proprietor, "I prefer to think that you have more serious furniture than that. . . ."

"What, the best from the Boule!"

"You understand that you must give me some guaranty for my rent."

"The devil, a palace doesn't suffice you for the rent of an attic?"

"No, sir, I want some furniture . . . some real furniture in mahogany!"

"Alas, sir, neither gold nor mahogany makes us happy, an ancient has said. And besides I cannot endure it. The wood is too ugly—everybody has it."

"But you must have some furnishings whatever they are, my dear sir?"

"No, it takes too much room in apartments. When there are chairs one never knows where to be seated."

"Surely you have a bed. Upon what do you rest?"

"I rest on God, sir."

"Pardon but one more question," said Bernard, "your profession, if you please?"

At this exact moment the young man's scout returning from his second trip entered the court. Among the objects with which he had filled his hooks could be seen an easel. "Ah, Monsieur," burst forth Durand, with terror, and he showed the easel to the proprietor, "he is a painter."

"An artist, I was sure of it," added in his turn Monsieur Bernard, and the hair of his wig stood on end from fright,—"an artist. Then you never got any information about the gentleman?" he returned, addressing the janitor. "You did not know what he did?"

"Well, you see," replied the poor soul, "he gave me five francs as a tip, could I doubt . . . ?"

"When you will have finished," demanded the young man in his turn.

"My man," resumed Bernard placing his spectacles perpendicularly on his nose, "since you have no belongings, you cannot move in. The law gives authority to refuse a tenant who has no guaranty."

"What about my word then?" the artist asked with great dignity.

"That isn't worth some furniture. . . . You can look for a lodging some place else. Durand will return you your tip."

"Huh?" the porter was aghast— "I have put it in the savings bank."

"But, sir," continued the young man, "I cannot find another lodging in a minute. At least give me hospitality for a day."

"Go stop in a hotel," answered Bernard. "Come to think of it," he quickly added on second thought, "if you wish,—I will rent you furnished the room that you were going to occupy and where you will find the insolvent tenant's furniture. Only you know that in this kind of renting the rent is paid in advance."

"I would like to know what you will demand for this dodge," said the artist forced to consider it.

"The room is very convenient, the rent will be twenty-five francs a month, considering the circumstances. One pays in advance."

"You said that before—it isn't worth saying twice," the young man growled as he fumbled in his pocket. "Have you change for five hundred francs?"

"Huh?" the proprietor was astounded, "you said?"

"Then,—the half of a thousand, there! have you never seen one?" added the artist, passing the bill before the eyes of the proprietor and janitor, who at the sight seemed to lose his balance.

"I shall have it for you," returned Bernard respectfully; "there will only be twenty francs taken out, since Durand will return the tip."

"He can have it," said the artist—"on condition that he will come every morning to tell me the day and date of the month, the quarter of the moon, what kind of weather it is and the form of government under which we are living."

"Ah, sir!" shouted Durand describing a circle of ninety degrees.

"That is good, fellow, you will serve as an almanac for me. Meanwhile, you will aid my scout to set up my housekeeping."

"Monsieur," said the proprietor, "I am going to get you your change."

The same evening, M. Bernard's new tenant, the painter Marcel, was set up in the runaway Schaunard's lodging, now transformed into a palace.

During all this time, the beforementioned Schaunard beat what he termed the call to arms of money in Paris. Schaunard had raised borrowing to the realm of an art. Foreseeing times when he would have to approach foreigners, he had learned how to borrow five francs in every language in the world. He had studied very deeply the list of ways in which money can escape those who look for it; and better than a pilot knows the hours of the tide, he knew the times when the waters were low or high, that is to say, when his friends and acquaintances were accustomed to receive money. There was a certain house even where, on seeing him enter a certain morning, they didn't say, "There is Monsieur Schaunard," but, "Well, this is the first or fifteenth of the month." In order to facilitate and equalize at the same time this kind of tithing he was going to levy, Schaunard had arranged in order of vicinity and districts an alphabetical table where could be found the names of all his friends and acquaintances. Opposite each name were marked the largest sums he could borrow in proportion to their means, the times when they were in cash and the hour of their dinner with the typical menu of the house. Beside this chart, Schaunard had a little pile of books perfectly in order upon which he kept track of the sums which were loaned to him up to the smallest fraction, for he did not wish to obligate himself beyond a certain sum which was still at the point of the pen of an uncle in Normandy, whose heir he was. When he owed twenty francs to one person, Schaunard closed his account and settled it entirely at one time, though to do so he had to borrow from those to whom he owed less. In this way he had constantly in the community a certain credit which he called his floating debt; and, as it was known that he was in the habit of paying when his personal resources permitted, people willingly helped him when they could. Now, since eleven in the morning when he had left his home to try to gather up the required seventy-five francs, he had only collected one small crown from the combination of the letters M. V. and R. of his famous list; all the rest of the alphabet, having like him, rent to pay, had kept him from his desired goal.

At six o'clock, a violent hunger rang the dinner gong in his stomach. He was then at the city walls of the Maine, where remained the letter U.—Schaunard mounted to the home of the letter U. where he had his napkin ring,—when there were napkins.

"Where are you going, sir?" the janitor stopped him in the passage.

"To the home of M. U." replied the artist.

"He isn't there."

"And Madame?"

"She isn't at home either; they told me to tell one of their friends who was going to call this evening that they had gone to the city for dinner; in fact, if it is you they expect," the janitor continued, "here is the address they left." And he handed to Schaunard a scrap of paper upon which his friend U. had written:

"We have gone to dine with Schaunard, rue, no . . . ; come there."

"Very well," said the latter going away, "when chance begins to meddle it makes strange vaudeville." Schaunard decided that he would go to a little pothouse just a few steps away where two or three times he had eaten very cheaply and he started forth towards that place, located in the alley of Maine, and known in lower Bohemia as the Mère Cadet. It is a pothouse whose ordinary clientele is composed of carters of the Orleans road, some singers of Montparnasse and some young beginners of the Bobino. In the fine season, the pupils of the numerous studios which are near the Luxembourg, the authors of unpublished books, the pamphleteers of unknown papers, came in a crowd to Mère Cadet, famed for its rabbit stews, its real sauerkraut, and a light white wine which smelled of gunpowder. Schaunard seated himself in the grove; so was called at Mère Cadet the sparse foliage of two or three rackety trees whose sickly verdure was used as a ceiling.

"My word, so much the worse," Schaunard said to himself. "I am going to increase my girth by having a private feast."

And without taking the first or second item, he ordered a soup, a half sauerkraut, and two half rabbit stews; he had noted that in dividing a portion one got at least a quarter more.

This order attracted to him the glances of a young woman dressed in white, with orange blossoms in her hair, and slippers on her feet, a veil in imitation—of imitation—rippled over her shoulders which should have certainly maintained the incognito. She was a singer of the Montparnasse theatre, whose corridors, so to speak, opened into the kitchen of the Mère Cadet. She had come for her dinner during an intermission of Lucia and was finishing at the moment with a demitasse a dinner made up exclusively of an artichoke with oil and vinegar.

"Two rabbit stews, by jove!" she said in an undertone to the girl who acted as waitress. "There is a young man who eats well. How much do I owe, Adele?"

"Four for the artichoke, four for the demitasse, and one sou for bread, that makes nine sous."

"There it is," said the singer, and she left humming, "This love that God gives me!"

"How she gives forth la," a mysterious creature then spoke, seated at the same table as Schaunard, half hidden by a wall of books.

"She gives it forth?" asked Schaunard; "for myself, I feel that she keeps it. Also you can never tell about that," he added pointing to the plate where Lucia di Lammermoor had eaten her artichokes,—"she has had her falsetto buried in vinegar."

"It is a strong acid," added the person who had just spoken. "The city of Orleans produces a brand which enjoys a great reputation."

Schaunard carefully studied this individual who so threw his hooks into the talk. The stare of his big blue eyes, which appeared to be constantly looking for something, gave to his expression the appearance of happy contentment which can be found among the seminarists. His skin had the colour of old ivory, except the cheeks, which were shaded the colour of powdered brick. His mouth seemed to have been designed by a student of first principles whose elbow had been jogged. The lips, slightly extended like those of the negroes, showed the teeth of a hunting dog, and his chin rested its two folds upon a white collar, one of the points of which challenged the stars while the other threatened to dig in the ground. From a bald felt hat, with an astonishingly wide rim, his hair escaped in blond ripples. He was dressed in a nut-coloured great coat with a cape whose material reduced to the woof, had the roughness of threadbareness. From the gaping pockets of this great coat bundles of papers and brochures escaped. Without being bothered by the scrutiny he tasted a garnished sauerkraut uttering very loud signs of satisfaction. While eating he read a magazine opened before him and upon which he made annotations from time to time with a pencil which he carried behind his ear.

"Come, come," shouted Schaunard suddenly tapping on his glass with his knife, "my rabbit stew."

"Monsieur," answered the girl, who appeared with a plate in her hand, "there is no more; here is the last and it is this gentleman who has ordered it," she added, putting the plate opposite the gentleman with the books.

"Oh dear," cried Schaunard. And there was so much unhappy disappointment in this "Oh dear" that the man with the books was touched inwardly. He moved aside the wall of tomes which separated them; and putting the plate between them both, he spoke in the sweetest tones:

"Monsieur, would I dare beg you to partake of this dish with me?"

"Monsieur," responded Schaunard, "I do not wish to deprive you."

"You will deprive me, then, of the pleasure of being agreeable to you."

"If that is the case, Monsieur . . ." and Schaunard moved his plate forward.

"Permit me to offer you the head," said the stranger.

"Ah, Monsieur," cried Schaunard, "I will not permit it . . ." but when he pulled back his plate he perceived that the stranger really had served him the disputed part.

"Oh well, what is he trying to teach me by all this politeness?" Schaunard growled to himself.

"If the head is the noblest part of man," the stranger went on, "it is the most unpleasant part of a rabbit. And there are a great many people who cannot bear it. As for me, it is just the opposite, I adore it."

"Then," said Schaunard, "I regret deeply that you have deprived yourself for me."

"What? I beg your pardon," said the man with the books, "but I have kept the head. I have even had the honour of observing to you. . . .'"

"Permit me," Schaunard said, shoving his plate under his nose. "What then is that piece there?"

"Just heavens, what do I see, ye gods! Another head! it is a two headed rabbit," cried the stranger.

"Two," said Schaunard.

"Cephale comes from the Greek. In fact Monsieur de Buffon, who indulges in sidenotes gives some examples of this peculiarity. But my word, it doesn't annoy me to partake of a phenomenon."

Thanks to this incident friendly relations were established. Schaunard, who did not wish to lack in politeness, ordered a litre of wine extra. The book man commanded another. Schaunard offered some salad, the book man countered with dessert. At eight o'clock there were six empty bottles on the table.

In talking, frankness, aroused by their indulgence in the wine, had moved each to tell the other his life's history, so that soon they knew each other as if it had been always. The book man, after having listened to Schaunard's confidences had told him that his name was Gustave Colline; he practised the calling of philosopher, and lived by giving lessons in mathematics, logic, botany, and several sciences ending in "ics." The little money he earned from going thus about teaching, he spent buying books. His nutbrown great coat was known by all the stall keepers on the quay from the Pont de la Concorde to the Pont St. Michel. What he did with all his books, too many to be read in the span of one man's life, nobody knew, and he had less idea than anyone else. But this bad habit had assumed the proportions of a real passion; and when he returned home in the evening without bringing a new book he revised for his purpose the saying of Titus, and said: "I have lost my day." His cajoling manners and his speech, which was a mosaic of every style, the terrible puns with which he punctuated his conversation, had seduced Schaunard, who demanded on the spot the permission to add his name to those who composed the famous list of which we have spoken.

They left the Mère Cadet at nine o'clock, both fairly tipsy, and having the deportment of those who have just had a debate with the bottles. Colline offered coffee to Schaunard, and the latter accepted on condition that he might provide the liqueurs. They entered a café in the street of Saint Germain l'Auxerrois, bearing the sign Momus, god of plays and of smiles.

At the moment when they entered the café, a lively argument had just started between two habitués of the place. One of them was a young man whose face was lost in the depths of an enormous bush of particoloured beard. As a direct antithesis to this mass of beard, a premature baldness had exposed his forehead, which resembled a knee, and a group of hairs so sparse that they could be counted tried in vain to cover the nakedness. He was dressed in a black suit which was out at the elbows, and showed when he raised his arm too high some practical ventilators at the armholes. His trousers had been black, but his shoes, which had never been new, appeared already to have made several trips around the world in the footsteps of the Wandering Jew.

Schaunard noticed that his new friend Colline and the youth with the great beard had greeted each other. "Do you know that man?" he asked the philosopher.

"Not really," responded the latter, "only I meet him occasionally at the library. I believe he is a man of letters."

"He has the appearance of one, at least," replied Schaunard.

The person with whom this young man was arguing was an individual of about forty years, fated for a stroke of apoplexy, as was indicated by his great head set closely on his shoulders without the transition of the neck. Tendency towards insanity showed itself in large letters by his depressed forehead, covered by a little black skullcap. He was called Monsieur Mouton and was employed at the Mayor's office of the Fourth District where he kept the register of the dead.

"Monsieur Rudolph," he cried with the voice of an eunuch, shaking the young man whom he had grabbed by a button of his jacket, "do you want me to tell you my opinion? Well, the newspapers are useless. Stop, suppose, I am the father of a family, am I not? Good . . . I come to have my game of dominoes at the café. Watch my reasoning closely."

"Continue, continue," said Rudolph.

"Well," continued père Mouton, accentuating each of his phrases by a blow of his fist which made the mugs and glasses on the table tremble,—"Well, I come across the papers, good . . . what do I see? One says white; the other, black;—pooh pooh. Now what does it do for me? I am a good family man who comes to play. . . ."

"This game of dominoes," said Rudolph.

"Every evening," continued Mouton. "Oh well, suppose; you understand. . . ."

"Very well," said Rudolph.

"I read an article which was opposed to my belief. It put me in a rage, and I swallow my wrath. Because you see, Monsieur Rudolph, all newspapers are liars. Yes, liars," he screeched in the sharpest falsetto, "and journalists are brigands, pamphleteers."

"But, Monsieur Mouton. . . ."

"Yes, pirates," continued the employee. "It is they who cause all the misery of the world; they have made revolution and paper money; witness Murat."

"Pardon," said Rudolph, "you mean Marat."

"Not at all, not at all," rejoined Mouton; "Murat, since I saw his burial when I was little. I assure you. . . . Even though there has been a play in the circle."

"Well, exactly," said Rudolph; "it is Murat."

"But what have I been telling you for the past hour?" shouted the obstinate Mouton. "Murat, who worked in a cellar. Well, suppose. Haven't the Bourbons done well with the guillotine since he has betrayed?"

"Who? Guillotined! Betrayed! What!" shouted Rudolph in his turn buttonholing Monsieur Mouton by his top coat.

"Well, Marat. . . ."

"No, no, Monsieur Mouton, Murat. My God, listen."

"Certainly, Marat, a scoundrel. He has betrayed the emperor in 1815. That is why I tell you all newspapers are the same," continued Mouton, resuming the theory of which he sought an explanation. "Do you know what I would like, I, Monsieur Rudolph? Well, suppose . . . I would like a good paper. . . . Ah, not big . . . good, which would not use sentences . . . there!"

"You are demanding," interrupted Rudolph, "a paper without sentences."

"Well, yes. Follow my idea."

"I will try."

"A paper which would give very simply the health of the king and the wealth of the earth. For, after all, of what use are all your newspapers, which no one understands? Suppose, I, I am in the office of the mayor, am I not? I keep my register, good! Well, it is as if someone came to tell me: 'Monsieur Mouton, you write the deceased. Well, do this, do that.' Well, what, what, that? Well, well, it is the same thing with the papers," he managed to conclude.

"Very evident," said a neighbour who had understood. And Monsieur Mouton having received the congratulations of some of the habitués who agreed with him, went to have his domino game.

"I have put him back in his place," he said pointing to Rudolph, who had returned to seat himself at the same table where Schaunard and Colline were.

"What a blockhead!" said the former to the two young men pointing to the employed one.

"He has a good head, with his eyelashes like the hood of a cab and his eyes like a lotto ball," said Schaunard taking out a short pipe marvelously coloured.

"My word, man," said Rudolph, "that is a very pretty pipe of yours."

"Oh, I have one much more beautiful to carry in society," Schaunard answered carelessly. "Give me some tobacco, Colline."

"What!" cried the philosopher, "I have no more."

"Permit me to offer you some," said Rudolph taking from his pocket a pouch of tobacco which he put on the table.

For this amenity, Colline thought he ought to offer a round of drinks in return. Rudolph accepted. Conversation turned to literature. Rudolph, questioned as to his profession already revealed by his clothes, confessed being in rapport with the muses and ordered another round. As the waiter went to fill the bottle Schaunard begged him to forget it. He had heard jingle in the pockets of Colline the silvern duet of two five franc pieces. Rudolph had soon attained the expansive level on which the two friends were and in his turn confided in them.

Doubtless they would have spent the night in the café if they had not been asked to leave. They had not taken six steps in the street, and it took them a quarter of an hour to do it, when they were surprised by rain in torrents. Colline and Rudolph lived at the opposite ends of Paris, one on the Isle of St. Louis, the other at Montmartre.

Schaunard, who had completely forgotten that he was without

a home, offered them hospitality. "Come home with me," he said, "I live near; we will spend the night bickering about literature and the fine arts."

"You can play music and Rudolph will say some of his verses," said Colline.

"Indeed yes," added Schaunard, "we must be merry as we have only once to live."

After Schaunard had arrived in front of the house, which he had some trouble in recognizing, he seated himself a moment upon a milepost while he waited for Rudolph and Colline, who had gone to a wine shop which was still open, to collect the essentials of a supper. When they returned Schaunard knocked several times at the door, for he remembered that the janitor had the habit of making him wait. The door was finally opened, and père Durand, sunk in the sweetness of first sleep, not remembering that Schaunard was no longer his tenant, was not at all upset to hear his name shouted through the shutter.

When all three had reached the top of the stairs which ascent had been both long and difficult, Schaunard, who walked ahead, uttered a cry of astonishment when he found the key in the door of his room.

"What's wrong?" demanded Rudolph.

"I don't understand at all," he murmured, "I find in the door the key which I took away this morning. Ah! we shall soon see. I had put it in my pocket. My word! there it still is!" he cried finding the other key.

"It is magic."

"It is phantasmagorical," said Colline.

"It is fantastics," added Rudolph.

"But," began Schaunard, whose voice betrayed the beginning of fright, "do you hear?"

"What?"

"What?"

"My piano;—which plays alone,—*la, mi, ré, do, la, si, sol, ré*— Scoundrel of *ré*, go, it is always false."

"But it surely isn't in your place," Rudolph said to him, and whispered in Colline's ear upon whom he was leaning heavily. "He is tipsy."

"I believe it. In the first place, it isn't a piano, it is a flute."

"But, you too, you are tipsy, my dear," responded the poet to the philosopher, who had seated himself upon the landing, "it is a violin."

"A viol . . . pooh. . . . Say, Schaunard," blustered Colline in pulling his friend by his legs. "That is good, that is. Here is a gentleman who pretends that it is a violin."

"My word," shouted Schaunard, about to be overcome, "my piano plays constantly, it is magic."

"Phantasmagory," stuttered Colline at the same time dropping one of the bottles which he held in his hand.

"Fantastics," squeaked Rudolph in his turn.

In the midst of this bedlam, the door of the room was opened suddenly and there appeared upon the threshold a being who held in his hand a three branched candlestick in which burned pink candles.

"What do you want, gentlemen?" bowing courteously to the three friends as he spoke.

"My heavens, what have I done? I am deceived, this isn't my home," Schaunard spoke.

"Sir," Colline and Rudolph spoke together, addressing the personage who had opened the door, "will you excuse our friend, —he is drunk, even as a third monk."

Suddenly a gleam of intelligence pierced Schaunard's drunkeness. He had just read upon the door a line written with chalk;

"I have come three times to look for my New Year's gifts. Phemie."

"Yes, yes, indeed, it is a fact, I am at home," he shouted. "There certainly is the visiting card Phemie has left to show that she came New Year's day. It is certainly my door."

"My God, sir," said Rudolph, "I am most confused."

"Believe me," added Colline, "on my part I join in with the acute embarrassment of my friend."

The young man could not keep from laughing. "If you wish to come in for a moment," he responded, "doubtless your friend will realize his error when he sees the place."

"Willingly," and the poet and the philosopher taking Schaunard by each arm, entered the room, or rather the palace of Marcel whom doubtless the reader has recognized. Schaunard looked vaguely around him murmuring:

"It is astonishing, how decorated my quarters are."

"Well, are you convinced now?" Colline demanded from him.

But Schaunard having perceived the piano went up to it and played some scales. "Oh, you others. Listen to that," making some chords resound. "Soon the animal recognized its master; *si, la, sol, fa, mi, ré,* that scoundrel of a *ré!* you will always be the same, —leave. I should certainly say it is my own piano."

"He insists," said Colline to Rudolph.

"He insists," repeated Rudolph to Marcel.

"And that also," added Schaunard, showing the skirt embroidered with stars, which was thrown over a chair, "it is not my embellishment perhaps!" and he looked down his nose at Marcel. "And that," he went on, taking from the wall the order to leave from the sheriff of which he had spoken earlier. And he began to read: 'Consequently, Monsieur Schaunard will be expected to empty these premises, and to leave them in the same condition he found them, April 8, before noon. And I have signed the present paper at a cost of five francs.' Ah, ah, then it isn't I who am Schaunard who has been put out by the bailiff,— with the formality of the stamp whose cost is five francs." And then again, recognizing his slippers on Marcel's feet, "Those are not then my turkish slippers, a present from one very dear? In your turn, Sir," said he to Marcel, "explain your presence among my household gods."

"Gentlemen," responded Marcel, addressing Colline and Rudolph more particularly, "the gentleman" and he pointed to Schaunard, "the gentleman is at home, I confess it."

"Ah," exulted Schaunard, "that is nice."

"But," continued Marcel, "I too, I am at my home."

"However, sir," interrupted Rudolph, "if our friend recognizes . . ."

"Yes," continued Colline, "if our friend . . ."

"And if on your part you remember," added Rudolph, "how he pretended!"

"Yes," broke in Colline,—echo,—"how he pretended!"

"Will you sit down, gentlemen," responded Marcel, "I will explain the mystery."

"Perhaps we might water the explanation?" hazarded Colline.

"And break a crust," added Rudolph.

The four young men seated themselves at the table and attacked a slice of cold veal which the wine seller had given to them.

Then Marcel explained what had happened during the morning between him and the proprietor, when he had come to move in.

"Then," said Rudolph, "the gentleman is perfectly right, we are at his house."

"You are in your own house," Marcel corrected politely.

But it required tremendous effort to make Schaunard comprehend what had happened. A comical incident took place then to complicate the situation further. Schaunard, searching for something in the sideboard, came across the five hundred francs which Marcel had changed for Monsieur Bernard. "Ah, I was positive of it," he cried, "that chance wouldn't abandon me. I remember now . . . that I left this morning to look for it. On account of the quarter's rent, it is true, it came during my absence. We have crossed each other's paths, that's it. How fortunate that I left the key in my drawer."

"Lovely folly," muttered Rudolph, seeing Schaunard arrange the money in equal piles.

"A dream, a lie, such is life," added the philosopher.

Marcel smiled. An hour later all four had fallen to sleep.

The next day at noon they woke up and seemed at first very astonished to find themselves together. Schaunard, Colline and Rudolph did not seem to recognize each other and addressed each other as Monsieur. Marcel had to remind them that they had arrived together the night before. At this point père Durand entered the room. "Sir," he said to Marcel, "today is the ninth of April, 1840, there is some mud in the streets and Louis Phillippe is always king of France and Navarre. What!" ejaculated père Durand perceiving his old tenant, "Monsieur Schaunard, where have you come from?"

"By telegraph," answered Schaunard.

"Oh say, you are joking, aren't you?" returned the porter.

"Durand," said Marcel, "I do not like to have the servants mingle in the conversation; go to a nearby restaurant and have a dinner for four sent up. Here is the order," he added, giving him a scrap of paper on which he had written the menu. "Gentlemen," Marcel continued to the three young men, "you brought me supper last night, permit me to offer you lunch this morning, not in my house, but in our house," he added extending his hand to Schaunard.

At the end of lunch, Rudolph begged to speak. "Gentlemen, permit me to leave."

"Oh, no," Schaunard responded sentimentally, "never leave us."

"That's true, they do us very well here," added Colline.

"To leave you a moment," continued Rudolph. "Tomorrow is due to appear the *Scarf of Iris*, a magazine of fashion of which I am editor-in-chief, and I must correct my proofs. I will return in an hour."

"The devil," said Colline, "that makes me think that I have a lesson to give to an Indian prince who has come to Paris to learn Arabic."

"Go tomorrow," said Marcel.

"Oh, no, the prince is going to pay me today. And then, I swear that this beautiful day would be ruined for me if I didn't make a small tour to the market for books."

"But you will return," begged Schaunard.

"With the speed of an arrow shot by a sure hand," replied the philosopher, who loved eccentric similes. And he went out with Rudolph.

"In fact," said Schaunard who remained alone with Marcel, "instead of coddling myself on a do-nothing pillow, I might search for some money to appease the avariciousness of Monsieur Bernard."

"You still count on permanently moving?" Marcel was very agitated.

"My word, yes, I must, since I am put out by the sheriff at a cost of five francs."

"But," continued Marcel, "if you move, will you take away your furniture?"

"I had that intention, not to leave one single hair, as Monsieur Bernard ordered."

"Oh dear, that is very annoying," said Marcel, "for I have rented your room furnished."

"That's so, isn't it? Oh pshaw," he was very melancholy, "there is nothing to warrant that I will find seventy-five francs today, or tomorrow, or ever."

"But hold on, I have an idea."

"Produce it," said Schaunard.

"Here is the situation. Legally this lodging is mine, for I have paid a month in advance."

"The lodging, yes, but the furnishings, if I pay, I may legally remove them; and if that were so I should even remove them extra legally," said Schaunard.

"In such a way you have furnishings and no lodging and I have a lodging and no furniture."

"There you are," said Schaunard.

"This lodging pleases me," Marcel continued.

"And me too," added Schaunard, "it has never pleased me more."

"What are you saying?"

"That it never pleased me more. Oh I know what I'm saying."

"Then, we can arrange this matter," said Marcel, "stay with me, and I will furnish the lodging if you will supply the furniture."

"And the terms?" asked Schaunard.

"Since I have money today I will pay it; the next time it will be your turn, think it over."

"I will not think it over, especially to accept a plan which is agreeable to me. I accept here and now; in fact, painting and music are sisters."

"Sisters-in-law," said Marcel.

At this moment Colline and Rudolph returned and Marcel and Schaunard informed them of their association.

"Gentlemen," cried Rudolph, rattling his purse, "I offer dinner to the company."

"That was precisely what I was going to have the honour to suggest," said Colline, pulling a gold piece from his pocket and fitting it in his eye. "My prince gave me this to buy a Hindustani-Arabian grammar, for which I have just paid six sous."

"And I," said Rudolph, "I had myself advanced thirty francs from the cash box of the *Scarf of Iris* under the pretext that I needed it to have myself vaccinated."

"This is the day of receipts," said Schaunard, "and only I have nothing, it is humiliating."

"I reassert my offer for dinner," said Rudolph.

"And I also," said Colline.

"Then," said Rudolph, "we are going to toss to see which will pay for the dinner."

"No," said Schaunard, "I have a better idea than that, infinitely better to overcome your embarrassment."

"Tell us."

"Rudolph will buy dinner and Colline will offer supper."

"That is what I would call the wisdom of Solomon," agreed the philosopher.

"It is worse than the marriage feast of Gamache," added Marcel.

The dinner took place in a Provençal restaurant famous for its literary waiters and its ayoli. As they had to leave room for the supper they had to drink and eat moderately. The acquaintance begun the day before between Colline and Schaunard and later with Marcel became more intimate. Each of the four young men hoisted the flag of his opinion on art; all four recognized that they had equal courage and even hope. In conversing and arguing they perceived that they were mutually sympathetic, that they all had the same cleverness of wits in fencing amusingly which livens without wounding, and that all the lovely qualities of youth had left no empty places in their hearts, easy to move by the sight or hearing of a beautiful thing. All four, having started from the same point to seek the same end, thought that there was in their meeting something more than the empty workings of chance, and this could easily be Providence also, natural protector of the abandoned, who put their hands in each other's and breathed very low in their ears the words of the evangelist which should be the only guide of humanity: "Support and love each other."

At the end of the repast which ended fairly solemnly, Rudolph rose to propose a toast to the future and Colline responded with a short talk which he had not taken from any book, nor which belonged at any point to beautiful style, and he spoke very simply the plain language of simplicity which made comprehensible what he said so badly.

"How foolish he is, this philosopher!" muttered Schaunard, who had his nose in his glass, "he forces me to put water in my wine."

After the dinner, they went to have coffee at the Café Momus where they had passed the evening before. From that day on the institution became uninhabitable for the other habitués.

After coffee and liqueurs, the Bohemian Club, formally established, returned to Marcel's room which took the name, Élysée Schaunard. While Colline went to order the supper which he had promised, the others got hold of some firecrackers, some sky-rockets, and other pyrotechnics and before going back to the table again they sent through the windows a superb artificial fire which put the whole house topsy-turvy and during which the four friends sang at the top of their lungs,

"Let us celebrate, let us celebrate, let us celebrate, this fine day."

The next morning, they found themselves together again, but without seeming surprised this time. Before each returned to his business, they went in company to breakfast frugally at the Momus where they planned to meet in the evening and where they could be found the greater part of every day. Such are the principal personages that will reappear in the little stories which make up this volume which is not a novel, and has no other pretension than that indicated by its title; for stories of Life in Bohemia are only in reality studies of manners, and their heroes belong to a class misjudged up to now, whose greatest fault is disorder; and yet they can give as an excuse for this same disorder—it is a necessity which life demands from them.

GIFT OF THE GODS

SCHAUNARD and Marcel, who had courageously set to work during the morning, suddenly stopped.

"Heavens! how hungry I am!" moaned Schaunard. And he added casually: "Do we eat today?"

Marcel seemed very astonished at this question, now more than ever embarrassing. "Since when have we been lunching two days in succession?" he asked. "Yesterday was Thursday." And he finished by describing with his painting stick this commandment of the Church:

> Friday do not eat
> Any kind of meat.

Schaunard had nothing to say to this and took up his painting which represented a plain inhabited by a red tree and a blue one whose branches shook hands with each other,—obvious allusion to the pleasures of friendship which did not really lead to any philosophical reflections. At this moment, the janitor knocked on the door. He brought a letter for Marcel.

"It is three sous," he said.

"You are sure of that?" asked the artist. "That's good, you will owe them to us." And he closed the door in his face.

Marcel had taken the letter and broken the seal. At the first words he began to leap about like an acrobat in the studio and to sing at the top of his voice the following famous ballad, a sign that he was at the peak of excitement:

> In the quarter there were four young men
> They were all four sick
> They sent them off to the hospital
> Tra la, tra lal, tra la, tra lal.

"Well, yes," said Schaunard, taking it up:

> And there they were put in a great big bed,
> Two at the foot and two at the head.

"We know that!"

Marcel resumed:

> There came a little nun that way
> Tra la, tra la, tra lay, tra lay.

"If you don't keep quiet," threatened Schaunard, who already noted symptoms of mental weakness, "I am going to perform for you the allegro of my symphony upon the 'Influence of Blue upon the Arts.'" And he went over to his piano.

That threat produced the effect of a drop of cold water fallen into a boiling liquid.

As if by magic Marcel became quiet.

"There," he said, giving the letter to his friend, "look."

It was an invitation to dinner from a deputy, an enlightened patron of the arts, and particularly of Marcel, who had painted a picture of his country home.

"It's for today," said Schaunard. "It's too bad that the note isn't good for two persons. But actually, come to think of it, your deputy belongs to the party in power, you cannot, you ought not accept; your faith forbids you to eat bread soaked in the sweat of the people."

"Bah!" Marcel was scornful. "My deputy is centre left; the other day he voted against the government. Furthermore, he is to get a commission for me, and he promised to introduce me to people; and then too, you understand, Friday or no Friday, I am overcome by an Ugolinian appetite, and I wish to dine today, and that's that."

"There are yet other difficulties," continued Schaunard, who could not help but be slightly jealous of the good luck which had befallen his friend. "You cannot go to dine in the city in a red blazer and a dock worker's hat."

"I shall borrow Rudolph's or Colline's suit."

"Foolish youth, do you forget that it is past the twentieth and that by this time the suits of these gentlemen are pawned and repawned?"

"I will certainly find one black suit in five hours," Marcel said.

"It took me three weeks to find one when I went to my cousin's wedding, and that was at the beginning of January."

"Oh well, I shall go like this," replied Marcel striding up and down. "No one can say that a wretched question of etiquette kept me from making my first bow to the world."

"Speaking of such things," interrupted Schaunard, taking great pleasure in arousing the discomfiture of his friend, "what about shoes?"

Marcel went out in a state of agitation impossible to describe. After two hours, he returned bearing one false collar. "That's all I could find," he sighed pitifully.

"It wasn't worth the trouble to dash around for so little," responded Schaunard. "We have enough paper here to make a dozen."

"But," groaned Marcel tearing his hair, "we must own something, oh the deuce!" And he began a lengthy search in every corner of the two rooms. After an hour of this research he collected a costume composed of the following:

One pair Scotch plaid pantaloons,
One grey hat,
One formerly white glove,
One black glove.

"If necessary that will make you two black gloves," consoled Schaunard. "But when you are dressed you will resemble the solar spectrum. After all that is what it is to go in for colour!"

Meanwhile, Marcel was trying the shoes.

Tragedy! They were both for the same foot!

The artist, in despair, spied in a corner an old shoe in which they put the trash. He took it.

"From Garrick to Syllabe," said his sarcastic companion; "the one is pointed and the other square toed."

"That will not be noticed, I will polish them."

"That's a good idea! Now you only want a correct black suit."

"Oh," sighed Marcel biting his fists, "I would give ten years of my life and my right hand to have one, you understand!"

Again they heard a knock at the door. Marcel opened.

"Mr. Schaunard?" asked a stranger, remaining on the door sill.

"I am he," replied the painter, motioning him to enter.

"Sir," said the unknown gentleman, who had one of those honest faces which are typical of the provinces, "my cousin has told me much about your talent for painting; and, being on the point of taking a trip to the colonies, where I have been sent as a delegate by the refiners of Nantes, I should like to leave a souvenir of myself to my family. That is why I came to see you."

"O blessed providence! . . ." murmured Schaunard. "Marcel, give a chair to M. . . ."

"M. Blancheron," replied the stranger; "Blancheron of Nantes, delegate from the sugar industry, former mayor of V. . . , captain in the National Guard, and author of a brochure on the subject of sugars."

"I am very honoured to be chosen by you," said the artist bowing before the representative of the refiners. "What kind of a portrait do you wish?"

"A miniature, like that," replied Blancheron, pointing to an oil portrait; for to the delegate as to a great many others, what is not building painting is miniature, there is no middle way. This simplicity gave the measure of the good man with whom he was doing business, especially when he had added that he desired that his portrait be painted with fine colours.

"I do not use any other," said Schaunard. "What size does the gentleman wish his portrait?"

"As large as that," responded Mr. Blancheron, pointing to a canvas of twenty feet. "But how much will that be?"

"From fifty to sixty francs; fifty without the hands, sixty with."

"Oh dear! my cousin told me about thirty francs."

"It goes according to the season," said the artist; "the colours are much more expensive at different times."

"Think of that! Just as sugar is?"

"Absolutely."

"Done then for fifty francs," concluded Mr. Blancheron.

"You are making a mistake, for ten francs more you will have hands in which I would place your brochure upon the sugar question. That would be pleasing."

"I declare, you are right."

"Confound it," Schaunard said to himself, "if he goes on, he will make me burst and one of my flying parts will wound him."

"Have you noticed?" Marcel whispered in his ear.

"What?"

"He has a black suit."

"I get you and I fall in with your idea. Leave it to me."

"Well, sir," asked the delegate, "when will we begin? It won't do to be slow as I leave soon."

"I, too, have a small trip to make; day after tomorrow I am leaving Paris. So if it is agreeable, we will commence at once. A good sitting will forward the job."

"But it will be dark soon and you cannot paint under lights," said Monsieur Blancheron.

"My studio is arranged so that I can work at any time," the painter went on. "If you will take off your suit and take the post, we will begin."

"Take off my suit! Why?"

"Didn't you say that you intended to give your portrait to your family?"

"Surely."

"Well then, you must be shown in your lounging costume, in a dressing gown. It is customary, besides."

"But I haven't a dressing gown here."

"But I have. That difficulty is provided for," said Schaunard, handing to his model a rag ornamented with paint stains, which made the simple man from the provinces hesitate at first.

"This garment is very odd," he said.

"And very precious," rejoined the artist. "A turkish vizier made a present of it to Monsieur Horace Vernet, who gave it to me. I am his pupil."

"You are a pupil of Vernet?" asked Blancheron.

"Yes sir, I boast of it."—"Horrors," he muttered to himself, "I am denying my gods."

"That's worth mentioning, young man," declared the delegate putting on the gown which had such a splendid origin.

"Hang the gentleman's suit on the coat-stand," Schaunard ordered his friend with a significant wink.

"Listen here," whispered Marcel as he hurled himself upon his booty and motioned to Schaunard. "It is really good! If you could keep a part of it."

"I will try! But that isn't the question, dress yourself quickly and run. Come back at ten, I will keep him till then. Above all bring me something in your pockets."

"I will bring you a pineapple," Marcel assured him, now that his troubles were over.

He dressed quickly. The suit fitted him like a glove, then he departed by the other door of the studio.

Schaunard set about his task. As night had come, Monsieur Blancheron heard six o'clock strike and remembered that he had not had dinner. He remarked about it to the artist.

"I am in the same position; but to oblige you I will do without tonight. Moreover, I was invited to a house in the faubourg Saint-Germain," added Schaunard. "But we cannot be disturbed as it would endanger getting a likeness." He began to work.

"After this," he said suddenly, "we can eat without upsetting our plans. Below there is an excellent restaurant which will send up whatever we wish."

And Schaunard observed the effect of his trio of plural pronouns.

"I am in favour of your suggestion," said Blancheron, "and in return I hope that you will do me the honour of being my guest."

Schaunard bowed.

"Indeed," he thought to himself, "he's a great man, a real gift from the gods. Will you choose the menu?" he asked his host.

"You will do me a favour if you will take charge of it," the other replied politely.

"You will not be sorry, Nicholas," caroled the artist, going downstairs four at a time.

He went in the restaurant, up to the counter and planned a

menu, the reading of which made the head waiter of the shop grow pale.

"Some ordinary Bordeaux."

"Who can pay?"

"Not I in all probability," answered Schaunard, "but one of my uncles whom you will see upstairs, a great connoisseur of food. So try to outdo yourself and let us be served in an half hour and above all use the china."

At eight o'clock Monsieur Blancheron already had experienced the need of pouring into the heart of a friend his ideas on the

sugar industry, and he repeated to Schaunard the brochure which he had written.

The latter accompanied him on the piano.

At ten o'clock Monsieur Blancheron and his friend were dancing the galop and calling each other by their first names.

At eleven o'clock, they swore never to leave each other and each made a will in which each reciprocated by leaving the other his fortune.

At midnight, Marcel returned to find them in each other's arms; they were buried in tears. Already there was water deep as half one's thumb in the studio. Marcel betook himself to the table and saw the splendid leftovers of a proud feast. He looked at the bottles. They were perfectly empty.

He wished to revive Schaunard, but the latter threatened to

kill him if he wanted to steal Blancheron, who now served as his pillow, from him.

"Ingrate!" growled Marcel as he took from his suit pocket a handful of nuts, "I, who procured dinner for him."

LENTEN LOVES

ONE evening during Lent, Rudolph went home quite early with the idea of working. But he had hardly sat down at his table and dipped his pen in the ink when he was distracted by a peculiar noise; so, putting his ear to the partition which was much too thin for privacy and which separated him from the next room, he heard perfectly a conversation punctuated with kisses and other amourous onomatopœics.

"Bother!" thought Rudolph, looking at his watch. "It isn't late . . . and my neighbour is a Juliet who generally keeps her Romeo long after the song of the lark. I shan't be able to work tonight." And taking his hat he departed.

While replacing his key in the box, he found the wife of the janitor half buried in the arms of a gallant. The poor woman was so startled that she could not open the door for five minutes.

"Evidently," mused Rudolph, "there are moments when janitresses are women." Opening the door he discovered in the corner of the threshold a fireman and a cook on holiday, clasping each other's hand and exchanging the dues of love.

"Dear me," said Rudolph, alluding to the warrior and his robust companion, "here are heretics who do not even dream that it is Lent." And he betook himself to the home of one of his friends in the neighbourhood.

"If Marcel is at home," he said to himself, "we will spend the evening talking about Colline. One must do something."

Even as he knocked violently the door was half-opened, and a young man simply clad in a monocle and a shirt appeared. "I cannot let you in," he said to Rudolph.

"Why?" demanded the latter.

"Look," said Marcel, pointing at a female head which had just appeared from behind a curtain: "there is my answer."

"She isn't beautiful," Rudolph added as the door was closed in his face.

"Well, now," he said again to himself as he regained the street, "what to do? If I went to see Colline? We would spend the evening talking about Marcel."

While passing along the rue de l'Ouest, generally dark and empty, Rudolph discerned a shadow walking along disconsolately and muttering rhymes between his teeth. "What ho! Who is this sonnet that dances attendance? Of all things, Colline!"

"Stop, Rudolph! Where are you going?"

"To your house."

"You will not find me at home."

"What are you doing here?"

"Waiting."

"What?"

"Ah," Colline was in a high mood, "for what does one wait when one is twenty and there are stars in the heavens, songs in the air?"

"Speak in prose."

"I am waiting for a woman."

"Good-evening," Rudolph went on his way, talking to himself. "Really," he murmured, "is this the feast day of Saint Cupid, and can I not take a single step without falling into the midst of lovers? It is immoral and scandalous. What are the police doing?"

As the Luxembourg gardens were still open, Rudolph took a short cut through them. In the midst of the deserted walks, several times he saw fleeting before him as if frightened by the sound of his steps, couples strangely bound together and seeking, as a poet has said: "The double pleasure of silence and shade."

"This is truly," remarked Rudolph, "an evening which has been copied from a romance." Meanwhile, permeated in spite of himself by a languorous charm, he sat down on a bench and sentimentally gazed at the moon. After a little, he was completely prey to a feverish hallucination. It seemed to him that the marble gods and heroes which peopled the garden were coming down from their perches to woo their neighbour goddesses and heroines; and he distinctly heard the great Hercules sing a madrigal to Velleda, whose tunic seemed strangly short. From the bench where he was sitting, he saw a swan from the fountain pursuing a nymph of the neighbourhood. "Oh good," thought

Rudolph, who believed all this mythology, "there goes Jupiter to keep a date with Leda. Providing the caretaker doesn't surprise them."

Then he buried his forehead in his hands and succumbed further to the gentle dominion of sentiment. But at this moment of sweet dreaming, Rudolph was cruelly awakened by a guardian who tapped on his shoulder.

"You must go," he said.

"That is fortunate," thought Rudolph. "If I remained here another five minutes I would have more forget-me-nots in my heart than there are on the banks of the Rhine or in the romances of Alphonse Karr."

And he beat a quick retreat from the Luxembourg humming quietly a sentimental ballad which for him was the Marseillaise of Love. An half hour later—I don't know how—he was at the Prado seated before some punch and chatting with a great man famous for his nose, which, by a peculiar grace, is aquiline as to profile and snub as to face,—a masterful nose which does not lack in wit and has had sufficient brave adventures to give wise advice about such matters and to be generally useful to a friend.

"Then," said Alexander Schaunard, the man of the nose, "you are in love?"

"Yes, my friend, it has attacked me just now, suddenly, like a bad toothache in the heart."

"Hand me some tobacco," said Alexander.

"Imagine," Rudolph continued, "since two o'clock I have only met lovers, men and women, two by two. I went into the Luxembourg where I saw every sort of wonder to unsettle me, which has affected my heart amazingly; there elegies came to me; I bleat and I coo; I am changed one half to a sheep, the other to a dove. Wait a minute, I must have some paper and pens."

"But what have you been drinking?" said Alexander disgusted. "You mystify me, you do."

"I assure you that I am sober," said Rudolph. "That is to say, I am not. But I will say this, and that is that I must hug something. You understand, a man must not live alone . . . in a word you must help me find a woman. . . . We will make a tour of the dance hall and the first woman I point out to you, you will tell her that I love her."

"Why can't you tell her yourself?" demanded Alexander in his magnificent nasal bass.

"Oh, my dear," said Rudolph, "I assure you that I have completely forgotten how one begins such things. Of all my novels of love, my friends have written the preface and of some even the dénouement. I never know how to begin."

"It is enough to know how to finish," said Alexander; "but I understand you. I saw a young lady who loves the oboe, perhaps you can meet her."

"Ah," sighed Rudolph, "I would so love to have her have white gloves and blue eyes."

"Oh lord, blue eyes. I cannot say . . . but white gloves . . . you know that one cannot have everything at the same time . . . well, let's be off to the haunts of aristocracy."

"Stop," said Rudolph on entering the room where were assembled the flower of the vicinity, "there's one who seems very attractive," and he pointed out a young girl sufficiently well turned out, who was standing in a corner.

"All right," responded Alexander, "you stay in the background; I shall hurl her the firebrand of passion for you. When it is meet for you to come, I will call."

For ten minutes Alexander chatted with the young lady who from time to time burst out in joyful shouts of laughter and ended by throwing a smile at Rudolph which was the equivalent of saying: come along, your lawyer has won your case.

"Go ahead," said Alexander, "victory is ours, the little girl doubtless is not cruel, but begin in a simple way."

"You do not need to advise me."

"Then, give me a little tobacco," said Alexander, "and go sit down with her."

"Dearie me," said the girl, when Rudolph had taken his place at her side, "how amusing your friend is, he speaks like a hunting horn."

"That is because he is a musician," answered Rudolph.

Two hours later, Rudolph and his lady had stopped before a house on the rue St. Denis. "This is where I live," she said.

"Well, my dear Louise, when and where shall I see you again?"

"At your place, tomorrow evening at eight."

"Are you really telling the truth?"

"Here is my promise," Louise answered, holding her fresh cheeks up to Rudolph who went so far as to taste those lovely fruits radiant with youth and health.

Rudolph returned home madly intoxicated. "Ah," said he walking with great steps up and down his room, "this must be commemorated; I must make a poem."

Next morning his janitor found thirty or more sheets of paper around his room and at the top of each sheet was majestically written the following solitary alexandrine:

O Love! O Love! The prince of youth!

This day, that is the next day, contrary to his habits, Rudolph had wakened at a very early hour, and although he had slept little he arose at once. "Oh," he shouted, "today indeed is the great day . . . but twelve hours to wait . . . How can I fill these twelve eternities?" And as his glance had rested on his desk, it seemed to him that his pen quivered, saying to him: "Work."

"Ah, certainly, I shall work, to hell with prose!! I cannot stay here, it smells of ink."

He installed himself in a café where he was sure not to meet any of his friends. "They will see that I am in love," he thought, "and will steal my ideal away." After a very quick lunch he tore to a station and jumped on a train. In an half hour he was in the woods of Ville d'Avray. Rudolph, at ease in a freshly rejuvenated world, spent the whole day walking and only returned to Paris at nightfall.

After having put in order the shrine which was to receive his idol, Rudolph made an impressive toilet, regretting a great deal that he couldn't dress in white. From seven to eight he was prey to the sharp fever of waiting. Slow torture which reminded him of ancient days and old loves which had given them charm. Then as was his habit he began picturing to himself even now a grand passion, a love affair in ten volumes, a real lyric with moonlight, setting suns, meetings under the willows, uneasiness, sighs, and all the rest. And he found himself in this state each time that chance brought a woman to his door, and not one had left him without bearing away on her brow an halo and around her throat a necklace of tears.

They would prefer a hat or some slippers, his friends told him; but Rudolph was obdurate and up to now the numerous schools which he had tried had not been able to cure him. He always expected a woman who wanted really to pose as an idol, an angel in a velvet robe to whom he could at his pleasure address his sonnets written upon willow leaves.

At last Rudolph heard the holy hour sound; and on the last stroke he believed he saw Love and Psyche, who decorated the top of his clock, entwine their alabaster bodies. At the same minute there were two timid knocks on the door. Rudolph went to open. It was Louise. "I am a person of my word, you see," she said. Rudolph closed the curtains and lighted a new candle. Meanwhile the girl had taken off her shawl and her hat which she placed upon the bed. The shining whiteness of its covers made her smile—and almost blush.

Louise was rather more charming than pretty; her fresh countenance presented an amusing mixture of simplicity and guile. It was quite like a motive of Greuze arranged by Gavarni. All the appealing youth of the girl was cleverly brought out by a toilet, which, although very simple, gave evidence that she possessed that inborn knowledge of coquetry which every woman has from her first swaddling clothes to her wedding dress. Louise, moreover, seemed to have studied particularly the theory of poses, and assumed before Rudolph, who looked at her through eyes of an artist, a series of seductive attitudes which were often more graceful than natural; her feet, well shod, were narrow enough . . . even for a romantic entranced by Andalusian or Chinese miniatures. As for her hands, their delicacy betokened indolence. Indeed, for six months, she had had no need to fear the pricks of her needle. To explain everything, Louise was one of these birds of passage which through fancy and often through need make their nest for a day or rather a night in the roofs of the Latin Quarter and rest there gladly some days, if one knows how to hold them by a whim or by ribbons.

After having talked an hour with Louise, Rudolph showed her as a suggestion the group of Love and Psyche.

"Is it not Paul and Virginia?" she asked.

"Yes," Rudolph responded, who did not wish to wound her so soon by contradicting her.

"They are well copied."

"Alas," Rudolph thought to himself, as he contemplated her, "the poor child knows no literature. I am sure that she limits herself to the spelling of the heart, which never adds s to the plural. I must buy her a grammar." Meanwhile, as Louise complained of being hurt by her shoe, naturally he helped her to unlace the strings.

Suddenly the light went out.

"I say," cried Rudolph, "who has blown out the candle?"

A joyous shout of laughter answered him.

Some days after Rudolph met one of his friends on the street. "What are you doing now?" the latter asked him. "No one ever sees you."

"I am living my poetry now," Rudolph responded.

The unfortunate one told the truth. He had wanted to ask from Louise more than the poor girl could give. Bagpipe, she had none of the sweetness of the harp. She used, so to speak, the jargon of love, and Rudolph absolutely demanded its lovely poetry from her. So they misunderstood each other completely. A week after, at the same dance hall where she had found Rudolph . . . Louise met a young blond who danced with her several times, and when the party was over he took her to his flat.

He was a second year student, he used the prose of pleasure very well, had nice eyes, and a deep purse. Louise borrowed paper and ink from him and wrote the following letter to Rudolph:

"Don't count on me no more, I embrase you for the last time. Farewell. Louise."

As Rudolph was reading this note that evening when he returned home, his light suddenly gave out.

"There now," said Rudolph reflectively, "that is the candle I lighted the evening when Louise came; it was fated to finish with our liaison. If I had known that, I should have chosen a longer one," he added in a tone half-irritated, half regretful, and he placed his mistress' note in a drawer which he sometimes called the cemetery of his love affairs.

One day, while visiting Marcel, to light his pipe Rudolph picked up a piece of paper upon which he recognized Louise's writing and spelling. "I have," said he to his friend, "an autograph from this same person; only it has two faults less than yours. Does that not prove that she loved me better than you?"

"That proves that you are a simpleton," Marcel growled; "white shoulders and white arms have no need of knowing grammar."

ALI-RUDOLPH OR TURK BY NECESSITY

Ostracized by an unfriendly landlord, Rudolph for some time had been living a life more fugitive than the clouds, and raising to its peak the art of going to bed supperless, or supping without going to bed; his housekeeper was called Chance, and often he lodged at the Beautiful Star Inn.

There were, however, two things which Rudolph never was without during these painful misfortunes, that is to say, his good humour and the manuscript of *The Avenger,* a drama which had had a resting place in every dramatic office in Paris.

One day, as Rudolph was being led to the lockup for indulging in a dance of death which was beyond the pale he found himself face to face with one of his uncles, M. Monetti, stovemaker and chimney builder, sergeant in the National Guard, whom he had not seen for an age.

Affected by the misfortunes of his nephew, Uncle Monetti promised to ease his situation, and we will see how, if the reader is not dismayed by the necessity of mounting six flights of stairs.

"Well, clutch the banister and up let us go. Ouf! One hundred twenty-five steps.—Here we are.—One step more and we are in the room,—another, and we will be out of it—It is small but high,—in addition good air and a good view."

The furniture consisted of several German stoves, two chimneys, some economical furnaces, economical above all when no fire burned in them, a dozen or more stove pipes in red iron or sheet iron, and a mass of heating displays; we must mention also, to complete the inventory, a hammock hung from two hooks in the wall, a garden chair with one leg lost, a chandelier trimmed with a bobeche and various other objects of art and fancy.

As for the second part—the balcony—two dwarf cypresses in pots transformed it into a park for the fine season.

When we enter, the host, a young man dressed as a comic

opera Turk, is partaking of a dinner where he flagrantly violates the law of the prophet, as is shown by what was once a hambone and a bottle recently full of wine. His feast over, the young Turk in oriental fashion threw himself on the floor and casually began to smoke a narghileh marked J. G. Completely under the spell of Asiatic bliss, from time to time he passed his hand over the back of a magnificent Newfoundland dog which doubtless would have responded to his caresses had it not been made of terra cotta.

Suddenly a noise of steps was heard in the corridor and the door of the room was opened permitting a person to enter who without a word went straight to one of the stoves which served as a secretary desk, opened the door of the oven and took from it a sheaf of papers which he studied attentively.

"What!" snorted the newcomer with a pronounced Piedmont accent, "you have not yet finished the chapter on ventilators?"

"If you please, my uncle," replied the Turk, "the chapter on ventilators is one of the most interesting of your work and demands careful study. I am studying it."

"Oh wretch, you tell me the same thing every time. And my chapter on Hot Air Stoves, where the deuce is it?"

"The hot air is going pretty well. But speaking of hot air, uncle, if you could spare me some wood, it wouldn't displease me. This is a small Siberia. I am so cold that if I only looked at the thermometer it would fall below zero."

"You mean you have already used one faggot?"

"Pardon me, uncle, but there are faggots and faggots and yours was very small."

"I will send you an economical lump of coal. That will keep the heat."

"That's just why there's none here."

"Well then," said the man from Piedmont as he was going out, "I will have a little faggot sent up. But I want my chapter on hot air tomorrow."

"When I get a fire I will be inspired," promised the Turk who had just been locked in by a double turn of the key.

If we were making a tragedy, this would be the moment to have a confidant appear. He would be called Noureddin or Osman and with a discreet and at the same time a protective attitude he would approach our hero and cleverly drag from his nose the secret with the help of the following:

> My lord, what fatal grief is troubling you?
> Why on your august brow this pallid hue?
> Has Allah toward your schemes been too severe,
> Or has fierce Ali sent out word austere
> To bear afar, aware of your heart's blaze,
> The beauty who knew how to charm your gaze?

But we aren't making a tragedy at all and in spite of the need we have for a confidant, we are forced to do without.

Our hero isn't at all what he seems to be, a turban doesn't make a Turk. The young man is our friend Rudolph, corralled by his uncle for whom he is really editing a manual on the perfect chimney builder. Actually, M. Monetti, devoted to his art, has given up his life to chimney building. This worthy Piedmontese had made for his own use a maxim almost a counterpart of that of Cicero. In moments of fine enthusiasm, he shouted "Nascuntur stovemakers." One day for the benefit of future races, he dreamed of formulating a theoretical code of the principles of an art in the practice of which he excelled and he had, as we have seen, selected his nephew to arrange the gist of his ideas in a form in which they could be understood. Rudolph was fed, slept, and lodged, etc., and was at the completion of the manual to receive a stipend of one hundred écus. At first to encourage his nephew at his work Monetti had generously advanced him fifty francs. —But Rudolph who had not seen so much money for a year departed half crazy, taking his écus with him and he stayed away three days; the fourth day he returned, alone!

Monetti, who was in a hurry to see his manual finished for he counted on winning a decoration, feared further escapades on his nephew's part; so to force him to work by making it impossible for him to leave he took all his clothes and left in their place the disguising costume in which we just now saw him.

Meanwhile the manual didn't proceed less slowly, as Rudolph utterly lacked certain necessary enthusiasm for this type of literature. The uncle got his revenge for this lazy indifference to stoves by forcing his nephew to undergo no end of annoyances. Ever so often he cut down on his dinners and often took away his smoking tobacco.

One Sunday, after painfully sweating blood and ink over the famous chapter on drafts, Rudolph broke his pen which was burning his fingers, and went to walk in his park.

As if to plague him and increase his longing even more he couldn't take a single glance around him without seeing at every window someone smoking. On the gilded balcony of a new house an elegant lion in a dressing gown chewed between his teeth a proud cigar. One floor above an artist blew smoke smelling of Turkish tobacco from a pipe with an amber stem. At the window of a taproom a big German's beer foamed and he exhaled with a mechanical precision dense clouds of smoke through a Cudmer pipe. On the other side a crowd of workmen returning to the outskirts of the city, were singing as they passed, a short-pipe in each one's mouth. As a last straw all the pedestrians who filled the street were smoking.

"Alas," said Rudolph enviously, "at this moment in the world everyone is smoking save me and the stoves of my uncle."

And Rudolph, his forehead buried on the railing of the balcony, meditated on the bitterness of life.

Suddenly he heard a great and prolonged shout of laughter below him. Rudolph leaned out a little to see whence came this burst of carefree joy and he perceived that he had been seen by the lodger just below, Mademoiselle Sidonie, young leading lady of the Luxembourg theatre.

Mademoiselle Sidonie came forward on the landing rolling between her fingers with all the skill of a Castilian, a little paper filled with light tobacco, which she took from an embroidered velvet bag.

"Oh the lovely tobacco girl," murmured Rudolph in thoughtful admiration.

"Who is this Ali Baba?" wondered Mademoiselle Sidonie at the same time.

And she thought very hard for a pretext for talking to Rudolph who on his part was searching for a similar excuse.

"Oh, dear!" exclaimed Mademoiselle Sidonie, as if talking to herself. "The devil, how irritating! To think I haven't a match."

"Mademoiselle, will you permit me to offer you some?" asked Rudolph as he let fall on the balcony two or three matches wrapped up in a paper.

"A thousand thanks," Sidonie responded as she lit her cigarette.

"I say, Mademoiselle" . . . Rudolph went on, "in exchange for the small service which my good angel has let me do for you, do I dare ask something from you?"

"Aha! he wants something so soon," thought Sidonie, looking at Rudolph more attentively.

"Oh," said she, "these Turks! they say they're fickle but most attractive. Speak, sir," she encouraged, raising her head toward Rudolph. "What do you wish?"

"For pity's sake, Mademoiselle, I beg a little tobacco from you; it has been two days since I've had a smoke. One pipeful only . . ."

"With pleasure, sir . . . But how? Will you trouble to come down?"

"Alas, that is not possible for me. I am locked in; but there remains the possibility of using a very simple strategem," said Rudolph.

And he tied his pipe to a piece of string and let it slide down to the next landing, where Mademoiselle Sidonie filled it very full. Rudolph began the ascension of his pipe at once with slowness and care; it arrived without mishap.

"Ah, Mademoiselle," he called to Sidonie, "how much better this pipe would seem had I been able to light it by the flame of your eyes."

This charming compliment was in at least its hundredth edition but Mademoiselle Sidonie found it no less gratifying.

"How you flatter me!" she felt she had to respond.

"But, Mademoiselle, I assure you that you seem beautiful as the three graces to me."

"Decidedly Ali Baba is most gallant," Sidonie thought. . . .
"Are you a real Turk?" she inquired of Rudolph.

"Not through choice but by necessity," he responded; "I am
a dramatic writer, Madame."

"And I a dramatic artist," continued Sidonie; then she added:
"Monsieur my neighbour, will you do me the honour of dining
and spending this evening with me?"

"Oh, Mademoiselle," sighed Rudolph, "though this invitation
gives me a view of heaven I cannot accept it. As I have the
honour of telling you, I am locked in by my uncle, M. Monetti,
stove and chimney maker, whose secretary I am really."

"You will dine none the less with me," replied Sidonie; "listen to this: I shall go in my room and knock on the ceiling. At
the spot where I knock look and you will find traces of a peep
hole which was formerly in existence and has been condemned
since; find the opportunity to remove the wood which stops
up the hole and although each of us will be at home we will almost
be together. . . ."

Rudolph began at once. After five minutes' toil, communica-
tion was established between the two rooms.

"Ah," lamented Rudolph, "the hole is small but there will
always be enough room for me to send my heart through to
you."

"Now," said Sidonie, "we will eat. Lay the cloth. I am going
to hand you the dishes."

Rudolph let his turban attached to a string slide down and
brought it back filled with things to eat, then the poet and the
actress began to dine together, each in his own corner. With his
teeth Rudolph devoured a patty and with his eyes Mademoiselle
Sidonie.

"Alas, Mademoiselle," said Rudolph when they had finished,
"thanks to you, my body has had nourishment. Won't you still
the hunger of my heart which has been fasting for so long?"

"Poor lad!" pitied Sidonie. And getting up on a chair she
raised her hand to Rudolph's lips for which he made a glove of
kisses.

"Oh," sobbed the young man, "what a misfortune that you

cannot do as Saint Denis, who could carry his head in his hands."

After dinner they commenced an exchange of talk on love and literature. Rudolph spoke of *The Avenger,* and Mademoiselle Sidonie demanded a reading. Suspended over the edge of the hole Rudolph began to declaim his play to the actress who to be nearer had seated herself in a chair mounted on a chest of drawers. Mademoiselle Sidonie pronounced *The Avenger* a great work; and as she was somewhat of a power in the theatre she promised to have his play accepted.

At the most touching point in the communion, Uncle Monetti was heard in the hall, his step light as a commander's. Rudolph had just enough time to close the hole.

"Here," Monetti addressed his nephew, "is a letter which has been following you for a month."

"Let me see," said Rudolph.—"Oh, Uncle," he shouted, "Uncle, I am rich! This letter announces that I have received a prize of three hundred francs from the Academy for floral games. Quick! My frock coat and my things, I must run to collect my laurels! They expect me at the Capitol."

"What about my chapter on ventilators?" asked Monetti coldly.

"Oh! Uncle, that is certainly not the question! Give me my things, I can't go out in this regalia."

"You will only leave when my manual is finished," said the uncle locking Rudolph in with a double turn of the key.

Left alone, it didn't take Rudolph long to make up his mind what to do. He tied a counterpane knotted into a rope very tightly to the railing, and in spite of the danger of the attempt he descended with the aid of this improvised ladder to Sidonie's balcony.

"Who's there?" she cried, hearing Rudolph knock on the shutters.

"Silence," he said, "open . . ."

"What do you want? Who are you?"

"How can you ask? I am the author of *The Avenger* and I am looking for my heart which I dropped in this room through the hole."

"Crazy man, you might have killed yourself."

"Listen, Sidonie," Rudolph went on, showing her the letter he had just received, "you see, fortune and fame are smiling on me. Let love do likewise."

The next morning, with the aid of a masculine disguise which Sidonie had provided, Rudolph managed to escape from his uncle's house. He hurried to the correspondent of the Academy

for floral games to receive a golden eglantine valued at one hundred écus, which survived almost as long as roses do.

A month later, M. Monetti was invited by his nephew to be present at the first night of *The Avenger*. Thanks to Mademoiselle Sidonie's talent his play was given seventeen times and the author received forty francs.

Some time later it was summer time, Rudolph was living on the avenue de Saint Cloud in the third tree on the left, the fifth branch, as one leaves the Bois du Boulogne.

THE CHARLEMAGNE CROWN

TOWARD the end of December the messengers of the Bidault agency were ordered to distribute about one hundred examples of an invitation, the following copy of which we swear is authentic.

Messrs. Rudolph and Marcel beg you to do them the honour of spending the evening with them, next Saturday, Christmas eve— It will be fun!

P. S. We only have one life to live.

Program of the Celebration.

At 7 o'clock, opening of the drawing-rooms; witty and lively conversation.

At 8 o'clock, entrance and promenade in the drawing-rooms of the spiritual authors of *The Mountain in Childbirth*, a comedy refused by the Odeon theatre.

At 8:30 o'clock, M. Alexander Schaunard, distinguished virtuoso, will perform upon the piano *The Influence of Blue on the Arts*, an imitative symphony.

At 9 o'clock, first reading of *The Bill on Abolition of Suffering from Tragedy*.

At 9:30 o'clock, M. Gustave Colline, hyperphysical philosopher, and M. Schaunard will begin a discussion of the comparison of philosophy and meta-politics. In order to avoid any collision between the two opponents they will be tied to each other.

At 10 o'clock, M. Tristan, man of letters, will speak of his first love affairs. M. Alexander Schaunard will accompany him on the piano.

At 10:30 o'clock, second reading of the *Bill on the Abolishment of suffering from Tragedy*.

At 11 o'clock, Recitation of *A Hunt for the Cassowary*, by a foreign prince.

Second half.

At Midnight, M. Marcel, historical painter, will be blindfolded and will improvise in white crayon the meeting of

Napoleon and Voltaire in the Champs Élysées. M. Rudolph will improvise likewise a similar meeting between the author of *Zaïre* and the author of the *Battle of Austerlitz*.

At 12:30, M. Gustave Colline, in a modest state of undress will imitate the athletic games of the fourth Olympiad.

At 1 A. M. third reading of the bill on the *Abolishment of Suffering from Tragedy* and an offering for the benefit of tragic authors who one day will find themselves without a job.

At 2 A. M., beginning of the games and organizing of the quadrilles which will last until morning.

At 6 o'clock, rising of the sun and final chorus.

During the whole fête ventilators will play.

N. B. Every person who would like to read or recite some poems will be at once thrown out of the drawing-rooms and given over to the police; you are also asked not to carry away the ends of the candles.

Two days later, copies of this letter were circulated widely in the lowest and humblest literary and art circles and created there a tremendous stir.

Meanwhile, among those invited, there were some who doubted the elegance foretold by the two friends.

"I doubt it much," one of the sceptical announced; "sometimes I have been at Rudolph's Wednesdays, rue de la Tour-d'Auvergne, where there were only spiritual chairs available, and where water slightly filtered in special jars was drunk."

"This time," said another, "it will be serious. Marcel showed me the prospectus of the entertainment and it's going to be tremendous."

"Will any ladies be there?"

"Yes, Phemie Teinturiere asked to be queen of the festival and Schaunard is to bring some ladies of the world."

In a few words the following is the origin of this party which caused such agitation in the Bohemian quarter beyond the bridges. For almost a year Marcel and Rudolph had been talking about this elegant entertainment which was always to take place the following Saturday; but unfavorable circumstances had forced them to make their promises for every week for fifty-two weeks so that it had come to a point where they could not take a step without having sarcastic remarks hurled at them from their friends, none of which was so exaggerated that they could find proper objections to them. When the business had reached the point when it was a bore the two friends decided to finish it by actually coming through with a party. For this reason they had issued the above invitation.

"Now," Rudolph had said, "there is no retreat, we have burned our bridges, there remain eight days for us to find the hundred francs necessary to do this well."

"Since we need them we will find them," Marcel replied.

And with the implicit faith that they had in Chance the two  friends went to sleep, sure that the hundred francs were on the road, the road of the impossible.

However, when nothing had happened, the day before the day for the party, Rudolph felt that perhaps it would be safe to assist Chance if he did not wish to be disgraced when the time came to light the lights. To make it easier the two modified little by little the elaborate program which they had planned. And from one deduction to another, after having deleted the word cakes, after having carefully gone over it again and diminished the refreshments, the total outlay they found could be reduced to fifteen francs. The problem was simplified but not quite solved.

"Let's see, let's see," said Rudolph, "we must use all our wits, for we can't fail this time."

"Impossible," agreed Marcel.

"How long has it been since I have heard the recitation of the battle of Studzianka?"

"Almost two months."

"Two months, grand, that's a real interlude. My uncle will have nothing to complain about. Tomorrow I will let him tell me the battle of Studzianka again. That will bring me five francs, surely."

"And I," said Marcel, "I will sell a Deserted Manor House

to old Medicis. That will bring five francs too. If I have time enough to add three towers and a mill perhaps it will bring ten francs and we shall have completed our budget."

And the friends went to sleep and dreamed that the princess Belgioioso begged them to change their reception day so as not to take away all her habitual guests.

Awakening in the early morning Marcel took a canvas and immediately began to make the abandoned Manor, a subject which was especially in demand by a second-hand man in the place du Carrousel. For his share, Rudolph went to call on his uncle Monetti, who excelled in the relation of the Retreat from Russia and to whom Rudolph when under serious pressure offered the satisfaction of telling his campaigns five or six times a year in consideration of a loan which the old stove and chimney maker never questioned if he showed enough enthusiasm for the rendition of these favourites.

After two hours, Marcel, head bowed and carrying under his arm the canvas, met, at the place du Carrousel, Rudolph who had just come from his uncle. His expression foretold bad news.

"Well," asked Marcel, "did you succeed?"

"No, my uncle went to see the Versailles museum. And you?"

"That beast of a Medicis no longer wants Ruined Castles. He asked for the Bombarding of Tangiers."

"Our reputation is gone if we do not have this party," wailed Rudolph. "What will my friend, the influential critic, think if I make him put on a white necktie and yellow gloves for nothing?"

And they both returned to the studio prey to the keenest worry. Just then four o'clock was striking on a neighbouring clock.

"We have only four more hours left," said Rudolph.

"But," pleaded Marcel going over to his friend, "are you absolutely sure that no money is left here? Huh?"

"Neither here nor any place else. Where would it come from, this money that is left?"

"If we looked under the furniture . . . in the chairs? They say that the refugees hid their valuables in Robespierre's time. Who knows! . . . Our arm-chair perhaps belonged to a refugee and then it is so hard that I have often thought it contained metal work. . . . Do you wish to make an autopsy?"

"This is a good show," Rudolph's tone was a combination of a severe and an indulgent one. Suddenly Marcel who had continued his excavations in every corner of the studio uttered a triumphant cry.

"We are saved," he shouted, "I was positive that there was treasure here. I say, look!"

And he showed Rudolph a piece of money as large as an écu and half eaten by rust and verdigris. The money came from the Carlovingian age and was of some value to collectors. Upon the face, luckily preserved, could be read the date of the reign of Charlemagne. "That, that is worth thirty sous," said Rudolph glancing disdainfully at his friend's find.

"Thirty sous well employed can work wonders," responded Marcel. "With twelve hundred men Bonaparte made ten thousand Austrians give up their arms. Skill helps. I shall go change this écu of Charlemagne at père Medicis'. Isn't there something else we can sell here? Say, in fact, if I took the cast of the tibia of Jacnowski, the Russian drum major, that would help."

"Take the tibia. But it is unfortunate that there won't be one single object of art left here."

During Marcel's absence, Rudolph, firmly resolved to give the party in spite of everything, went to see his friend Colline, the hyperphysical philosopher who lived just two steps away.

"I've come to beg you to do me a favour. In my position as host it is absolutely necessary for me to have a black suit and I haven't one. Lend me yours."

"But," Colline hesitated a bit, "in my capacity as guest I need my black suit too."

"I will let you come in your frock coat."

"I never had a frock coat, you know well."

"Well, listen, it can be managed differently. If necessary you needn't come to my party; then you could lend me your black suit."

"That is very unsatisfactory; then too, I am on the program. I can't be absent."

"There are certainly other things which will be," countered

Rudolph. "Lend me your black suit and if you want to come, come as you like—in shirt sleeves—you will pass as a faithful servant."

"No, no," said Colline blushing. "I will wear my nut-coloured overcoat—but really all this is very unpleasant."

And as he saw that Rudolph had already possessed himself of the famous black suit, he begged:

"But wait a minute. There are a few little things in it."

Colline's suit deserves notice. Frst, this suit was completely blue, but it was customary for Colline to say his black suit. And as he was at the time the only one of the group owning a suit, his friends likewise were accustomed to refer to the philosopher's state clothing as Colline's black suit. Furthermore, this famous garment had a special shape, just as strange as anyone could see: the tails, very long, attached to a very short body had two pockets, real abysses in which Colline was in the habit of keeping thirty or so books, which he eternally carried with him, which fact made his friends say that during the closed season of the libraries, students or literary men could look up information in the pockets of Colline's suit—a library always open to readers.

Strange to say, this day Colline's suit contained but one quarto volume of Bayle, a treatise on the hyperphysical mind in 3 volumes, a tome of Condillac, two volumes of Swedenborg and Pope's *Essay on Man*. When he had emptied his suit library he let Rudolph dress in it.

"See here," the latter said, "the left pocket is still heavy—you have left something."

"Oh," said Colline, "that's so; I forgot to empty the pockets of the foreign language section." And he took out two Arabic grammars, a Malayan dictionary and a *Perfect Bouvier* in Chinese, his favourite reading.

When Rudolph got home he found Marcel playing quoits with three five franc pieces. At first Rudolph refused the hand his friend offered him—he feared a crime.

"Hurry, hurry," said Marcel. "We have the fifteen francs needed. This is how: I met an antiquarian at Medicis'. When he saw my sample he didn't think it so bad. It was the only one lacking in his medal cabinet. He has sent everywhere to fill up this gap and had lost all hope. So, when he had examined my écu well he didn't hesitate a moment to offer me five francs. Medici nudged me with his elbow, his look supplied the rest. He meant: We divide the spoils of this sale and I will out-bid him. We raised it to thirty francs. I gave the Jew fifteen and here is the rest. Now our guests can come—we are equipped to dazzle them. Oh say, you have a black suit?"

"Yes," said Rudolph, "Colline's suit."

And as he fumbled in his pocket to find his handkerchief Rudolph let fall a little volume in Manchurian, forgotten in the section on foreign language.

The two friends began their preparations at once. One arranged the studio, one made a fire in the stove;— a canvas frame ornamented with candles was hung from the ceiling in lieu of a chandelier. A chest of drawers was placed in the centre of the studio to serve as a platform for the orators. In front of it they put the only chair, which was to be occupied by the influential critic, and they scattered on a table all the volumes, romances, poems, leaflets, whose authors were to honour the occasion by their presence. To avoid any friction between the different groups of literary lights, the studio throughout had been divided in four sections, at the entrance of each of which upon four placards hastily made could be read—

RESERVED FOR POETS   ROMANTIC
RESERVED FOR PROSE WRITERS   CLASSIC

The women were to have a place practically in the centre.

"Oh, dear, how we need chairs," said Rudolph.

"Oh!" said Marcel, "there are several on the landing fastened to the wall—if we could get them."

"Indeed we must get them," said Rudolph as he went after the benches which belonged to some neighbours.

It struck six. The two went to dine very speedily and returned to proceed with the lighting of the drawing-rooms. They themselves were dazzled.

At seven Schaunard appeared accompanied by three women who had forgotten to bring their diamonds and their hats. One of them had a red shawl stained with black. Schaunard designated her especially for Rudolph.

"She is a very proper lady," he said, "an English woman forced into exile by the fall of the Stuarts. She lives simply by giving English lessons—her father was chancellor under Cromwell, according to what she told me. You must be polite to her and don't call her by her first name too often."

Numerous steps were heard on the stairs. The guests were arriving. They seemed astonished to see fire in the stove. Rudolph's black suit met the ladies and he kissed their hands in true regency style.

When twenty people had come Schaunard asked if there would not be some kind of refreshment.

"In a minute," said Marcel. "We are waiting for the influential critic to arrive to light the punch."

At eight the guests were all assembled and the program was begun. Each act was alternated with a round of something—no one ever knew what.

Toward ten the white front of the influential critic appeared; he stayed only an hour and was very temperate in his drinking. At midnight, as there was no more wood and it was very cold, the guests who were seated drew lots to see who would throw his chair in the fire.

At one everyone was standing.

A friendly gaiety never ceased to exist among the guests. There were no mishaps to regret, except a hole made in the foreign language department of Colline's suit and a smack Schaunard gave the daughter of Cromwell's chancellor.

This memorable party was the talk of the quarter for a week and Phemie Teinturiere who had been queen of the ball was in the habit of saying when referring to it to her friends—"It was superbly beautiful; they had a candle, my dear."

MADEMOISELLE MUSETTE

MADEMOISELLE MUSETTE was an attractive twenty year old girl, who, a short time after her arrival in Paris, had become what pretty girls do become when they have a fine body, lots of coquetry, some ambition, and no spelling. After having been the joy of suppers in the Latin Quarter for a long time, where she had made a name for herself by singing with a voice continually fresh, if not always true, rustic table songs, which the finest connoisseurs of rhymes have since praised, Mademoiselle Musette suddenly left the rue de la Harpe to go to live on the Cytherean heights of the Breda Quarter. She was not slow in becoming one of the queens of the aristocracy of pleasure and little by little made her way toward that goal of fame which consists in being mentioned in the Paris newspapers or having one's pictures on sale at all print dealers.

However, Mademoiselle Musette was an exception to the women among whom she lived. It was her nature, instinctively refined and poetic, like all women who are truly women, to love luxury and all the pleasures luxury brings in its wake. Her coquetry had flaming desires for whatever was beautiful and distinguished; daughter of the people, she had never once been out of her element in the midst of the most regal splendours. But Mademoiselle Musette, who was young and beautiful, would never be willing to be the mistress of a man who was not as young and handsome as she. She had been once seen refusing courageously the splendid offers of an old man, so rich that he was called the Peru of the Chaussée d'Antin, and he had built a gold stairway for Musette's whimsical feet. Sensible and clever, she had a horror of fools and simpletons whatever their age, title, or name. She was a fine and beautiful girl was this Musette, who in love adopted in part the famous epigram of Champfort: Love is the interchange of two whims. Furthermore, never had her liaisons been preceded by one of those shameful bargains

which dishonour modern chivalry. As she said herself, Musette played fair and demanded that she be paid in the currency of sincerity.

But if her whims were violent and sudden, they were never sufficiently lasting to reach the pitch of passion. And the great elasticity of her feelings, the little attention she paid to the purses, and to the rank of those who wished to court her, gave a great mobility to her life, which was perpetually alternating between blue coupés and omnibuses, mezzanines and the fifth floor, silk gowns and Indian cotton dresses. O lovely girl! Living poem of youth, with the deep laugh and the gay song! Heart full of pity, beating for the whole world underneath the revealing blouse. O Mademoiselle Musette! You who are the sister of Bernerette and of Mimi Pinson! It would take the genius of Alfred de Musset to describe worthily the carefree and wandering way you took through the flowery paths of youth; and surely he would have liked to praise you too, if like me he had heard you sing with your sweet false notes the rural couplet of one of your favourite roundelays!

The tale we are going to tell is one of the most charming episodes in the whole career of this charming adventuress who has hurled so many bonnets over so many mills.

At one time when she was the mistress of a young state's councillor who had munificently put into her hands the key to his inheritance, Mademoiselle Musette was in the habit of giving a reception once a week in her lovely drawing-room on the rue de la Bruyère. These receptions were like most Parisian receptions with the difference that here everyone enjoyed himself; when there was no place left to sit down they sat on each other, and it was often necessary for two people to use the same glass. Rudolph, who was Musette's friend and only a friend (neither one ever knew why), asked Musette permission to bring his friend Marcel with him; a talented young man, he added, for whom the future is busy embroidering an academician's robe.

"Fetch him along," said Musette.

The evening when they were to go to Musette's Rudolph went to Marcel's to take him. The artist was dressing himself.

"What," asked Rudolph, "are you going out in society in a coloured shirt?"

"Does that wound custom?" asked Marcel quietly.

"Does it wound it? Why it's enough to draw blood, simpleton."

"The devil," said Marcel looking at his shirt which had a white background with pictures representing wild boars followed by a pack of hounds, "I have no other here. Oh bother, so much the worse; I will use a false collar, and as Methuselah buttons up to the neck no one will see the colour of my shirt."

"What, you are still wearing Methuselah?" Rudolph was worried.

"Alas!" sighed Marcel. "It is necessary; God and my tailor too wish it; still there is a garniture of new buttons and I have darned it just now with some fishing line."

Methuselah was simply Marcel's suit; he so called it because it was the oldest member of his wardrobe. Methuselah was made in the latest fashion of forty years ago, furthermore it was of a terrific green colour, but in the lights Marcel swore that it looked black.

After five minutes, Marcel was dressed, dressed in the most perfect bad taste; the outfit of a dauber going into society.

Casimir Bonjour will never be as astonished the day he is told of his nomination to the Institute as Marcel and Rudolph were on arriving at Musette's house. This is the reason. Mademoiselle Musette, who for some time had been quarrelling with her lover, the state's councillor, had been deserted by him at a very critical moment. As she was pursued by her proprietor and her creditors, her belongings had been seized and removed to the courtyard to be taken away and sold the next day. In spite of this event, Mademoiselle Musette never thought of telling her guests not to come and did not give up her reception. She solemnly turned the courtyard into a drawing-room, put a rug on the pavement, got everything in readiness as usual, dressed herself to receive, and invited all the lodgers to her little party, to the splendour of which God kindly volunteered to provide illumination.

This joke was tremendously successful. Never had any of

Musette's receptions had such animation and gaiety; they were still dancing and singing when the agents came to take away the furnishings, rugs, and divans, and perforce the guests had to go home.

Musette sang as the party dispersed:

> They'll talk a long while, la ri ra,
>   Of my Thursday evening party—
> They'll talk a long while—la ri ri.

Marcel and Rudolph were left alone with Musette who mounted to her apartment where nothing remained but the bed.

"Ah me," sighed Musette, "my adventure isn't so amusing now; I'll have to go lodge at the Beautiful Star Inn. I know it well, that inn; there are terrible drafts."

"Ah! madame," said Marcel, "if I had the powers of the God Pluto I would give you a temple more beautiful than Solomon's. But . . ."

"You are not Pluto, my friend. It doesn't make any difference, I appreciate the idea. Oh well," she added glancing around at her apartment, "all this bores me here, and then the furniture was old. I've had it almost six months. But that isn't the worst of it all; after the ball one sups, I suppose."

"Let us sup . . . pose then," said Marcel who had the disease of punning especially in the morning, when he was horrible.

As Rudolph had won some money at poker, which he had played during the evening, he took Musette and Marcel into a restaurant which was just opening.

After lunch, the three friends, who had no wish to sleep, discussed spending the day in the country, and as they were near a railroad they took the first train to leave and got off at Saint Germain.

All day they strolled through the woods and did not return to Paris until seven that evening and then in spite of Marcel, who insisted that it must only be twelve-thirty and if it was growing dark it was because the weather was cloudy.

During the night of the reception and all the rest of the day Marcel whose heart was an explosive which one glance could ignite, had been smitten with Mademoiselle Musette and had made violent love to her, as he said to Rudolph. He had been just about to offer to buy the beautiful girl surroundings more beautiful even than her old ones with the income from the sale of his famous picture of the *Crossing of the Red Sea.* So the Artist saw with pain the time arrive when he would have to separate from Musette, who in permitting him to kiss her hands, her neck, and various other accessories, limited herself to shoving him gently away every time that he wished to force an entry to her heart.

On arriving at Paris, Rudolph had left his friend with the young girl who begged the artist to accompany her to her door.

"Will you let me come to see you?" Marcel asked. "I will do your portrait."

"My dear," said the pretty girl, "I cannot give you my address since perhaps I will have none tomorrow but I will come to see you and I will mend your suit which has such a big hole in it that one could walk out of it without paying."

"I will look for you as for the Messiah," promised Marcel.

"It won't be long," laughed Musette.

"What a lovely girl," mused Marcel as he walked slowly away. "She is the incarnation of gaiety. I will make two holes in my suit."

He had not gone thirty feet when he was tapped on the shoulder; it was Musette.

"My dear Mr. Marcel," she said, "are you a French knight?"

"I am Rubens and my lady, that is my device."

"Well then, listen to my tale of woe and have pity, noble sire," began Musette, who was slightly affected by literature, although her slaughter of grammar amounted to a St. Bartholomew's massacre; "my proprietor has taken my apartment key and it is eleven o'clock: do you understand?"

"I understand," said Marcel offering his arm to Musette. He

took her to his studio, situated along the Quai des Fleurs. Musette was drooping with sleep, but she had still enough strength to say to Marcel as she pressed his hand: "You remember what you have promised me."

"O Musette! charming girl," said the artist in a slightly strained tone, "you are here under a friendly roof, sleep in peace, I am going away."

"Why?" asked Musette, her eyes almost closed; "I have no fear, I promise you; besides there are two rooms. I will sleep on your sofa."

"My sofa is too hard to sleep on; there are cobblestones in it. I am giving you my bed; I will ask for one for myself from a friend who lives on my landing. It is more prudent," he said. "I ordinarily keep my word, but I am twenty-two and you are eighteen, O Musette . . . and I am going away. Goodnight."

The next morning at 8 o'clock Marcel came back with a pot of flowers which he had bought at the market. He found Musette asleep where she had thrown herself on the bed, still dressed. At the noise he made she woke up and held out her hand to Marcel.

"Good boy," she said to him.

"Good boy," repeated Marcel, "aren't you making fun of me?"

"Oh, why do you say that?" asked Musette. "That isn't nice of you; instead of saying unpleasant things, offer me that pretty pot of flowers."

"That's really why I brought them up. Take them and in return for my hospitality sing me one of your lovely songs; the echo of my roof will perhaps keep a bit of your voice and I shall still hear you after you have gone."

"Oh so! you want to put me out?" asked Musette. "And if I don't want to go! Listen Marcel, I haven't mounted thirty-six steps not to say what I think. You please me and I please you. It isn't love but it is perhaps the beginning. Well, I am not going to leave, I stay and I will stay here as long as the flowers which you just gave me do not fade."

"Ah!" Marcel cried, "but they will be withered in two days. If I'd only known I would have bought immortelles."

For two weeks Musette and Marcel had lived together and led, though often without money, the most lovely life in the world. Musette felt for the artist a tenderness which had no relation to her former passions, and Marcel began to fear that he was seriously in love with his mistress. Not knowing that she was at all worried over being too fond of him, he looked every morning to see the condition the flowers were in whose death was to bring to end their liaison, and he couldn't explain their freshness each day. But he soon found the secret of the mystery. One night on waking, Musette was no longer at his side. He got up, went into the room, and saw his mistress who was taking advantage of his sleep every night to water the flowers and keep them from dying.

RIVERS OF GOLD

IT was the nineteenth of March. . . . And were he to attain the advanced age of M. Raoul Rochette, who had seen the building of Nineveh, Rudolph will never forget that date for it was that very day of Saint Joseph at three o'clock in the afternoon when our friend left the bank where he had just drawn a sum of five hundred francs in hard current cash.

The first use Rudolph made of this small fortune which had just fallen into his pocket was not to pay his debts, as he had sworn to himself to be economical and not to do anything extra. Moreover on this subject he had some extremely fixed ideas, and said that before considering luxuries he had to think of necessities. That is why he paid none of his creditors and bought instead a Turkish pipe which he had coveted for a long time.

Fortified by this purchase he started for the lodging of his friend Marcel, who had been putting him up for some time. As he entered the artist's studio, Rudolph's pockets jingled like a village chime on a grand holiday. Hearing this unusual noise, Marcel supposed it was one of his neighbours, a great bear operator, going over the proceeds of his killing and he complained:

"There is that plotter next door at his schemes again. If this keeps up I am going to give notice. There is no chance of working in such a tumult. It makes one think of substituting for the state of poor artist that of the forty thieves."

And not having the slightest idea in the world that his friend Rudolph had been changed into a Croesus, Marcel set at his painting of the *Crossing of the Red Sea,* which canvas had been on the easel now for three years.

Rudolph, who had not yet said a word, meditating quietly on an experiment he was going to make on his friend, said to himself:—"We will soon have a good laugh. My God, how jolly it will be!"

And he dropped a five franc piece on the floor.

Marcel raised his eyes and regarded Rudolph, who appeared as solemn as an article in the *Revue des Deux Mondes*.

The artist picked up the money with a most satisfied air and pocketed it very graciously, for, although a mere dauber, he knew how to live and was very polite to strangers. Knowing, also, that Rudolph had gone out to look for money, Marcel, seeing now that his friend had succeeded in his foray, limited himself to admiring the result without asking by aid of what resources it had been obtained. He again started back to his work without a word, and managed to drown an Egyptian in the waves of the Red Sea. As he was achieving this murder, Rudolph dropped a second five franc piece. And when he saw the expression of the painter's face he started to smile in his beard, which as everyone knows is particoloured.

At the low metallic sound Marcel, as if shocked by electricity, jumped up quickly and shouted:

"What! Is there a second verse?"

A third piece rolled on the floor, then another, still another; finally a flock of écus began to dance a quadrille in the room.

Marcel commenced to give visible signs of going mad, and Rudolph laughed as they do in the orchestra seats of the Theatre-Français at the first performance of *Jeanne of Flanders*. Suddenly, and without reserve, he fumbled with both hands in his pockets and the écus began a fabulous steeple chase. It was the inundation of Pactolus, Jupiter's revel with the Danaë.

Marcel was still, silent, his eye glazed; his agitation little by little effected a change in him similar to that of Lot's wife when long ago she was a victim of curiosity. And as Rudolph threw on the floor his last pile of one hundred francs, one-half of the artist's body had already turned to salt.

As for Rudolph, he continued to laugh. And compared with this thundersome hilarity, the roars of an orchestra of M. Sax would have seemed like the sighs of a nursing infant for the breast of its mother.

Overcome, stifled, dumb with emotion, Marcel believed that

he was dreaming; and to chase away the nightmare which possessed him he bit his finger till blood came, which pained him so terribly that he had to cry.

He was sure then that he was thoroughly awake; and seeing the oceans of gold at his feet he moaned as in a tragedy: "Can I believe my eyes?" Then he added, taking Rudolph's hand in his: "Explain this mystery to me."

"If I explained it to you, there wouldn't be one any longer."

"But please do."

"This gold is the fruit of my labours," said Rudolph, as he gathered up the money, which he arranged on the table, then retreating a few steps he gazed with respect at the piles of five hundred francs and thought to himself:

"Is it really now that my dreams will come true?"

"There must be not much less than six thousand francs," Marcel said as he contemplated the écus which trembled on the table. "I have an idea. I am going to make Rudolph buy my *Passage of the Red Sea.*"

Suddenly Rudolph assumed a theatrical pose and with a very solemn gesture and tone he addressed the artist:

"Listen to me, Marcel, the fortune which I made glitter under your eyes is not in the least the result of evil moves. I have not trafficked with my pen, I am rich but honest. This money was given me by a generous hand and I have sworn to use it to achieve through work a dignified position for a virtuous man. Work is the most holy of duties."

"And the horse is the most noble of animals," Marcel interrupted Rudolph. "But say!" he added, "what does this talk mean, where do you get your ideas? From studying the careers of the common-sense school, doubtless."

"Don't interrupt me and cease your shots of impertinence," warned Rudolph, "they would moreover glance off my helmet of invulnerable goodwill in which I am clothed hereafter."

"Here, here, that's enough of a prologue. What are you aiming at?"

"This is my plan. Protected from the real difficulties of living, I am going to do serious work; I will accomplish my great labour

and establish myself solidly in public opinion. First, I am re-
nouncing Bohemia. I am dressing like everyone else. I shall have
a black suit, and I shall frequent drawing-rooms. If you wish to
follow in my wake we shall go on living together but you will
have to do as I do. Strictest economy will rule our life. Knowing
how to manage, we shall have three months of work assured
with no further bother attached. But economy is necessary."

"Friend," urged Marcel, "economy is a science only for those
who have means, a fact which makes you and me ignorant
of its first principles. Yet if you will advance six francs from
the common fund, we can buy the works of M. Jean Baptiste
Say, a very distinguished economist,
and he perhaps will instruct us in
the practice of this art. . . . Look,
you have a Turkish pipe, you?"

"Yes," Rudolph said, "I bought
it for twenty-five francs."

"My God, you spend twenty-
five francs for a pipe . . . and still
you talk of economy."

"And this is a real economy,"
Rudolph contended: "Every day I
break a two sous pipe. By the end
of the year that means an outlay
much greater than this that I have just made. . . . You see it
is an actual saving."

"Why, you are right," said Marcel. . . . "I would never have
thought of that."

At this point a neighbouring clock struck six.

"Let's get dinner over quickly," remarked Rudolph, "I want
to begin this evening. But, speaking of dinner, I've just had a
thought: Each day while we prepare our meals we are losing
precious time; and time means money to the worker, therefore,
we must save it. Beginning with today we will dine in the
city."

"Yes," encouraged Marcel, "twenty steps from here there is
an excellent restaurant, a little expensive, to be sure, but as it

is so close the time going will be short and we will make on the saving of time."

"We will do so today," Rudolph agreed; "but tomorrow or after, we will consider a scheme even more economical,—instead of going to a restaurant we will get a cook."

"No, no," Marcel interrupted, "rather a general servant who will do the cooking. Look at a few of the advantages which will follow. First, our housekeeping will always be done, he will clean our boots, he will wash our brushes, he will do our errands. I shall try even to develop in him a taste for the beautiful and I shall make a pupil out of him. We shall save at least six hours a day in trouble and in annoyances which would be injurious to our work."

"Oh," Rudolph chimed in, "I have another thought, I have. . . . . But let's go eat."

Five minutes later, the two friends were settled in one of the booths of the neighbouring restaurant, and were busy thinking of further economy.

"Now this is my idea,—if instead of getting a servant we get a mistress?" It was Rudolph who launched this.

"A mistress for two!" Marcel was astonished, "that would be avarice carried to an extreme and we would waste all we could save by buying knives to cut the other's throat. I prefer the servant; but we must think it over."

"Actually we will get us an intelligent man servant," Rudolph went on, "and if he has even a smattering of spelling I shall teach him how to write."

"That would be a solace for him in his old age," murmured Marcel, who was adding up the bill which came to fifteen francs. "There, that's dear enough. Generally we dine for thirty sous for the two of us."

"Yes," Rudolph responded, "but we dined so insufficiently that it was necessary to have supper in the evening. Taking it all in all, it is certainly a saving."

"You are, like the strongest," murmured the artist, overcome by this logic, "you are ever right. Shall we work this evening?"

"Heavens, no. I am going to see my uncle," said Rudolph.

"He is a good man, I shall apprise him of my new station and he will give me good advice. And you, where are you going, Marcel?"

"Me, why I shall go to old Medicis to ask him if he has any pictures to be restored which he will entrust to me. By the way, give me five francs."

"What to do?"

"To cross the Pont des Arts."

"Say, that's a foolish expense, although too small to be considered, it is foreign to our principle."

"I am wrong, indeed," said Marcel, "I will go by the Pont Neuf . . . but I will take a carriage."

And the two friends left, each taking a different direction which by a strange chance led both to the same place where they met again.

"What, you didn't find your uncle?" asked Marcel.

"You didn't see Medicis?" demanded Rudolph.

And they burst out laughing.

Moreover they returned home at a very early hour the next day.

Two days later, Rudolph and Marcel were absolutely changed. Both dressed like first class husbands,—they were so handsome, so shining, so chic that when they met on the street they were slow in recognizing each other. Their plan of economizing, moreover, was in full swing. But the organization of work was indeed slow to be put in practice. They had found a servant. He was a fine servant, thirty-four years old, of Swiss origin, and had an intelligence which made one think of Jocrisse. Further, he was not born to be a servant; and if one of his masters entrusted to him a fairly large package, Baptiste blushed with rage and had a messenger take it to its destination. But Baptiste had his virtues; for instance, give him a hare and if necessary he could make a stew of it. Again, as he had been a distiller before becoming a valet, he still had a great love for his art and used a large part of the time which he owed to his masters searching for the secret to a new and better specific which he wanted to bear his name; in addition he succeeded with a walnut brandy. But where Baptiste was without a rival was in the art of smoking

Marcel's cigars and lighting them with Rudolph's manuscripts.

One day Marcel wanted to have Baptiste pose as Pharaoh for his picture of the *Crossing of the Red Sea*. To this plan Baptiste absolutely refused and demanded his wages.

"It's just as well," said Marcel, "I will have your wages for you this evening."

When Rudolph returned his friend announced that they had to dismiss Baptiste.

"He's good for absolutely nothing," he said.

"That's true," responded Marcel, "he is a living object of art."

"He is a rotten cook."

"He is lazy."

"He must go."

"Let us fire him."

"But he has certainly some good qualities. He makes a very good stew."

"And there is the walnut brandy. He is the Raphael among walnut brandy makers."

"Yes, but he is only good at that, and that isn't enough for us. We waste so much time in our arguments with him."

"He keeps us from working."

"He is the reason for my not finishing the *Crossing of the Red Sea* for the Salon. He refused to pose as Pharaoh."

"Thanks to him, I haven't accomplished the work expected of me. He didn't want to go to the library to look up some notes I needed."

"He is ruining us."

"Definitely we can't keep him."

"Let's send him away . . . But then we'll have to pay him."

"We will pay him but he must go; give me some money to count out his wages."

"What! money! But it isn't I who holds the purse, it's you."

"Not at all, it's you. You are entrusted with the general management," said Rudolph.

"But I assure you that I have no money!" exclaimed Marcel.

"Do you mean to say there isn't any more! That's impossible, you can't spend five hundred francs in a week, especially when you live as we have, with the most rigid economy, limiting ourselves to what is only strictly necessary." (He ought to have said strictly superfluous.) "We must go over our accounts," Rudolph went on, "we will find the error."

"Yes," said Marcel, "but we won't find the money. That's all right, let's examine the expense books."

Here is a specimen of this expense which had been begun under the auspices of holy Economy:

"19 March—Received 500 francs. Expenses: one Turkish pipe, 25 francs; dinner, 15 francs; miscellaneous, 40 francs."

"What were those miscellaneous items?" Rudolph questioned Marcel who was reading.

"You know very well," the latter replied, "that was the evening when we didn't get home till morning. But that saved us wood and candles."

"After, go on."

"From 20 March—Lunch, 1 fr. 50; Tobacco 1 fr. 50; Dinner, 2 frs.; Eyeglass, 2 fr. 50. Oh," said Marcel, "that was your bill wasn't it, the eyeglass? Why do you need an eyeglass? You can see perfectly."

"You know very well that I had to give an account of the Salon in the *Scarf of Iris;* it is impossible to be a critic of paintings without an eyeglass; that was a legitimate expense.—Next."

"A malacca stick."

"Ahem, that is your item," said Rudolph, "you didn't need a stick."

"That's all that was spent on the 20th," was Marcel's only reply. "The 21st we lunched in town, dined also, and had supper too."

"We didn't spend so much that day!"

"Actually very little— Hardly 30 francs."

"But what more? Go on."

"I don't know any more," said Marcel. "It is marked under the heading Miscellaneous."

"A vague and untrustworthy title," Rudolph interrupted.

"The 22nd. That is the day of Baptiste's coming. We gave him on account 5 francs for his salary; for the Barbary organ, 50 centimes; for the ransom of 4 little Chinese babies condemned to be thrown in the Yellow River by parents of incredible cruelty, 2 fr. 40."

"Oh yes!" said Rudolph, "explain a slight contradiction evident in this list. If you give to Barbary organs, why do you insult barbarian parents? Moreover, why ransom little Chinese? If they had only been in brandy."

"I was born generous," replied Marcel, "get on; up to now we haven't gotten too far away from the rule of economy."

"23rd—Nothing is marked down—24th—the same. They were two good days. . . . 25th—Given to Baptiste, on account for his salary, 3 francs. It seems to me that he gets money often enough," Marcel reflected.

"We'll owe him less," responded Rudolph— "Continue."

"26th March—Diverse and useful expenses from the point of view of Art. 36 fr. 40."

"Now what could we have bought that was so useful?" enquired Rudolph. "I can't remember. 36 francs 40, what could that be?"

"What, you don't remember? That was the day we went up the Notre Dame tower to have a bird's eye view of Paris."

"But that cost eight sous to go up in the towers," said Rudolph.

"Yes, but when we came down we went to dine at St. Germain."

"That item is at fault through its clearness."

"For the 27th, there is no notation."

"Good, we economized that day."

"For the 28th, given to Baptiste, payment on his salary, 6 francs."

"Ah, this time, I am sure that we owe nothing more to Baptiste. It might even be that he owes us. . . . We shall see."

"29th—Look, the 29th isn't noted; the place for the note is taken up with the beginning of an article on manners."

"The 30th—Ah, we had company for dinner; enormous outlay for the 30th; 55 francs. The 31st, that's today, we haven't spent anything yet. You see," said Marcel, as he finished, "that the expenses have been kept very exactly. The total doesn't come to five hundred francs."

"Then there must be money in the drawer."

"We can look," said Marcel opening a drawer. "No, there is nothing more, only a spider."

"A spider in the morning as good as a warning," was Rudolph's response.

"Where the devil can so much money have disappeared to?" growled Marcel astonished that the drawer was empty.

"My word, it's all very plain," said Rudolph, "Baptiste has received all of it."

"Look here," cried Marcel mulling around in the drawer when he spied a paper. "The bill for the last quarter rent."

"Pshaw," growled Rudolph, "how did it get there?"

"And even paid," added Marcel; "then it's you who paid the proprietor."

"I? Get out," objected Rudolph.

"Then, what does it mean?"

"But, I promise you. . . ."

"But what is the meaning of this?"

"Quel est donc ce mystere," they choired together, the tune of the finale of "La Dame Blanche."

Baptiste, who adored music, appeared at once.

Marcel showed him the bill.

"Oh yes," Baptiste was casual, "I forgot to tell you, the proprietor came this morning while you were out. I paid him to save him the trouble of returning."

"Where did you find the money?"

"Oh, Monsieur," Baptiste went on, "I took it from the drawer which was open; I even supposed that you gentlemen had left it open for this purpose; and I said to myself: 'My masters have forgotten to say to me, 'Baptiste, the proprietor will be here for the quarter's rent, he must be paid;' and so I acted as if I really had been told."

"Baptiste!" Marcel was in a white rage, "you have overstepped your orders; beginning with today you are no longer a part of our household. Baptiste, return your uniform."

Baptiste took off the oil cloth cap which made up his livery, and gave it to Marcel.

"That's all right," said the latter, "now you can leave."

"And my wages?"

"What are you saying, foolish one? You have already had more than we owe you. I gave you fourteen francs in barely two weeks. What are you doing with so much money? You are carrying on with a dancing girl?"

"A rope dancer," supplemented Rudolph.

"Then I shall be abandoned," wailed the unhappy servant, "without a roof to cover my head."

"Take back your livery," replied Marcel, moved in spite of himself. And he returned Baptiste's cap.

"So it's that wretch who has dissipated our fortune," said Rudolph, watching poor Baptiste take his departure. "Where will we dine today?"

"We shall know that tomorrow," Marcel replied.

THE COST OF A FIVE FRANC PIECE

ONE Saturday evening, at the time when he was still living with Mademoiselle Mimi, who will appear soon, Rudolph made the acquaintance at his humble dining place of an agent for toilet articles named Mademoiselle Laura. Having learned that Rudolph was editor-in-chief of the *Scarf of Iris* and of the *Castor*, fashion papers, the dressmaker, in the hope that she would obtain some sales for her wares, determinedly set her cap for him. To these advances Rudolph had responded by a pyrotechnical display of songs which would have made Benserade, Voiture, and every Ruggieri of the noble style jealous; and dinner over, Mademoiselle Laura when she had discovered that Rudolph was a poet, gave him clearly to understand that she was not loath to accept him as her Petrarch. Without any beating around the bush she even granted him an engagement for the next day.

"Dear me," Rudolph said to himself after he had taken Mademoiselle Laura home. "She is a very charming person. She seems to know her grammar and to have a fairly expensive wardrobe. I am rather inclined to make her happy."

When she arrived at the door of her house, Mademoiselle Laura loosed Rudolph's arm, thanking him for the trouble which he had taken to escort her such a distance.

"Oh, Madame," Rudolph said as he bowed to the ground, "I could wish that you lived in Moscow or the East Indies that I might have the pleasure of being your guide for a longer time."

"That's rather far," simpered Laura.

"We ought to have gone by way of the boulevards, Madame," said Rudolph. "Permit me to kiss your hand by way of your cheek," he asked as he saluted his companion upon the lips before Laura could object.

"Oh, sir," she exclaimed, "you are too quick."

"That I may arrive sooner," responded Rudolph. "In love the first relays must be fresh for the galop."

"Queer fellow," the dressmaker thought to herself as she entered her room.

"Pretty lady," Rudolph said to himself as he went away.

When he arrived home he went to bed very quickly and had the sweetest dreams. He saw himself with Mademoiselle Laura on his arm in the dance halls, in the theatres, along the promenades, clothed in gowns more splendid than ones longed for in the land of fairy tale.

The next day at 11 o'clock, as was his habit, Rudolph got up. His first thought was of Mademoiselle Laura.

"She is a very fine woman," he murmured, "I'm sure she has been raised in St. Denis. At last I am to know the happiness of having a mistress who is not pockmarked. I will make some definite sacrifices for her. I'm off to collect my money from the *Scarf of Iris,* I will buy gloves and take Laura to dinner at a restaurant where there are napkins.—My suit isn't very handsome," he remarked while dressing; "but pooh, black is so very stylish."

And he went out to the office of the *Scarf of Iris.* While walking up the street he met an omnibus upon the sides of which was a poster which read as follows:

TODAY, SUNDAY, THE FOUNTAINS AT VERSAILLES.

Thunder falling at Rudolph's feet would not have made a stronger impression on him than the sight of that poster.

"Today, Sunday, I had forgotten it," he exclaimed, "I won't be able to get any money. Today, Sunday! ! ! And all the écus there are in Paris are on the way to Versailles."

However, impelled by one of those vain hopes to which man is ever prey, Rudolph hastened to his office hoping that a happy chance would have brought thither the bookkeeper.

Actually, M. Boniface had come for a moment but had left at once.

"To go to Versailles," the office boy told Rudolph.

"Well," said Rudolph, "it's all over. But wait a minute," he thought, "my engagement isn't until evening. It is noon, I have still five hours to find five francs, twenty sous an hour, like the horses in the Bois de Boulogne . . . I must begin."

As he chanced to be in the section where a journalist, whom he called the influential critic, lived, Rudolph decided to begin his efforts there.

"I am sure of finding him at home," he encouraged himself as he went up stairs; "it is the day for his article, there's no danger that he's gone out; I shall borrow five francs from him."

"So, it's really you!" thus the man of letters greeted Rudolph. "You came most opportunely; I have a small favour to ask of you."

"How fortunate that is!" thought the editor of the *Scarf of Iris*.

"Were you at the Odeon, yesterday?"

"I always go to the Odeon."

"Then you've seen the new play."

"Who would have seen it? The audience of the Odeon, and I'm it."

"That's so," agreed the critic; "you are one of the caryatides of this theatre. Rumour has it that you provide the subsidy for it. Well, this is what I want from you: the report of the new play."

"That's easy; I have the memory of a creditor."

"Who wrote the thing?" asked the critic, thinking that Rudolph had done so.

"It is by a gentleman."

"He must not be strong."

"Weaker than a Turk, certainly."

"Then he isn't robust. The Turks, you know, have usurped the claim of strength. They could not come from Savoy."

"What could hinder them?"

"Because every man from Savoy is of Auvergne, and the

Auvergnians are all errand boys. And then there aren't any Turks now, except at masked balls in the outskirts of the city and the Champs-Élysées, where they sell dates. The Turk is a myth. One of my friends knows the East and he tells me that all nationalities are first originated in the rue Coquenard."

"What you say is charming," said Rudolph.

"You think so?" asked the critic. "I am going to put that in my article."

"Here is my story; it is written straightforwardly," explained Rudolph.

"Yes, but it's short."

"Adding some hyphens and your criticism will take some space."

"I have no time at all, my dear, and then my opinion won't take enough space."

"Put an adjective every three words."

"Couldn't you introduce into your story a little or rather a long estimate of this play, eh?" begged the critic.

"Sure," said Rudolph, "I certainly have my ideas about the tragedy but I warn you that I have printed them three times in the *Castor* and the *Scarf of Iris*."

"That doesn't matter. How many lines will your ideas take up?"

"Forty."

"Confound it, you have big ideas, you have. Well, lend me your forty lines, will you."

"Oh good," thought Rudolph. "If I give him copy worth twenty francs he can't refuse me five. I must warn you," he said to the critic, "that these ideas aren't absolutely new. They are a little worn at the elbows. Before printing them, I have preached them in every café in Paris and there isn't a waiter who doesn't know them by heart."

"Oh, that doesn't bother me! After all, is there anything really new under the sun, goodness excepted?"

"There you are." Rudolph gave it to him as soon as he had finished it.

"Thunderbolts and lightning! There are still two columns to

be filled. How can I fill this void?" despaired the critic. "While you are here, give me some paradoxes."

"I haven't any with me now," said Rudolph, "but I can lend you some. Only they don't belong to me; I bought them for fifty centimes from one of my friends who was in despair. They have only been used a little."

"All right," agreed the critic.

"Ah," thought Rudolph as he began to write again. "I am certainly going to ask him for ten francs. In these days paradoxes are as dear as young partridge." And he wrote about thirty lines of humbug upon pianos, red fish, the school of good sense, and Rhine wine, which he called only fit for dressing rooms.

"That's very good," said the critic. "Do me now the kindness of adding that the convict prison is the place in the world where one finds the most honest people."

"But, why that?"

"To make two more lines. Good, that's done," said the influential critic, calling his servant to carry his article to the press.

"Now's the time to strike," thought Rudolph, and he solemnly stated his request.

"Oh, my friend, I haven't a sou here," the critic was regretful. "Lolette takes all my money for lip salve and just now she has stripped me of my last ace to go to Versailles to see the Nereids and bronze monsters vomit watery streams."

"At Versailles. Oh so that's it! Indeed," said Rudolph. "It's an epidemic."

"But why do you need money?"

"I'll sing my song," Rudolph went on. "At 5 o'clock this evening I have an engagement with a woman of the world, a distinguished person who only goes forth in an omnibus. I should like to unite her and my destinies for a few days and it seems only decent to me to let her taste the sweetnesses of life. To dine, dance, to promenade, etc., but I need five francs absolutely, and if I don't find them French literature is degraded in me."

"Why wouldn't you borrow this amount from the woman herself?" suggested the critic.

"The first time, that isn't possible, at all. You are the only person who can help me."

"By all the mummies of Egypt I swear by my word of honour that there isn't a sou here with which to buy a pipe or a virginity. But I do have some old books which you could turn into cash."

"Today, on Sunday, that's impossible. Mother Mansut, Lebigre, and all the bookstalls of the quays and of the rue St. Jacques are closed. What are your old books? Volumes of poetry, with the portrait of the author in spectacles. But those things won't sell."

"Unless one is condemned to it by the court of assizes," said the critic. "But here are still some novels and some concert tickets; if you take them and are clever you might perhaps make some money."

"I would prefer something else, a pair of pants for instance."

"See here," the critic urged, "take this Bossuet and this plaster cast of M. Odile Barret; my word on it, it is the widow's mite."

"I see that you are full of good will," said Rudolph. "I will take the treasures but if I get thirty sous for them I will consider it as the thirteenth labour of Hercules."

After having gone to about four places, Rudolph, with the aid of an eloquence of which he had the secret at crucial moments, succeeded in having himself loaned two francs by his laundress upon the deposit of the books of verse, the novels, and the portrait of Barret.

"Well, that's that," he said to himself as he traversed the bridges, "I have the sauce; now it's necessary to find the stew. Perhaps I might go to my uncle!"

An half hour later he was at his uncle Monetti's who read in his nephew's face what he was about to ask. So he put himself on guard, and foresaw every demand with a series of recriminations such as this:—The times are hard, bread is dear, creditors don't pay, rents come due, business is in a bad way, etc.,—all the hypocritical songs of shopkeepers.

"Would you believe," asked the uncle, "that I was forced to borrow money from my shopboy to pay a bill."

"You ought to have come to me," said Rudolph. "I would have loaned you money. I received two hundred francs three days ago."

"Thanks, my boy, but you need what you have. But while you are here, you could indeed, as you have such a lovely hand, copy some bills which I wish to send."

"These five francs will cost me dear," sighed Rudolph as he set himself at the task which he accomplished as quickly as possible.

"My dear uncle," he addressed Monetti, "I know how you love music, and I brought you some concert tickets."

"You are very kind, my boy. Do you wish to dine with me?"

"Thanks, my uncle, I am ex-pected to dinner in the fau-bourg St. Germain, I am rather annoyed because I haven't time  to go home to get some money to buy gloves."

"You haven't any gloves? Do you want me to lend you mine?" asked the uncle.

"Thanks, we haven't the same size hand; only you would oblige me if you would lend me . . ."

"Twenty-nine sous to buy some? Certainly, boy, there they are. When one goes in society one must be well dressed. Better excite envy than pity, your aunt always said. Well, I see that you are launching out, so much the better. I would have given you more," he went on, "but that is all I have in my till. I must go up at once. I cannot leave the store alone; at every minute buyers come in."

"You said business wasn't good."

Uncle Monetti made a pretence of not hearing and said to his nephew who pocketed the twenty-nine sous: "Don't hasten to return them."

"What a miser!" Rudolph muttered as he made his escape.

"Look at that; it still lacks thirty-one sous. Where can I find them? But, I know, I shall go to the cross roads of Providence."

So Rudolph called the most central spot in Paris, that is, the Palais Royal. A place where it is almost impossible to stay ten minutes without meeting ten of one's acquaintances, especially one's creditors. So Rudolph went to stand on guard at the entrance to the Palais Royal. This time, Providence was slow to come. At last Rudolph could see her. She wore a white hat, a green overcoat, and a stick with a gold knob; a Providence very well turned out indeed.

It was an agreeable and rich youth, although a phalansterian.

"I am thrilled to see you," she greeted Rudolph; "now come and walk with me a bit and we can talk."

"Well, I must submit to the attentions of the phalanstery," murmured Rudolph as he fell in step with the owner of the white hat, who talked shop without mercy.

As they were approaching the Pont des Arts, Rudolph remarked to his companion, "I must leave you as I have nothing to pay the toll."

"That's all right," said the other clutching Rudolph and tossing two sous to the guard.

"Now the moment has arrived," thought the editor of the *Scarf of Iris* as they crossed the bridge; and having arrived at the end, before the Institute clock, Rudolph stopped short, pointed to the dial with a despairing gesture and groaned:

"My God! a quarter to five! I am ruined!"

"What's up?" the other was astonished.

"It's this," said Rudolph, "thanks to you who have led me on this far in spite of myself I have missed a rendezvous."

"Important?"

"I think so, some money that I was to go get at five . . . at the Batignolles . . . I will never get there . . . oh lord! what shall I do? . . ."

"For mercy's sake," said the phalansterian, "that's simple, come home with me, I will lend you some."

"That's impossible, you live at Montrouge and I have business at six o'clock near Chaussée d'Antin . . . oh lord . . ."

"I have a few sous with me," Providence announced timidly, "but very few."

"If I only had enough to take a carriage perhaps I would arrive in time at the Batignolles."

"Here's all that I have, my friend, thirty-one sous."

"Give them to me quickly and I am saved," urged Rudolph, who had just heard five o'clock strike, and he started to run toward his meeting place.

"That's been hard to collect," he decided as he counted his

money. "One hundred sous, good as gold. At last I am saved, and Laura will see that she has to do with a man who knows how to live. I don't want to bring home one centime tonight. One must revive literature and show that money is the only thing it needs to be rich."

Rudolph found Laura at the trysting place.

"That's something like it," said he. "For exactitude, she is a female clock."

He spent the evening with her and boldly melted five francs in the crucible of generosity. Mademoiselle Laura was delighted with his manners, and took pains not to notice that Rudolph was not taking her home until the time when he was leading her into his room with him.

"What I do is wrong," she said. "Don't let me repent of it by an inconstancy which is native to your sex."

"Madame," protested Rudolph, "I am known for my constancy. It's gotten to a point that my friends are so astonished at my faithfulness they give me the sobriquet of the 'General Bertrand of Love.' "

VIOLETS FROM THE NORTH POLE

A T this time, Rudolph was terribly in love with his cousin Angela, who could not bear him, and the temperature of the perfect lady's man registered twelve degrees below zero.

Mademoiselle Angela was the daughter of M. Monetti, the stove and chimney maker whom we have had reason to mention before. Mademoiselle Angela was eighteen years old, and had come from Burgundy where she had spent five years with a relative who was going to leave her her fortune when she died. This relative was an old woman who had never been young or beautiful, but had always been ill-natured in spite or because of being pious. Angela, who, when she left home, was a lovely child whose adolescence promised a delightful youth, returned after five years transformed into a beautiful, but cold, repressed, and indifferent person. The secluded life of the provinces, the practice of an assumed devoutness, and the training in narrow principles, which she had received, had filled her mind with vulgar and unreasonable prejudices, cramped her imagination, and reduced her heart activity to the simple function of breathing. Angela had, so to speak, holy water instead of blood in her veins. When they met she received her cousin with an icy reserve, and he wasted his time at every attempt to play on the strings of her memories of the time when they had sketched anew the romance of Paul and Virginia, which is traditional between cousins.

Meanwhile Rudolph was terribly in love with his cousin Angela, who could not bear him; and, having learned one day that the young girl was soon to attend the wedding ball of one of her friends, he was bold enough to promise Angela a bunch of violets to wear to this party. After she had gained her father's permission Angela accepted her cousin's gallantry, insisting, however, that the violets be white.

Rudolph, radiant because of his cousin's graciousness, skipped and sang when he returned to his Mt. St. Bernard. So he named his residing place. You can see why in a trice. As he was crossing the Palais Royal passing before the shop of Madame Prevost, the famous florist, Rudolph saw some white violets in the window and through curiosity went in and asked their price. A decent bouquet would cost not less than ten francs and there were some which cost more.

"The devil," said Rudolph, "ten francs and only a week for me to find this fortune. It will be a hard pull, but just the same my cousin will have her flowers. I have an idea."

This adventure took place during Rudolph's literary apprenticeship. Then he had no revenue but an income of fifteen francs a month which was given him by a friend, a great poet who, after a long stay in Paris, had become with the aid of patrons the master of a school in the provinces. Rudolph, whose godmother's name was Spendthrift, used his income in four days; and, as he was unwilling to give up the holy and unremunerative calling of elegiac poet, he lived the rest of the month on the chance manna which drops haphazardly from Providential baskets. This lenting didn't bother him; he lived through it gaily, thanks to a stoical sobriety, and to the resources of his imagination which he called upon daily until the first of the month came. This Easter day which ended his fast. At this time Rudolph was living in the rue Contrescarpe-Saint Marcel, in a great building which was called in former days the hotel de l'Eminence grise, because Father Joseph, Richelieu's confidant, had lived there, so it was said. Rudolph roomed at the very top of this house, one of the highest in Paris. His room in the shape of a belvedere was incomparable in the summertime, but from October to April it was a little Kamchatka. The four cardinal winds which leaked through the four windows piercing each side congregated there to execute regal quartets as long as the cold season lasted. Ironically enough, there was still a fireplace whose enormous flue seemed to be the entrance of honour for West Wind and all his train. At the first suggestion of cold weather, Rudolph indulged in a special plan of heating; he chopped systematically the few furnishings he had, and at the end of the week, his household goods were considerably reduced,—there remained only the bed and two chairs; one must add that these pieces were made of iron and so, naturally preserved from fire. Rudolph called this form of heating, breaking up housekeeping through the chimney.

It was, at the time of this story, January, and the thermometer which marked twelve degrees at the Quai des Lunettes, would have been two or three lower if it had been taken to Rudolph's terrace which he had named Mt. St. Bernard, Spitzberg, Siberia.

The evening that he had promised the white violets to his cousin, Rudolph was overcome with a terrible anger when he returned home; the four winds had again broken a pane of glass while playing about the room's four corners. It was the third insult of this kind in two weeks. And Rudolph gave vent to infuriated oaths against Aeolus and his whole family of winds. After having patched up this new break with a picture of one of his friends, Rudolph entirely dressed got into bed between the two thinly padded boards which he called his mattress, and the whole night long he dreamed of white violets.

After five days Rudolph had not yet found any way of bringing his dream to pass, and it was the day after the morrow when he was to give the bouquet to his cousin. Meanwhile the thermometer had continued to fall, and the unhappy poet was in despair, fearing that the violets would perhaps become dearer. Finally, Providence had pity on him, and this is the way.

One morning Rudolph, as a last resort, went to beg luncheon from his friend, the painter Marcel, and he found him conversing with a woman in mourning. She was a widow from the vicinity; she had lost her husband recently and had come to ask how much it would cost to paint upon the tomb, which she had had raised to the memory of the deceased, a man's hand, below which would be inscribed:

My darling wife, I wait for thee.

To obtain the work at the best figure, she had even informed the artist that at the time when God would send her to join her husband he would have to paint a second hand, adorned with a bracelet, with a new thought which would be as follows:

At last united now are we . . .

"I will put this proviso in my will," said the widow, "and I will see to it that you have this commission."

"Since that is so, Madame," responded the artist, "I accept the price you offer me . . . but it is in consideration of the eventual clasp of the hands. You will not forget me in your will."

"I could wish that you give me this as soon as possible," said the widow; "however, take your time and do not forget the scar on the thumb. I want a lifelike hand."

"It will be a speaking likeness, Madame, you may rest assured," said Marcel as he accompanied the widow to the door. But as she was about to leave she turned around.

"I have another bit of advice to ask you, Mr. Artist; I would like to have written on my husband's tomb a thingummy in verse, where would be recounted his good behaviour and the last words which he uttered on his death-bed. Is that the correct thing?"

"It is most correct; that is called an epitaph, it is very chic."

"You would not know someone who could do that for me cheaply enough? There is my neighbour, M. Guerin, the public scribe, but he would steal my eyes from their sockets."

At this point Rudolph winked at Marcel who understood at once.

"Madame," said the artist pointing to Rudolph, "a happy chance has brought here the one person who can be useful to you in this sad business. Monsieur is a distinguished poet and you could not find a better."

"I insist on something very sad," resumed the widow, "and on very correct spelling."

"Madame," urged Marcel, "my friend knows spelling to the tip of his fingers; at college he took every prize."

"There," said the widow, "my nephew-in-law has had a prize too; however he is only seven."

"A precocious child," averred Marcel.

"But," the widow continued, "does the gentleman know how to write sad verses?"

"Better than anyone, Madame, for he has had a great many trials in his life. My friend excels in sad poetry, that is why the papers constantly criticize him."

"What!" exclaimed the widow, "he is mentioned in the papers; then he is as learned as M. Guerin."

"Oh, even more so. Trust in him, Madame, you will not regret it."

After having explained to the poet the substance of the poetic epitaph she wished to have put on her husband's tomb, the widow consented to give Rudolph ten francs if she was satisfied; only she wanted the verses very quickly. The poet agreed to send them to her the very next morning by his friend.

"Oh lovely fairy, Artemisia," chuckled Rudolph when the widow had gone, "I promise you you will be satisfied; I will give you good measure in your funereal lyric and the spelling will be better than that of a duchess. Oh good old lady, to reward you may heaven let you live to be seven hundred, like good brandy."

"I object to that," interposed Marcel.

"That's so," said Rudolph, "I forgot that you have still her hand to paint after her death and that such longevity would make you lose money." And he raised his hands as he beseeched: "O Heaven, do not heed my prayer. How lucky for me to come here," he added.

"Actually, why did you want me?" asked Marcel.

"Thinking it over, and now especially that I must pass the night writing this poem, I cannot refrain from asking you for what I came seeking: First, dinner; second, tobacco, a candle; and third, your polar bear costume."

"Do you mean that you are going to the masked ball? This evening is the first, to be sure."

"No, but just as you see me I am as frozen as the grand army during the retreat from Russia. Doubtlessly my overcoat of green lasting and my pants of plaid merino are very handsome but they are too springlike, and good for living over the equator; when one sleeps over the pole as I do, a polar bear costume is more suitable,—I would go farther, it is essential."

"Take Bruin," said Marcel, " that's an idea; it is hot as a stove and you will be as warm in it as bread in an oven."

Rudolph at once donned the furry costume. "Now," said he, "the thermometer is going to be terribly fooled."

"Do you mean that you are going to go out like that?" Marcel asked his friend after they had managed a sketchy enough dinner served in the pan marked at five centimes.

"Heavens," said Rudolph, "I care not for public opinion, moreover it is the beginning of the carnival season today." And he crossed the whole of Paris with the serious demeanour of the quadruped whose skin he wore. Passing by Engineer Chevalier's thermometer, Rudolph thumbed his nose at it.

Arrived home, not without having frightened the janitor greatly, the poet lit his candle and took great care to protect it with thin paper, to frustrate any of the tricks of the North Wind, and at once started upon his task. But he was not long in discovering that even if his body was almost perfectly protected from the cold his hands were not; and he had not written two lines of his epitaph when a terrific numbness had overcome the fingers so that they could not grip the pen.

"The most courageous man cannot struggle against the elements," said Rudolph, falling exhausted on his chair. "Caesar crossed the Rubicon, but he would not have crossed the Beresina."

Suddenly the poet uttered a cry of joy from the depths of his bear heart, and he jumped up so quickly that he upset a part of his ink upon the white expanse of fur: he had had an idea borrowed from Chatterton.

Rudolph dragged from beneath his bed a considerable mass of papers among which were about ten enormous manuscripts of his famous drama of *The Avenger*. This drama, on which he had laboured two years, had been written, destroyed, and written again so many times that the copies taken together

weighed fifteen pounds. Rudolph put aside the most recent
version and arranged the others before the fireplace. "I was sure
that I would ultimately place these," he said, "if I had patience.
This is certainly a fine potboiler. Ah, if I had foreseen what
is happening, I would have made a prologue and today I would
have more to burn. . . . But, pshaw, one can't foresee everything."

And he lit some sheets of the manuscript in his fireplace
by the flames of which he removed the numbness from his hands.
At the end of five minutes, the first act of *The Avenger* had
been played and Rudolph had written three lines of his epitaph.

No one in the world would be able to paint the astonishment
of the four winds of heaven when they saw smoke coming out
of the chimney.

"That's an illusion," breathed the North Wind, which was
amused to rub Rudolph the wrong way. "If we should blow
down the chimney flue," continued another wind, "it would
make the chimney smoke."

But as they were about to commence harassing poor Rudolph,
the South Wind perceived M. Arago at the window of the
Observatory from where the learned man was shaking his finger
at the four winds.

So the South Wind shouted to his brothers: "Let us save
ourselves quickly,—the almanac shows calm weather for tonight; we are opposing the Observatory and if we haven't retired
by midnight M. Arago will have us put in gaol."

During all this, the second act of *The Avenger* burned with
the greatest success. And Rudolph had written ten lines. But
he could only write two during the third act.

"I have always thought this act was too short," murmured
Rudolph, "but it is only when it is presented that one can see
a failing. Fortunately this will last longer; there are twenty-three
scenes, of which the throne scene was to be the peak of my
glory" . . . the last tirade of the throne scene disappeared in
smoke and Rudolph had still six lines to write.

"We will pass to the fourth act," he said, taking a light.
"It will last five minutes, it is all a monologue." He passed to
the climax which burst into flame and went out. At the same

minute, Rudolph framed in a magnificent flight of fancy the last words of the deceased in whose honour he had just been working. "These will do for another performance," he said shoving the rest under his bed.

The next day, at eight in the evening, Mademoiselle Angela made her entrance at the ball, carrying in her hand a splendid bunch of white violets, in the midst of which opened up two roses, white also. The whole night this bouquet won for the young girl compliments from the ladies, and songs from the men. Consequently Angela was a little grateful to her cousin who had procured all these little balms for her pride, and she would have perhaps thought more of him had it not been for the gallant persecutions of an admirer who had danced several times with her. He was a blond young man, wearing one of those pairs of superb curling mustaches which are so alluring to tender hearts. The young man had already asked Angela to give him the two white roses which remained from her bouquet, which had been despoiled by everyone. . . . But Angela had refused, only at the end of the ball to forget the two flowers upon a bench from where the blond youth quickly retrieved them. At this instant it registered fourteen degrees in the gallery where Rudolph, leaning against his window, watched aslant the city wall of the Maine the lights of the ballroom where his cousin Angela, who couldn't bear him, was dancing.

THE CAPE OF STORMS

THERE are in the months which are the beginning of each new season some appalling moments;—the first and the fifteenth generally. Rudolph, who could not see one or the other of these two days approach without dismay, called them "The Cape of Storms." On that day it isn't Aurora who opens the gates of the East, it is creditors, proprietors, bailiffs, and other creatures with money bags. That day begins with a shower of reminders, orders to leave, bills, and ends with a hail of protests,—*Dies iræ!*

But, on the morning of April fifteenth, Rudolph was sleeping very quietly and was dreaming that one of his uncles had bequeathed him a whole province in Peru with some Peruvians included.

As he was swimming in the very midst of an imaginary river of gold, a noise of a key turning in the lock interrupted the heir presumptive at the most radiant moment of his golden dreams.

Rudolph sat up in bed, his eyes and wits still drowsy, and he looked around him. Then he vaguely saw standing in the middle of the room, a man who had just entered, and what man?

This morning stranger wore a three-cornered hat, on his back a money bag, and in his hand, a large bill case; he was dressed in a French suit of flax grey, and seemed very out of breath from having climbed the five flights of stairs. His manners were very agreeable, and his step as heavy as that of a money changing counter should it begin to move. For a moment Rudolph was perturbed at the sight of the three-cornered hat and suit for he thought he was seeing a policeman.

But the sight of the money bag indifferently filled made him realize his error.

"Ah, I have it now," he thought, "it is a payment on my inheritance, this man comes from the Islands. . . . But still

he isn't a negro." Motioning to the man, he spoke to him as he
pointed to the sack:

"I know what it is. Put it there. Thanks."

The man was a messenger from the Bank of France. At
Rudolph's invitation, he responded by putting under his eyes
a bit of paper covered with hieroglyphics and many coloured
stamps.

"You wish a receipt," asked Rudolph. "That's right. Hand me
the pen and ink. There, on the table."

"No, I have come to receive," returned the boy with the bill,
"a sum of one hundred and fifty francs. Today is April 15."

"Ah!" murmured Rudolph as he examined the bill. "A bill
from Birman. He is my tailor. . . . Alas," he added in a melancholy tone, bringing his gaze to bear first on his frock coat
thrown on the bed and then on the bill, "the causes disappear
but the effects remain. What did you say? Today is the fifteenth
of April? Why, that's extraordinary! And I haven't had any
strawberries to eat yet!"

The collector, bored by these delays, left, saying to Rudolph
as he did so: "You have until four o'clock to pay."

"That's not enough time for honest people," answered Rudolph. "The schemer," he added regretfully as he continued
to watch the financier in his three-cornered hat, "he is taking
his sack away."

Rudolph drew his bed curtains, and tried to resume the road
to his inheritance but he lost the way, and very much elated,
began to dream that the director of the Théâtre Français with
hat off came to him to ask for a play for his theatre, and Rudolph
who knew the ropes asked for a payment first. But just at the
moment when the director seemed willing to give it over, the
sleeper was again half wakened by the entrance of a new person,
another product of April 15.

It was M. Benoit—wrongly named—the proprietor of the
furnished lodgings where Rudolph roomed. M. Benoit was at
the same time proprietor, bootmaker, and money lender for
his lodgers; this morning M. Benoit radiated a frightful odour
of bad brandy and expired leases. He had in his hand a bag which
was empty.

"The devil!" thought Rudolph. "This is no longer the director of the theatre . . . he would be wearing a white necktie and his bag would be full!"

"Good day, Monsieur Rudolph . . ." began M. Benoit as he came toward his bed.

"Monsieur Benoit. . . . Good day to you. What fortune gives me the pleasure of this call?"

"Well, I came to tell you that today is the fifteenth of April."

"So soon! How time flies! It is extraordinary; I will have to buy some nankeen trousers. April 15th! Ah! To think of that. And I would never have dreamed that it was had it not been for you, M. Benoit. How grateful I am to you! !"

"You owe me one hundred sixty-two francs," replied M. Benoit; "and it's about time to settle this little account. . . ."

"I'm not absolutely in need, you needn't worry yourself, Monsieur Benoit, I will give you further time . . . little accounts will grow into big. . . ."

"But," objected the proprietor, "you have already put me off several times."

"In that case, let us settle, let us settle, Monsieur Benoit, it makes absolutely no difference to me, today or tomorrow, and then we are all of us mortal . . . let us settle."

A happy smile radiated the face of the proprietor, and there was nothing, even including his empty money bag, which wasn't inflated with hope.

"What do I owe you?" asked Rudolph.

"First, there is three months' rent at twenty-five francs; total, seventy-five francs."

"Errors excepted," Rudolph. "What else?"

"Second, three pairs of shoes at twenty francs."

"One moment . . . one moment, Monsieur Benoit, let's not get mixed up; I am not dealing with my proprietor now but with the bootmaker; I wish a separate account. . . . Bills are a serious matter, we mustn't get entangled in them."

"As you like," agreed M. Benoit, sweetened by the hope that he was going to put an end to this account. "Here is a separate bill for the shoes. Three pairs of boots at twenty francs; total, sixty francs."

Rudolph cast a pitying glance at a pair of ruined shoes. "Alas!" thought he, "they might have been used by the Wandering Jew and not have been any worse for it. . . . Moreover they have been so worn out by pursuing Marie. . . . Go on, Monsieur Benoit."

"We said sixty francs," he resumed. "Again, money loaned twenty-seven francs. . . ."

"Stop there, Monsieur Benoit. We have agreed that each saint must have a separate niche. It is in the role of friend that you have loaned me money. So then, if you will, let us leave the realm of bootmaking and enter that of trust and friendship which demands a new account. To what extent has your friendship gone for me?"

"Twenty-seven francs."

"Twenty-seven francs. You have a very inexpensive friend, Monsieur Benoit. Finally, let us count up now, seventy-five, sixty, and twenty-seven . . . that comes to?"

"One hundred sixty-two francs," said Monsieur Benoit as he gave him the three bills.

"One hundred sixty-two francs," commented Rudolph . . . "that's extraordinary. What a beautiful thing addition is! Oh well, Monsieur Benoit, now that the account is settled both of us can be tranquil, we know what to count upon. Next month, I will ask for your receipt, and as, during this time, the trust and friendship that you have in me can only increase, in the event that it may be necessary you can grant me a further delay. Moreover, if the proprietor and the bootmaker are too exigent I will beg the friend to make them listen to reason. It's extraordinary, Monsieur Benoit; but every time that I consider your triple character of proprietor, bootmaker, and friend, I am tempted to believe in the holy trinity."

As he listened to Rudolph, the steward had become red, green, yellow and white all at once; and at each new pleasantry of his lodger, this rainbow of anger buried itself deeper and deeper in his face.

"Monsieur," he said, "I don't like to be made fun of. I have waited long enough. . . . I now give you notice and if by this evening you haven't given me any money, I will see what measures I must take."

"Money! money! Is it money that I'm begging from you?" demanded Rudolph. "Even if I had some I wouldn't give it to you Friday, it would bring bad luck."

Monsieur Benoit's wrath became tempestuous; and if the furniture hadn't belonged to him doubtless he would have broken the legs of a chair. So he departed breathing threats.

"You've forgotten your bag," Rudolph cried after him.

"What a life!" murmured the unhappy young man when he was left alone. "I would prefer to tame lions."

"But," Rudolph went on as he jumped out of bed and dressed himself quickly, "I can't stay here. The invasion of the allies will continue. I must flee, I must even lunch. Well, if I should call on Schaunard, I could ask him for lunch and borrow a few sous from him. One hundred francs would be enough. Yes, I shall go to see Schaunard."

Going downstairs, Rudolph met Monsieur Benoit who had just undergone further defeats from his other lodgers, as his empty sack testified. It was now but an object of art.

"If anyone asks for me, tell them that I am in the country . . . in the Alps," said Rudolph. "Or better, say that I no longer live here."

"I will tell the truth," Monsieur Benoit stressed his words most significantly.

Schaunard lived in Montmartre. There was the whole of Paris to cross. This journey was very hazardous for Rudolph. "Today," he said, "the streets are paved with creditors." However, he didn't keep to the outer boulevards as he wanted. A fantastic hope led him on the contrary to follow the dangerous roads in the centre of Paris. Rudolph thought that, on a day when millions of francs were walking the public highways on the backs of collectors, it might easily be possible that a note for a thousand francs lost on the way awaited its Vincent de Paul. So Rudolph walked slowly, his eyes on the ground. But he only found two pins. After two hours he arrived at Schaunard's.

"Ah! It's you," the latter greeted him.

"Yes, I have come seeking lunch."

"Oh! my dear fellow, your arrival is ill timed; my mistress has just come and I haven't seen her for two weeks; if you had arrived only ten minutes sooner. . . ."

"But you haven't a hundred francs you could lend me?" asked Rudolph.

"What! you too," Schaunard was overcome with astonishment . . . "you come asking me for money! You have joined with my enemies!"

"I will return them Monday."

"Or on Trinity. My dear, you forget really what day this is? I can't do anything for you. But there is no reason to despair, the day isn't over yet. You may still run into Providence, she doesn't get up before noon."

"Oh!" Rudolph replied. "Providence has too much to do caring for the little birds. I shall go to see Marcel."

At that time Marcel was living on the rue de Breda. Rudolph found him very sad as he contemplated his great painting which was to represent the Crossing of the Red Sea.

"What's wrong?" inquired Rudolph as he went in. "You seem very subdued."

"Alas!" said the painter speaking in metaphors. "I have been experiencing holy week for a fortnight."

To Rudolph this reply was as clear as spring water.

"Salt herring and black radishes! Very well! I remember now." (Actually Rudolph had still a salty memory of the time when he had been reduced to eating exclusively this fish.)

"Lord! Lord!" he went on, "this is serious! I came to borrow a hundred francs."

"One hundred francs!" repeated Marcel. "You must be up to some joke to come to ask me for this mythical sum, at a time when everyone is crossing the equator of necessity! You've been taking hashish. . . ."

"Alas! I have taken nothing at all," and Rudolph left his friend on the edge of the Red Sea.

From noon till four o'clock Rudolph rounded the cape again and again at every house of his acquaintance; he traversed the forty-eight sections and covered about eight leagues but without any success. The influence of April fifteenth made itself felt everywhere with an equal rigour; meanwhile dinner time was approaching, but dinner wasn't approaching with the time, and it seemed to Rudolph that he was upon the raft of the Medusa.

As he crossed the Pont Neuf, suddenly he had an idea. "Oh! Oh!" he said to himself turning in his steps. "April 15. . . . April 15. . . . But I have an invitation for today." Fumbling in his pocket he pulled out a ticket printed as follows:

Barrière de la Villette

AU GRAND VAINQUEUR

Room for 300 persons

Anniversary Banquet
In honour of the birth of
the
Humanitarian Messiah
April 15, 184 . . .
Good for one person.

N.B. There is only a half bottle of wine for
each person.

"I am not of the opinion of the disciples of the Messiah." Rudolph said to himself. "But I will partake willingly of their food." And fleet as a bird he covered the distance which separated him from the barrier.

When he arrived at the drawing rooms of the Grand Vainqueur, the crowd was immense . . . the room for three hundred persons held five hundred. A vast horizon of veal with carrots revealed itself to Rudolph.

Finally they began to serve the soup.

As the guests were carrying their spoons to their mouths five or six of the bourgeoisie and several policemen broke into the room, an officer at their head.

"Gentlemen," said the officer, "by order of the higher authority, the banquet cannot take place. I summon you to with-draw."

"Oh!" regretted Rudolph, leaving with the rest. "Oh, the sad fate which has just upset my soup!"

He sadly resumed his way home and arrived there at eleven in the evening.

Monsieur Benoit was waiting for him. "So, it's you," the proprietor greeted him. "Have you thought of what I told you this morning? Have you brought me some money?"

"I am to receive some tonight; I will give it to you tomorrow morning," responded Rudolph as he felt for his key and the candle in its pigeonhole. He found nothing.

"Monsieur Rudolph," Monsieur Benoit continued, "I am very regretful but I have rented your room, and I have no other available, you will have to search somewhere else."

Rudolph had a great soul and a night under the stars did not dismay him. Furthermore in case of bad weather he could sleep in a stage box at the Odeon, a thing which he had done before. Only, he asked for his possessions from Monsieur Benoit, which possessions consisted of a bundle of papers.

"That's true," remarked the proprietor, "I have no right to hold your things from you. They were left in the desk. Come up with me; if the person who has your room has not retired, we can enter."

The room had been rented during the day to a young woman who was called Mimi and with whom Rudolph had at one time begun a love duet.

They recognized each other at once. Rudolph whispered to Mimi and pressed her hand gently. "See how it rains!" said he calling attention to the storm which had just begun.

Mimi went straight to Monsieur Benoit who waited in a cor-ner of the room.

"Monsieur," she said pointing to Rudolph, "Monsieur is the person I expected this evening. My door is closed to anyone else."

"Ah!" Monsieur Benoit made a face. "I understand."

While Mimi was hastily improvising supper, midnight sounded.

"Ah," said Rudolph to himself. "The fifteenth of April has passed, I have finally doubled my Cape of Storms. Dear Mimi," said the young man as he took the beautiful girl in his arms and kissed her on the nape of her neck, "you couldn't have put me out. You have a large bump of hospitality."

A CAFÉ IN BOHEMIA

THROUGH the following combination of circumstances Carolus Barbemuche, man of letters, and platonic philosopher, became a member of Bohemia in the twenty-fourth year of his age.

At this time, Gustave Colline the great philosopher, Marcel the great painter, Schaunard the great musician, and Rudolph the great poet, so they regularly addressed each other, patronized the café Momus, where they were spoken of as the four musketeers, as they were always seen together. Indeed, they came and went together, played together, and sometimes too did not pay their bill together, always with a harmony worthy of the Conservatory orchestra.

They had elected to forgather in a room where forty persons

had been comfortable, but they were always found alone, for they had succeeded in making the place insupportable to the habitual visitors.

The passing guest who ventured into this den from the moment of his entrance became the victim of this wild quartet, and most of the time fled before he got hold of a newspaper or of his after dinner coffee, the cream of which was often turned by the strange epigrams on art, sentiment, and political economy. The conversations of the four friends were of such a character that the waiter who was in the habit of serving them had gone crazy in the flower of his youth.

Moreover the situation reached such a difficult point that the proprietor of the café finally lost patience and appeared one evening to state seriously his grievances:

1. Monsieur Rudolph was in the habit of coming at breakfast time and taking into "his" room all the newspapers of the establishment; he even considered it unreasonable and became angry when he found the covers broken, which proceeding made the other clients, who were deprived of the journals of opinion, wait until dinner, ignorant as carps of politics. The frequenters of the café hardly knew the names of the last cabinet members.

Monsieur Rudolph had even forced the café to subscribe to *Castor* of which he was editor-in-chief. The proprietor had at first refused; but as Monsieur Rudolph and his companions called for the waiter every quarter of an hour and demanded at the top of their lungs: "The *Castor*, bring us the *Castor*," some of the other habitués whose curiosity was aroused by these rabid demands also asked for the *Castor*,—magazine for the hat trade, which was published every month, decorated with a vignette and an article on philosophy, an extra by Gustave Colline, in the column called "Varieties."

2. The aforementioned Monsieur Colline and his friend Monsieur Rudolph found relaxation from their mental labours by playing backgammon from ten o'clock in the morning to midnight; and as the establishment only possessed one backgammon board the other guests found their passion for this game unsatisfied by the monoply of the gentlemen who each time that someone asked them for it limited themselves to replying:

"The backgammon is in use; come back tomorrow."

The guests of Bosquet were then reduced to telling each other about their first loves or to playing piquet.

3. Monsieur Marcel, unmindful that a café is a public place, had seen fit to carry his easel there, his paint box and all the instruments of his art. He even made bold to have models of both sexes come there. Which behaviour wounded the feelings of the Bosquet clients.

4. Following the example of his friend, Monsieur Schaunard

talked of having his piano moved to the café and had no reticence about having sung by a choir there a motif taken from his symphony,—*The Influence of Blue on The Arts.* Monsieur Schaunard went even farther,—he slipped in the lamp which served as a signboard for the café a transparency sign on which could be read:

FREE COURSE IN SINGING AND INSTRUMENTAL
MUSIC FOR BOTH SEXES
INQUIRE AT THE DESK

What happened was that the aforementioned desk was crowded every evening by persons of a negligent appearance, who came to ask where to go.

Moreover, Monsieur Schaunard had many rendezvous there with a woman who was called Phemie Teinturiere, who always forgot her hat.

So Monsieur Bosquet the younger declared that he would never put foot in an establishment where the bounds of nature were so outraged.

5. Not satisfied with only a very moderate order these gentlemen tried to moderate it still more. As a pretext they discovered that the coffee of the establishment was adulterated with chicory, so they brought a filter for spirits of wine and distilled their coffee themselves, which they sweetened with sugar bought outside at a low price. This was an insult to the kitchen.

6. Corrupted by the talk of these gentlemen, the waiter Bergami (so named on account of his whiskers), forgetful of his humble birth and casting aside all discretion, saw fit to address to the woman at the desk a bit of verse in which he urged her to forget her duties as a mother and a wife;—from the licentiousness of his style, it could be seen that this letter had been written under the pernicious influence of Monsieur Rudolph and his school.

Consequently, and in spite of the regret that he had, the head of the establishment found it necessary to ask the Colline party to choose another place where they might carry on their revolutionary conferences.

Gustave Colline, who was the leader of the group, assumed the speakership and 'a priori' proved to the proprietor of the café that his grievances were ridiculous and not substantiated; that they had done him a signal honour in choosing his place as a seat of their wit; that his departure and that of his friends would cause the ruin of the café, raised by their presence to the rank of artistic and literary centre.

"But," said the proprietor, "you and those who come to see you, you drink so little."

"This sobriety of which you complain is an argument in favour of our habits," replied Colline. "Moreover it rests only with you whether or not we spend more; it is only necessary for you to open an account for us."

"We will provide the book," added Marcel.

The proprietor didn't have the appearance of listening, and demanded enlightenment on the subject of the provocative letter which Bergami had addressed to his wife. Rudolph, accused of having acted as secretary for this illicit passion, proved his innocence with vivacity.

"Furthermore," he added, "the virtue of Madame was a sure proof against. . . ."

"Oh," said the proprietor . . . with a smile of pride, "my wife was educated at St. Denis."

In short Colline managed to ensnare him completely by his insidiously eloquent replies, and all was adjusted by the promise of the four friends that they would no longer consider the café all theirs, that the café from now on would receive the *Castor* free, that Phemie Teinturiere would wear a hat; that the backgammon table would be given up to the other Bosquet habitués every Sunday from noon until two o'clock, and especially that they wouldn't ask for further credit.

All went well for a few days.

The night before Christmas, the four friends arrived at the café in the company of their sweethearts.

There were Mademoiselle Musette; Mademoiselle Mimi, Rudolph's new mistress, an adorable creature whose burning voice had the timbre of cymbals; and Phemie Teinturiere, the idol of Schaunard. That evening Phemie had a hat. As for Madame

Colline, who was never seen, she had as usual remained at home, busily putting commas in her husband's manuscripts. After coffee, which was, oddly enough, accompanied by a battalion of little glasses, someone asked for punch. Little accustomed to these fine manners, the waiter had to repeat the order twice. Phemie, who had never been at the café, seemed thrilled and ravished to drink out of glasses with a stem. Marcel argued with Musette on the subject of a new hat, whose origin he suspected. Mimi and Rudolph, still in the honeymoon period of their union, were dallying together alternating their chat with

strange sounds. As for Colline, he went from woman to woman, declaring from an overflowing heart all the gallant gems of style gathered from the Almanac of the Muses.

While this jocund company gave itself over to play and laughter, a strange person seated at the end of the room at a separate table watched the gay picture which passed before him with eyes whose expression was strange. For almost two weeks he had come every evening; he was of all the patrons the only one who could stand the terrific noise which the Bohemians made. Their proudest saws found him invulnerable; he stayed there all evening, smoking his pipe with mathematical regularity, his eyes fixed as if he guarded a treasure and his ear open to all that was said around him. For the rest he seemed nice and well to do, for he had a watch held in bondage to his pocket by a gold chain. And one day when Marcel ran into him at the desk he had surprised him changing a louis to pay for his drink. From that moment the four designated him by the name of Capitalist.

Suddenly Schaunard who had excellent sight remarked that the glasses were empty.

"Dear me," said Rudolph, "tonight is Christmas eve, we are all good Christians, we must have an extra."

"My word, yes," added Marcel; "let's ask for something strange."

"Colline," added Rudolph, "ring for the waiter."

Colline shook the bell with frenzy.

"What shall we have?" asked Marcel.

Colline bent himself in two like an arc and said, pointing to the women:

"It belongs to these women to rule the order and appearance of the refreshments."

"I," said Musette, smacking her lips, "I would not fear champagne."

"Are you crazy?" exclaimed Marcel. "Champagne, in the first place, isn't wine."

"So much the worse, I love it, it is noisy."

"For me," said Mimi, fondling Rudolph with a glance, "I prefer beaune, in a little basket."

"Have you lost your mind?" asked Rudolph.

"No, I wish to lose it," Mimi responded, upon whom beaune had a special effect.

Her lover was overwhelmed by the thought.

"I," said Phemie Teinturiere giving a bounce on the elastic divan, "I would like perfect love. It's good for the stomach."

Schaunard spoke a few words in his nasal tone, which made Phemie tremble upon her foundations.

"Oh pshaw," said Marcel, "let's spend 100,000 francs, one time for luck."

"And then," added Rudolph, "the desk complains that we don't drink enough. We must astonish him."

"Yes," said Colline, "let us give ourselves over to a supurb feast! Moreover we owe these ladies the most passive obedience, love lives on devotion, wine is the essence of pleasure, pleasure is the duty of youth, women are flowers, they must be watered. Let us water them. Waiter, waiter," and Colline pulled on the bell rope in feverish excitement.

The waiter appeared as quick as the wind.

When he heard them talk of champagne, and of beaune, and of various liqueurs, his face showed all the degrees of surprise.

"I have holes in my stomach," said Mimi, "I would indeed like some ham."

"And I some sardines and butter," added Musette.

"And I some radishes," suggested Phemie, "with a little meat around . . ."

"Why don't you say at once that you wish supper then?" asked Marcel.

"That would be enough for us," the girls replied.

"Waiter, bring us whatever is needed for supper," Colline ordered solemnly.

The waiter had gone into three colours from surprise. He slowly went down to the desk and informed the proprietor of the café of the strange things that had just been ordered.

The proprietor believed that it was a joke, but at another ringing of the bell he himself went up and spoke to Colline for whom he had a certain respect. Colline explained that they wished to celebrate the festival of Christmas eve and he wished to have served what had been ordered.

The proprietor didn't answer, but went out backwards, tying knots in his napkin. For a quarter of an hour he advised with his wife, and thanks to the liberal training she had received at St. Denis, this woman, who had a weakness for the arts and letters, persuaded her husband to have the supper served.

"In fact," said the proprietor, "they might have some money once by chance."

And he gave the order to the waiter to take whatever they had asked for. Then he buried himself in a game of piquet with an old customer.—Fatal imprudence!

From ten to midnight the waiter went up and down stairs. Every moment he was asked for extras. Musette had herself served English fashion and changed the cutlery at every mouthful. Mimi drank wine from every glass. Schaunard had in his throat an unredeemable Sahara; Colline cast about him amorous glances, all the while tearing his napkin with his teeth, and pinched the leg of the table, which he mistook for Phemie's knees. As for Marcel and Rudolph, while they maintained their bold front, they saw not without disquietude the hour of settlement approaching.

The stranger viewed this scene with a solemn curiosity; from time to time his mouth would open as if to smile; then was heard a sound similar to that of a window which rattles when it is closed. It was the stranger who was laughing inside.

At a quarter before midnight the lady at the desk sent the bill. It reached the prodigious heights of twenty-five francs seventy-five.

"See here," said Marcel, "we will draw lots to see who will go argue with the proprietor. This is going to be serious. Let's take the dominoes and whoever draws the highest."

Chance unfortunately marked Schaunard as mediator. Schaunard was an excellent virtuoso, but a bad diplomat. He arrived at the counter just as the proprietor had lost to his old customer. Trembling under the shame of three defeats, Momus was in a dreadful humour, and at Schaunard's first overtures he became violently angry. Schaunard was a good musician but he had a deplorable disposition. He replied with some impertinences with double meanings. The quarrel became more and more lively and the proprietor went upstairs to inform them that he must be paid or else no one should leave. Colline attempted to intervene with his thoughtful eloquence; but seeing the napkin of which Colline had made rags, the wrath of the proprietor was doubled, and as a guarantee he even seized with a profane hand the nut-brown overcoat of the philosopher and the women's pelisses. A volley fire of insults was exchanged between the Bohemians and the master of the café.

The three women talked of love affairs and trinkets.

The stranger roused himself from his impassiveness, slowly got up, took one step, then another, and seemed at last alive; he approached the proprietor, took him aside and spoke to him in a low voice. Rudolph and Marcel followed him with their glances. The proprietor finally left saying to the stranger:

"Assuredly, I consent, M. Barbemuche, assuredly; arrange it with them."

Monsieur Barbemuche returned to his table to find his hat, put it on his head, turned to the right and in three steps was before Rudolph and Marcel, took off his hat, bowed to the men, acknowledged the ladies with a salute, drew out a handkerchief, blew his nose, and began to talk in a timid voice:

"Pardon, gentlemen, the indiscretion which I am about to commit," he said. "For a long time I have burned to make your acquaintance, but I have not found any favourable opportunity to establish myself with you. Permit me to seize this which is presented tonight?"

"Certainly, certainly," said Colline, aware of his approach.

Rudolph and Marcel bowed without saying anything.

The too exquisite delicacy of Schaunard just failed to spoil everything.

"Permit me, Monsieur," he spoke vivaciously, "you haven't the honour of knowing us, and conventions are opposed to this. . . . Would you have the kindness to give me a pipeful of tobacco? Moreover, I shall be of the same opinion as my friends. . . ."

"Gentlemen," continued Barbemuche, "I, like you, am a disciple of the arts. As I have been able to tell in hearing you talk, our tastes are the same. I have the most lively desire to be one of your friends, and to be able to join you here each evening. The proprietor of this place is a brute but I have said two words to him and you are free to go away. I dare hope you will not refuse me the chance to find you here again in accepting this small favour that. . . ."

An indignant blush mounted to Schaunard's face.

"He is trading on our position," he said; "we cannot accept. He has paid our bill; I am going to play him at billiards for the twenty-five francs and I will give him points."

Barbemuche accepted the scheme and had the good taste to lose; but this good trait won him the esteem of the Bohemians.

They parted planning to meet the next day.

"So," said Schaunard to Marcel, "we owe him nothing; our dignity is safeguarded."

"And we can almost demand another supper," added Colline.

A RECEPTION IN BOHEMIA

THE evening in a café when he had paid out of his own cash the bill for a supper eaten by the Bohemians, Carolus had managed in such a way as to leave in the company of Gustave Colline. Since he had been present at the meetings of the four friends in their eating place where he had relieved them from embarrassment, Carolus had particularly observed Colline, and already felt a real sympathy for this Socrates of whom he was later to become the Plato. That is why he had chosen him at first to be his mediator in this group. As they walked along, Barbemuche asked Colline to enter a café which was still open to have a drink. Not only did Colline refuse but even redoubled his steps as he passed before the aforementioned café and pulled his hyperphysical hat carefully down over his eyes.

"Why don't you wish to go in there?" asked Barbemuche, insisting with the politeness that good taste demands.

"I have my reasons," replied Colline; "there is at the desk of that establishment a woman who studies the exact sciences a great deal, and I could not avoid having a very prolonged discussion with her, which I try to avoid by never passing through this street at noon nor at any other hour. Oh! it's plain," Colline answered simply, "I used to live in this section with Marcel."

"But I would have very much liked to offer you a glass of punch and to chat a moment with you. Perhaps you know a place somewhere in the environs where you could enter without being stopped by the difficulties of . . . mathematics?" added Barbemuche, who deemed himself most witty.

Colline meditated for a moment.

"Here is a little place where my situation is clearer," he said. And he pointed out a wine store.

Barbemuche made a face and seemed to hesitate.

"Is this a proper place?" he asked.

Having seen his cold and reserved manner, his rare words, his discreet smile, and particularly his chain with charms and his watch, Colline had imagined that Barbemuche was employed in an embassy, and he assumed that he feared to compromise himself by going into a cabaret.

"There is no danger of our being seen," he said, "at this time all the diplomatic corps have gone to bed."

Barbemuche decided to go in, but in the bottom of his soul he would have liked to have had a false nose. For greater security, he demanded a private room and took care to spread a napkin over the panes of the glass door. Having taken these precautions he seemed less nervous and had them bring a bowl of punch. Slightly stimulated by the heat of the beverage, Barbemuche became more communicative; and after having given certain details about himself he dared state the hope that he had conceived of being an official member of the Bohemian Club, and he begged Colline's support to aid him in the successful conclusion of this ambitious project.

Colline responded that personally he was on Barbemuche's side, but he could assure him of nothing absolutely.

"I promise you my vote," he said, "but I cannot take upon myself the disposal of those of my comrades."

"But," asked Barbemuche, "for what reasons would they refuse to admit me as one?"

Colline put on the table the glass which he had just started to raise to his lips, and with a very solemn manner spoke almost exactly as follows to the bold Carolus:

"Do you cultivate the fine arts?" asked Colline.

"I labour modestly in those noble fields of knowledge," replied Carolus, who was beginning to add to the colours of his style.

Colline thought the phrase was well turned and bowed:

"Do you know music?" he asked.

"I have played the double bass."

"That's a philosophic instrument, it makes solemn sounds. Then if you know music, you understand that one cannot without wounding the laws of harmony introduce a fifth performer into a quartet; then it ceases to be a quartet."

"It becomes a quintet," answered Carolus.

"What did you say?" asked Colline.

"Quintet."

"Exactly, in the same way if to the Trinity, that divine triangle, you add another person, it would no longer be the Trinity, it would be a square, and behold a whole religion is destroyed in its principle!"

"Permit me," said Carolus, whose wits were commencing to be foggy among all the ramifications of Colline's reasoning, "I do not quite see . . ."

"Look now and follow me," continued Colline, "do you know any astronomy?"

"A little; I am a bachelor."

"There is a little song about that," said Colline: "Bachelor, said Lisette. . . . I no longer remember the tune. Then, you must know that there are four cardinal points. Well, if a fifth cardinal point should arise, all the harmony of nature would be destroyed. That would be what one calls a cataclysm. Do you understand?"

"I am waiting for the conclusion."

"Actually the conclusion is the end of the sermon, even as death is the end of life, and as marriage is the end of love. Well, my dear sir, I and my friends are accustomed to live together, and we are afraid of seeing the harmony which reigns in our union of manners, opinions, tastes and characters, destroyed by the admission of another. We are to be some day the four cardinal points of contemporary art; I say this to you without reserve; and accustomed to this idea it would annoy us to see a fifth cardinal point!"

"Meanwhile, when one is four, one can just as well be five," hazarded Carolus.

"Yes, but then one is no longer four."

"That is a futile plea."

"There is nothing futile in the world, all is in all, the little brooks make great rivers, short syllables make alexandrines, and mountains are made of grains of sand; that is in the 'Sagesse des Nations,' there is a copy of it on the quay."

"You think then that these gentlemen will make some difficulties before they will admit me to the honour of their intimate companionship?"

"I fear so indeed," replied Colline, who never missed making this joke.

"What did you say?" asked Carolus astonished.

"Pardon . . . that was a jewel!" And Colline resumed: "Tell me, my dear sir, what in the noble fields of knowledge is the furrow that you work by choice?"

"The great philosophers and the good classic authors are my models; I nourish myself from studying them. Telemachus first inspired me with the passion which devours me."

"Telemachus, there are a great many copies on the quay," said Colline. "I found one there just recently, I bought it for five sous, because it was a bargain; however, I would consent to give it up to oblige you. In addition, good workmanship, good edition, considering the season."

"Yes, sir," Carolus went on, "high philosophy and healthy literature, that is what I aspire to. In my opinion, art is a calling."

"Yes, yes, yes," said Colline, "there is a song about it too." And he began to sing:

Yes, art is a calling
And we know how to make use of it.

"I think that that is from Robert le Diable," he added.

"I was saying just now that, art being a solemn calling, writers must unceasingly. . . ."

"Pardon me, sir," Colline interrupted as he heard a late hour striking, tomorrow morning is about to be here and I am afraid of disturbing a person who is dear to me; moreover," he muttered to himself, "I had promised her to return . . . It's her birthday!"

"Indeed it is late," replied Carolus; "let us go."

"Do you live far away?" asked Colline.

"Rue Royale-Saint-Honoré, Number 10."

Colline at one time had had occasion to go in that house and remembered that it was a magnificent hotel.

"I will speak about you to these gentlemen," he said to Carolus as he took leave of him, "and you may be sure that I will use all my influence to make them like you. . . . Oh yes! Let me give you a bit of advice."

"Speak," said Carolus.

"Be friendly and gallant to Mademoiselles Mimi, Musette and Phemie; these women exercise a certain power over my friends, and in knowing how to make them use their influence on Marcel, Schaunard and Rudolph, you will manage more easily to obtain what you want."

"I will try," said Carolus.

The next day, Colline happened into the midst of the Bohemian communal life; it was the hour for luncheon, and luncheon had arrived with the hour. The three households were at table and gave themselves up to an orgy of artichokes with pepper sauce.

"Confound it!" said Colline, "one lives very well here, but that can't last. I come," said he finally, "as the ambassador of the generous being whom we met at the café last night."

"Does he send so soon to demand the money that he advanced for us?" questioned Marcel.

"Oh!" cried Mademoiselle Mimi, "I wouldn't have believed that of him, he has such a proper air!"

"That isn't the question," responded Colline; "this young man wishes to be one of us, he wishes to take an active part in our society and to share the rewards, you understand."

The three Bohemians raised their heads and looked at each other.

"There you are," Colline ended; "now the discussion is open."

"What is the social position of your protégé?" inquired Rudolph.

"He isn't my protégé," replied Colline; "last night as I left you, you begged me to follow him; on his side he invited me to accompany him, so it worked out perfectly. And I went with him; a part of the night he showered me with attentions and fine liqueurs, but in spite of it I kept my independence."

"Very well," said Schaunard.

"Enumerate to us some of his leading characteristics," suggested Marcel.

"Greatness of soul, austere habits, he is afraid of entering wine merchants' shops, bachelor of letters, candid, he plays the double bass, a nature which occasionally changes five francs."

"Very well," said Schaunard.

"What are his aims?"

"I have just told you, his ambition has no limits; he aspires to be intimate with us."

"That is to say, he wishes to use us," replied Marcel. "He wishes to be seen riding in our carriages."

"What art does he pursue?" asked Rudolph.

"Yes," Marcel took it up, "on what does he play?"

"His art?" repeated Colline. "On what does he play? Literature and philosophy mixed."

"Who are his philosophic acquaintances?"

"He practices a departmental philosophy. He calls art a calling."

"He said calling?" Rudolph was overcome.

"He did."

"And in literature what is his path?"

"He pursues Telemachus."

"Very well," said Schaunard as he chewed the choke of the artichoke.

"What! Very well, idiot?" interrupted Marcel; "don't dare to repeat that in the street."

Schaunard, irritated by this reprimand, kicked Phemie underneath the table as he had just caught her making inroads on his sauce.

"One thing more," said Rudolph, "what is his worldly situation? How does he live? His name? His dwelling place?"

"His condition is honourable; he is a professor of everything in the bosom of a rich family. His name is Carolus Barbemuche, he consumes his revenues by his luxurious habits and lives on the rue Royale, in a hotel."

"A furnished hotel?"

"No, he has some belongings."

"I would like to have the floor," said Marcel. "It is evident to me that Colline is deceived; he has sold his vote in advance for a certain number of liqueurs. Don't interrupt me," continued Marcel, seeing the philosopher getting up to protest, "you can reply in a minute. Colline, a mercenary soul, has presented this stranger to you under a light too favourable to be true. I tell you, I understand the designs of this stranger. He wishes to use us. He has said to himself: 'There are some fine fellows who are making their way; I must creep into their pockets. I will arrive with them before the gateway to renown.' "

"Very well," said Schaunard; "can it be that there is no more sauce?"

"No," replied Rudolph, "the edition is exhausted."

"On the other hand," Marcel went on, "this insidious being whose patron Colline is aspires perhaps to the honour of our friendship with only questionable intentions, guilty ideas. We are not alone here, gentlemen," continued the orator casting an eloquent glance at the ladies; "and the protégé of Colline by introducing himself to our hearthstone under the mantle of literature, could easily be nothing but a villainous seducer. Reflect! For myself, I vote against his admission."

"I wish to speak to make a correction only," said Rudolph. "In his remarkable impromptu speech, Marcel said that the aforementioned Carolus wished, for the purpose of dishonouring us, to introduce himself in our homes under the mantle of literature."

"It was a parliamentary figure of speech," Marcel rejoined.

"I find fault with that figure; it is bad. Literature has no coat."

"Since I am performing here the function of reporter," said Colline as he got up, "I will uphold the conclusions of my report. The jealousy which devours him is impairing the senses of our friend Marcel, the great artist is insane . . ."

"Come to order," growled Marcel.

"Insane, to the point that he, such a good designer, has just introduced into his discourse a figure, the incorrectness of which the intelligent orator who has succeeded me to this chair has just pointed out."

"Colline is an idiot," shouted Marcel as he gave a violent blow of his fist on the table, thereby creating a profound disturbance among the plates. "Colline understands nothing of the nature of the affections, he is incompetent to discuss the question, he has an old bookshop in place of a heart."

(Prolonged shouts from Schaunard.)

During all this confusion, Colline seriously shook out the waves of eloquence stored in the plaits of his white cravat. When silence was established he thus continued his discourse:

"Gentlemen, I will in a word dispel from your minds the chimerical fears which Marcel's suspicions would have aroused there in regard to Carolus."

"Try a bit to dispel them," Marcel laughed.

"It will be no more difficult than this," responded Colline as he extinguished with a breath the match with which he had just lit his pipe.

("Speak, speak," they all cried together, Schaunard, Rudolph, the girls, to whom the debate offered great amusement.)

"Gentlemen," said Colline, "although I have been personally and violently attacked within these walls, although I have been accused of selling the influence which I have with you for alcoholic spirits, clean is my conscience. I will not respond to the attacks which have been made on my integrity, my loyalty, my morality." (Emotion.) "But, there is one thing I wish to have respected, I." (The orator gave himself two punches in the stomach.) "It is my prudence which is well known to you that has been doubted. I am accused of wishing to have penetrate into our midst a being who designs to be an enemy to the happiness of your affections. This idea is an insult to the virtue of these women, and moreover an insult to their good taste. Car-

olus Barbemuche is very ugly." (Visible denial on the face of
Phemie Teinturiere, noise under the table. It is Schaunard who
is reprimanding by kicks his young friend's compromising
frankness.)

"But," continued Colline, "what will reduce to powder the
wretched argument out of which my adversary has made a
weapon against Carolus by arousing your fears, is that the
aforementioned Carolus is a platonic philosopher." (Sensation
on the men's bench, tumult on the ladies' bench.)

"Platonic, what does that mean?" asked Phemie.

"It is an illness of men who dare not kiss the ladies," said
Mimi. "I had a lover like that. I kept him for two hours."

"How foolish!" said Musette.

"You are right, my dear!" Marcel told her, "a platonist in
love, it is the same as water in wine, do you understand? Let's
drink our wine pure."

"And long live youth!" added Musette.

Colline's statement had started a favourable reaction in
Carolus' favour. The philosopher wished to profit by the good
will aroused by his eloquent and skilful censure. Now he continued: "I can't see what actually would be the objections that
could be raised against this young person, who, after all, has
served us. As for me, who have been accused of acting rashly
in wishing to introduce him into our midst, I consider that
opinion in contempt of my dignity. I have behaved in this matter with the prudence of a serpent; and if a ratifying vote
doesn't confirm this prudence I offer my resignation."

"Would you be willing to put the question to the cabinet?"
asked Marcel.

"I put it," responded Colline.

The three Bohemians consulted together and with common
accord it was decided to restore to the philosopher his character
of extreme prudence which he demanded. Colline gave the
platform at once to Marcel who, inclined a bit toward his objections, declared that perhaps he would vote for the conclusions
of the reporter. But before taking a deciding vote which would
grant to Carolus the intimacy of Bohemia, Marcel had brought
to a vote the following amendment: As the introduction of a

new member in the group was a very serious matter, as a stranger could introduce to it elements of discord because of his ignorance of the manners, characters and opinions of his comrades, each of the members would spend a day with the said Carolus and would devote himself to a study of his life, his tastes, his capacity for literature and his wardrobe. The Bohemians would communicate at once with each other as to their particular impressions, and afterwards his admission or refusal would be granted. Furthermore, before this admission, Carolus was to undergo a novitiate of a month, that is to say, that he would not have the right before this period elapsed of calling them by their first names or of taking their arms on the street. The day of his reception, a splendid ball would be given at the new member's expense. The budget for the celebration could not amount to less than twelve francs.

This amendment was adopted by a majority of three to one, Colline, who decided that not enough confidence was being placed in him and that this amendment again questioned his prudence.

The same evening, Colline expressly arrived at the café at an early hour in order to be the first to see Carolus. He did not wait long; Carolus soon arrived bearing in his hand three enormous bunches of roses.

"What!" Colline was astonished. "What do you plan to do with this garden?"

"I remembered what you told me yesterday, your friends will doubtless come here with their ladies and it is for them that I have brought the flowers; they are very beautiful."

"Certainly . . . They must be worth at least fifteen sous."

"You think so?" objected Carolus. "In the month of December! Now if you had said fifteen francs."

"Oh, heavens!" exclaimed Colline, "a trio of écus for these simple gifts from Flora, how foolish! Then you are a relative of the Cordillieri? Well my dear sir, there is fifteen francs that we will be forced to throw out the window."

"What! What do you mean?"

Colline then recounted the jealous suspicions which Marcel had aroused in his friends, and informed Carolus of the violent discussion which had taken place that morning among the Bohemians on the subject of his entrance into their club. "I swore that your intentions were pure," added Colline, "but the opposition was none the less active. So keep from again arousing the jealous suspicions that will come if you are too gallant to the ladies and to begin let us hide the bouquets." And Colline took the roses and hid them in a cupboard which served as a refuge for waste. "But that isn't all," he went on; "these gentlemen wish before uniting themselves intimately with you, to hold each one separately an inquest over your character, your tastes, etc." Then that Barbemuche wouldn't run too foul of his friends Colline outlined rapidly for him a mental portrait of each of the Bohemians. . . . "Try to agree with each one of them separately," added the philosopher, "and in the end they'll be all for you."

Carolus agreed to everything.

The three friends soon came in accompanied by their consorts.

Rudolph was very polite to Carolus, Schaunard was familiar, Marcel remained reserved. As for Carolus, he endeavoured to be gay and friendly with the men and very indifferent to the women. As they separated for the evening, Barbemuche invited Rudolph to dine the next day. Only he begged him to come at noon. The poet accepted.

"Good," he said to himself, "it's I who will commence the inquest."

The next day at the appointed hour Rudolph appeared at Carolus' residence. Barbemuche actually lived in a very beautiful hotel on the rue Royale, and occupied in it a room in which a certain degree of comfort reigned. Only Rudolph seemed astonished to see that although it was midday, the shutters were closed, the shades were drawn and two candles were lit on the table. He asked Barbemuche to explain.

"Study is the daughter of mystery and silence," responded the latter. They seated themselves and conversed. At the end of an hour's talk, Carolus with infinite patience and oracular cleverness introduced a sentence which in spite of its simple form was nothing less than a summons to Rudolph to listen to a pamphlet which was the fruit of Carolus' labour. Rudolph realized that he was caught. Curious, however, to see the colour of Barbe-muche's style he bowed politely and assured him that he was enchanted. Carolus didn't wait for the end of the sentence.—He hastened to bolt the door of the room, locked it with a key on the inside and came back to Rudolph. He at once took a little notebook whose narrowness and slimness brought a smile of satisfaction to the poet's face.

"Is that the manuscript of your work?" he asked.

"No," answered Carolus, "it is the catalogue of my manu-scripts, and I am looking for the number of the one you will permit me to read you. . . . Here it is: *Don Lopez, or The Fatality; No. 14.* It is on the third shelf," said Carolus and he opened a small cupboard in which Rudolph, almost overcome, perceived a large quantity of manuscripts. Carolus took one, closed the cupboard and sat down opposite the poet.

Rudolph glanced at one of the four notebooks of which the work was made up, written on paper with a Champ de Mars water mark.

"What," he asked himself, "it isn't in verse! But it is called Don Lopez."

Carolus took the first volume and thus commenced the reading:

"On a cold night in winter, two cavaliers, wrapped in the folds of their cloaks and mounted on lazy mules, traversed side by side one of the roads which invade the hideous solitude of the deserts of the Sierra Morena. . . ."

"Where am I?" thought Rudolph, overwhelmed by this beginning. Carolus thus continued to read the first chapter, all written after this fashion. Rudolph listened vaguely and searched for a chance to escape. "There is the window," he said to himself; "but even if it weren't closed, we are on the fourth floor. Ah, now I understand all these precautions."

"Well, what do you think of my first chapter?" asked Carolus, "I beg of you do not spare me your criticisms."

Rudolph thought he remembered hearing some scraps of

blatant philosophy on suicide, offered by the man named Lopez, hero of the novel, and he answered on a chance:

"The great figure of Don Lopez is developed conscientiously; it calls to mind the 'Profession of Faith of a Savoyard Priest'; the description of Don Alvar the mule pleases me tremendously; it could be an outline by Gericault. The landscape calls forth some lovely lines; as for the ideas, it is the seed of J. J. Rousseau sowed in the soil of Lesage. Only let me make an observation. You use too many commas, and you abuse the word 'henceforth'; it is a nice word, effective if used from time to time, it gives colour but one mustn't abuse it."

Carolus took his second notebook and read again the title *Don Lopez or The Fatality*.

"I formerly knew a Don Lopez," said Rudolph; "he sold cigarettes and Bayonne chocolate, he was a relative of yours perhaps . . . continue. . . ."

At the end of the second chapter the poet interrupted Carolus. "Doesn't your throat hurt a little?" he asked him.

"Not at all," replied Carolus; "you will now hear the story of Inesilla."

"I am most curious. Only if you are tired," said the poet, "you mustn't . . ."

"Chapter three!" read Carolus in a clear tone.

Rudolph scrutinized Carolus carefully and perceived that he had a very short neck and a florid colour. "I have one hope still," thought the poet when he had made this discovery. "That is apoplexy."

"We are going on to Chapter four. You will oblige me by telling me what you think of the love scene." And Carolus resumed his reading.

At a moment when he glanced at Rudolph to read in his face what effect the dialogue produced, Carolus saw the poet bent forward in his chair extending his head in the position of a man who listens for distant sounds.

"What's wrong?" he asked.

"Shhh!" said Rudolph; "don't you hear? It seems to me that someone called fire! We might go see?"

Carolus listened a moment but heard nothing.

"My ears must be tingling," said Rudolph, "go on; Don Alvar interests me tremendously; he is a noble young man."

Carolus went on reading and put all the music possible in this speech of the young Don Alvar:

"O Inesilla, whoever you are, angel or devil, whatever your country, my life is yours, and I will follow you whether it be to heaven or hell."

At this moment there was a knock on the door and a voice called Carolus from outside.

"That's my janitor," he said as he unbolted the door. Actually it was the janitor; he brought a letter; Carolus opened it anxiously. "Bother the interruption," he said; "we will have to put off the reading to another time; I am in receipt of news which forces me to leave at once."

"Oh," Rudolph thought, "that's a letter which falls straight from heaven; I recognize the seal of Providence."

"If you wish," resumed Carolus, "we will go together to the place where this message calls me and after we will dine."

"I am at your command," said Rudolph.

That evening when he returned to the club, the poet was questioned by his friends on the subject of Barbemuche.

"Are you pleased with him? Did he treat you well?" demanded Marcel and Schaunard.

"Yes, but it cost me a lot," replied Rudolph.

"How? Did Carolus make you pay?" asked Schaunard, his indignation growing.

"He read me a novel in the midst of which the characters are named Don Lopez and Don Alvar, and the young heroes call their mistresses Angel or Demon."

"How horrible!" choired the Bohemians together.

"But otherwise," asked Colline, "literature aside, what do you think of Carolus?"

"He is a good young man. Moreover you can make your own personal observations: Carolus is counting on entertaining us one after the other. Schaunard is invited for dinner tomorrow.

Only," added Rudolph," when you go to Barbemuche's home, distrust the manuscript cupboard, it is a dangerous piece of furniture."

Schaunard was prompt at the meeting place, and gave himself over to an examination worthy of an auctioneer and bailiff making a seizure. And he returned in the evening, his mind filled with notes, as he had studied Carolus from the point of view of personal equipment.

"Well," they asked, "what is your opinion?"

"Oh," responded Schaunard, "this Barbemuche is filled with good qualities, he knows the names of every wine, and only eats delicate things, the kind they have at my aunt's on feast days only. It seems to me that he is intimately connected with tailors of the Vivienne and booters from the Panoramas. I noticed furthermore, that he is almost the size of all of us, which means that at need we could lend him our suits. His manners are less severe than Colline said; he has let himself be taken wherever I wished to take him, and has paid for a dinner in two acts, the second of which took place in the cabaret in the market, where I am known for having indulged in divers orgies during the carnival. Carolus went there like a real man. There you have it! Marcel is invited for tomorrow."

Carolus realized that Marcel, of the Bohemians, offered the greatest obstacle to his being received in the group; so he treated him with particular care; but he made himself most pleasing to the artist when he gave him hope that he would procure some commissions for him from his pupil's family. When it was Marcel's turn to report, his friends found no longer that determined hostility which he had shown at first against Carolus. The fourth day, Colline told Barbemuche that he was admitted.

"What! I am received?" shouted Carolus, overcome with joy.

"Yes," replied Colline, "but with restrictions."

"What do you mean by that?"

"I mean that you still have a quantity of small vulgar habits which you must correct."

"I will do everything to imitate you," replied Carolus.

During the whole time of his novitiate the platonic philosopher attended the Bohemians assiduously; and, giving himself over to studying their habits more deeply, he sometimes experienced tremendous shocks. One morning, Colline entered Barbemuche's room, his face radiant. "Well, well, my dear fellow," he said to him, "you are actually one of us, it is all over. Now there only remains to settle the day of the great fête and the place where it will take place; I have come to arrange with you."

"But that can be arranged perfectly," replied Carolus; "the parents of my pupil are at the moment in the country; the young viscount, whose teacher I am will lend me their apartment for one evening; there, we will be more comfortable; only we will have to invite the young viscount."

"This is a delicate situation," replied Colline; "we will open new literary horizons to him. But do you think he will consent?"

"I am sure of it."

"Then it remains only to set the day."

"We will plan that at the café," said Barbemuche.

Carolus went at once to his pupil and announced to him that he had just been received into a rare literary and artistic society and that to celebrate his reception he counted on giving a dinner followed by a little party; he planned to have him be one of the guests; "and as you cannot return late and as the party will last well into the night for our convenience," added Carolus, "we will give this small gala affair here, in your apartment. François, your servant, is discreet, your parents will know nothing, you will have made the acquaintance of the wittiest people in Paris."

"Have they been published?" asked the young man.

"Published, assuredly; one is the editor in chief of the *Scarf of Iris* which your mother receives; these are very distinguished people, almost celebrated. I am their intimate friend; they have charming ladies."

"There will be ladies?" asked Viscount Paul.

"Ravishing," answered Carolus.

"Oh, my dear teacher, I thank you; to be sure, we will give the party here; all the chandeliers will be lighted and I will have the covers taken from the furniture."

That evening at the café Barbemuche announced that the party would take place the following Saturday.

The Bohemians invited their mistresses to think of their dresses.

"Don't forget," they told them, "that we are going to real drawing rooms. So now prepare for it; simple costumes, but elegant."

Beginning with that day the whole street was informed that Mademoiselles Mimi, Phemie and Musette were launching into the world.

This is what happened on the morning of the great occasion. Colline, Schaunard, and Rudolph went in a group to Barbemuche, who seemed astonished to see them so early.

"Has some accident occurred which obliges us to postpone the celebration?" he asked with a certain nervousness.

"Yes and no," answered Colline. "Only, this is the way it is. Among ourselves we never go in for ceremony; but when we are to be among strangers we wish to maintain a certain decorousness."

"Yes?" said Barbemuche.

"So," Colline went on, "as we are to foregather this evening with the young gentleman who is opening his drawing rooms to us, out of respect to him and to us, as our almost slovenly appearance might compromise us, we have simply come to ask you if you would not for this evening lend us some clothes to cut a certain dash. It is almost impossible for us, you must realize, to come in blazer and great coat to the sumptuous surroundings of this residence."

"But I haven't four black suits," said Carolus.

"Ah," said Colline, "we will manage with what you have."

"Look it over," Carolus said as he opened a wardrobe sufficiently well stocked.

"But here you have an arsenal filled with elegance."

"Three hats!" Schaunard was ecstatic. "Can one have three hats when one has only one head!"

"And shoes," cried Rudolph, "have a look at them!"

"Now those are shoes!" roared Colline.

In a twinkling of an eye they had each chosen a complete outfit. "Until this evening," they said to Barbemuche as they took their leave; "these girls are planning to be dazzling."

"Oh see here," said Barbemuche as he cast a glance over his completely empty clothes press, "you have left me nothing. How shall I receive you?"

"Oh, for you it's different," said Rudolph, "you are the master of the house. You need pay no attention to form."

"Be that as it may," complained Carolus, "there is only left one dressing gown, one pair of pantaloons, a flannel waistcoat and some slippers; you have taken everything."

"It doesn't matter. We pardon you in advance," the Bohemians responded.

At six o'clock a very fine dinner was served in the dining-room. The Bohemians arrived. Marcel limped a bit and was in bad humour. The young viscount leapt to the ladies' side and led them to the best places. Mimi had a very fantastic toilet. Musette was gowned with provocative taste. Phemie resembled a coloured glass window, she didn't dare sit down at the table. The dinner lasted two hours and a half and the gaiety was immense.

The young viscount Paul tramped furiously on Mimi's foot, who was his neighbour, and Phemie asked for something twice at each course. Schaunard was in his cups. Rudolph improvised sonnets and broke glasses as he accented the metre. Colline talked to Marcel, who was very irritable.

"What's wrong?" he asked.

"My feet hurt me horribly and that makes me cross. That Carolus has the foot of a small mistress."

"But," comforted Colline, "he need only to understand that things can't go on like this and in the future he is to have his shoes made several sizes larger; rest assured, I will manage it. But let's go in to the drawing rooms where the liqueurs from the islands call us."

The festivities were renewed with greater spirit. Schaunard sat down at the piano and executed with tremendous verve his new symphony: "The Death of the Young Girl." The fine fragment of the march of the "Creditor" won for the author the honour of being recalled three times. There were two strings broken in the piano.

Marcel was still sulky, and as Carolus approached to chide him he responded: "My dear sir, we will never be intimate friends and this is the reason. Physical differences are nearly always a certain indication of a moral difference, philosophy and medicine agree to that."

"What!" exclaimed Carolus.

"So!" answered Marcel pointing to his feet. "Your shoes are much too narrow for me and indicate to me that we haven't like characters; otherwise your little party was charming."

At one o'clock in the morning the Bohemians departed and after making long detours arrived at home. Barbemuche was sick and carried on a senseless conversation with his pupil who, for his part, dreamed of Mademoiselle Mimi's blue eyes.

THE HOUSEWARMING

THE following took place sometime after the poet Rudolph began to live with young Mademoiselle Mimi; and for a week, the whole Bohemian group was in great sorrow over Rudolph's disappearance, which had suddenly become inexplicable. They had searched for him in every place where he was in the habit of going and everywhere they had received the same answer: "We haven't seen him for a week." Gustave Colline, especially, was seriously disquieted and this is the reason: Several days before, he had entrusted to Rudolph an article on deep philosophy which the latter was to insert in the column "Varieties" in *Castor*, a review of elegant head gear of which he was editor in chief. This philosophical article, had it appeared to the eyes of astonished Europe? Such was the question that the unhappy Colline asked himself; and his anxiety can be understood when it is known that the philosopher had not yet had the honour of appearing in the press, and that he burned with the desire to see what effect his prose printed in pica type would produce. To procure this satisfaction to his pride, he had already spent six francs to enter every reading room in Paris without finding a *Castor*. Not being able to bear it longer Colline swore to himself that he would not rest a moment until he had put his hand on the elusive editor of this magazine.

Aided by chances too long to be recounted the philosopher had kept his word. Two days later he knew Rudolph's abiding place, and appeared there at six in the morning.

Rudolph was inhabiting then a furnished hotel on a deserted street in the Saint Germain district, and he roomed on the fifth floor because there wasn't a sixth. When Colline came to the door he found no key in it. He knocked for ten minutes with no response from within; the early racket even attracted the janitor who came to beg Colline to be quiet.

"You can see that the gentleman is asleep," he said.

"That's why I wish to waken him," replied Colline as he rapped again.

"He doesn't want to answer you then," remarked the janitor as he placed at Rudolph's door a pair of polished boots and a pair of woman's slippers which he had just shined.

"See here," said Colline as he examined the male and female shoes, "polished shoes that are very new! I have mistaken the door, it isn't here that I wish to do business."

"Actually," asked the janitor, "whom are you searching?"

"A woman's shoes!" Colline muttered to himself as he meditated on the austere habits of his friend. "Yes, I certainly am deceived. This isn't Rudolph's room."

"Pardon me, sir, but it is here."

"Then you too are deceived, my man."

"What do you mean?"

"I mean that you are wrong," Colline pointed to the polished shoes. "What is that?"

"They are Monsieur Rudolph's shoes, why is that so astonishing?"

"And those," Colline pointed to the slippers, "are those Monsieur Rudolph's too?"

"They are his lady's," replied the janitor.

"His lady!" Colline was stupefied. "Ah, the voluptuary! That's why he won't open."

"Ahem!" thought the janitor. "This young man is outspoken!" Then aloud, "If the gentleman will leave his name I will tell Monsieur Rudolph."

"No," said Colline. "Now that I know where to find him I shall come back."

And he departed at once to announce the great news to his friends.

Rudolph's polished boots were generally accepted as products of Colline's rich imagination and they agreed that his mistress was a paradox. However, this paradox was a truth; for that same evening Marcel received a letter written for all the friends. This letter went as follows:

Monsieur and Madame Rudolph, men of letters, beg you to do them the honour of dining with them tomorrow evening at exactly five o'clock.

N.B. There will be plates.

"Gentlemen," Marcel went to communicate the contents of the letter to his comrades. "The news is confirmed; Rudolph actually has a mistress; furthermore he invites us to dine," and Marcel went on, "A postscript promises dishes. I will not hide it from you that this paragraph seems to me to be poetic licence; however we will see."

The next day at the time designated Marcel, Gustave Colline, and Alexander Schaunard, famished as if it were the last day of Lent, appeared at Rudolph's where they found him playing with a red cat while a young woman was laying the table.

"Gentlemen," said Rudolph as he shook his friends' hands and indicated the young woman, "permit me to present to you the mistress of the house."

"It is you who are the house, isn't it?" asked Colline, who had a weakness for this type of joke.

"Mimi," replied Rudolph, "I present my best friends to you and now go serve the soup."

"Oh, Madame," Alexander Schaunard hurled himself at Mimi, "you are fresh as a wild flower."

And after he had convinced himself that there actually were plates on the table, Schaunard found out what there was to eat. He even indulged his curiosity to the point of removing the covers of the dishes in which the dinner was cooking. The presence of a lobster made a deep impression upon him. As for Colline, he had taken Rudolph aside to demand news of his philosophic article.

"My dear, it is at the press. *Castor* appears next Thursday."

We give up painting the philosopher's joy.

"Gentlemen," Rudolph addressed his friends, "I beg your pardon for remaining away so long without giving you news; but I was on my honeymoon." And he related the story of his marriage with this charming creature who had brought him a dowry of eighteen years and six months, two china cups and a red cat which was called Mimi too.

"And now, friends," he added, "we will have a housewarming for my establishment. I warn you, however, that we will have a simple repast; the truffles will be replaced by the sincerest friendliness."

In reality that amiable goddess didn't cease to reign over the convivial spirits, who discovered furthermore that the afore-mentioned frugal repast did not lack a certain style. Rudolph, actually, had spent some money. Colline had to remark that the plates were really changed, and declared at the top of his lungs that Mademoiselle Mimi was worthy the blue scarf with which empresses of the kitchen are decorated, a sentence which was perfect Sanskrit to the young girl, and which Rudolph translated to her as: she would make a very good cook.

The appearance on the scene of a lobster caused general wonder. Under the pretext that he had studied natural history, Schaunard demanded that he cut it up; he even profited by this situation to break a knife and to appor-tion the largest part to himself, which aroused popular indignation. But Schaunard had no pride at all, especially in the matter of lobster; and as a portion of it yet remained he had the audacity to put it to one side explain-ing that it would serve as a model for a still life picture he had in mind. Indulgent friendship pretended to believe this lie, a result of immoderate gourmandry.

As for Colline, he reserved his enthusiasms for the dessert and was very firm, even violently so, about not exchanging his share of the rum cake for an entrance ticket to the orangery at Versailles which Schaunard offered him. Meanwhile the con-versation began to be animated. Three bottles of red seal were followed by three of green seal in the midst of which was soon seen to appear a flask which, by its neck surmounted by a silver casque, could be recognized as forming a part of the Royal Champenois regiment, a fancy champagne gathered in the vineyards of Saint Ouen and sold at Paris for two francs a bottle because the merchant pretended he was selling out his busi-ness.

But it isn't the country that makes the wine, and our Bohemians accepted as authentic the liqueur which was served them in special glasses; and in spite of the small anxiety the cork showed to escape from its prison, they were thrilled over the excellence of the vintage when they saw the quantity of froth. Schaunard used what courage he had left to mix up the glasses and to take Colline's, who was solemnly moistening his cracker with mustard as he explained to Mademoiselle Mimi the philosophy article which was to appear in *Castor*. Then suddenly he became pale and asked permission to go to the window to watch the sun set, although it was ten at night and the sun had set and had been sleeping for some time.

"It is very unfortunate that the champagne isn't chilled," remarked Schaunard as he again tried to substitute his empty glass for his neighbour's full one, an attempt which met with no success.

"Madame," Colline who had given up taking the air addressed Mimi, "champagne is chilled with ice, ice is made by the condensation of water, 'aqua' in Latin. Water freezes at two degrees and there are four seasons, summer, autumn and winter, the latter caused the retreat from Russia. Rudolph, give me a hemistich of champagne."

"What did your friend say?" Mimi, who didn't understand, asked Rudolph.

"It's just a word," responded the latter; "Colline means a half glass."

Suddenly Colline tapped Rudolph's shoulder briskly and said to him in an embarrassed tone, which seemed to make dough of the syllables: "Tomorrow is Thursday, isn't it?"

"No," replied Rudolph, "tomorrow is Sunday."

"No, Thursday."

"No again, tomorrow is Sunday."

"So! Sunday," Colline murmured as he swung his head, "more often tomorrow is Thursday." And he fell asleep letting his head droop in the cream cheese which was left on his plate.

"Why does he sing about Thursday?" asked Marcel.

"Oh! I know now," Rudolph began to understand the philosopher's insistence, he who was gripped by one idea; " it is because of his *Castor* article. Listen, he is dreaming out loud."

"Good," Schaunard remarked, "he won't get any coffee, will he, Madame?"

"Speaking of such things," Rudolph began, "serve the coffee, Mimi."

She was about to get up when Colline, having recovered a bit of his boldness, grasped her around the waist and whispered confidentially to her:

"Madame, coffee originated in Arabia where it was discovered by a goat. Its use passed to Europe. Voltaire drank seventy-two cups a day. For me, I like it without sugar, but I like it very hot."

"Heavens, how learned the man is!" thought Mimi as she fetched the coffee and pipes.

Meanwhile it was getting later; midnight had passed long ago and Rudolph tried to make his comrades understand that it was time to go home. Marcel who had remained entirely sober got up to leave.

But Schaunard perceived that there was still a bit of brandy in a bottle and declared that it wouldn't be midnight as long as a drop remained in a flask. As for Colline he sat astride his chair and muttered in a deep voice: "Monday, Tuesday, Wednesday, Thursday."

"Dear me!" Rudolph was most annoyed. "I certainly can't keep them here all night; in other days it could be done; but now it's entirely different," he added as he sought Mimi's sweet glance, which seemed to demand solitude for the two.

"But what can we do? Marcel, give me a bit of advice. Invent a trick to get them out."

"No, I won't invent one," said Marcel, "but I will use an old one. I remember a comedy where an intelligent valet took the opportunity of putting out of his master's house three rogues drunk as Silenus."

"I remember that," said Rudolph, "it's in Kean. Actually the situation is the same."

"Well," continued Marcel, "we shall see if the theatre is nature. Wait a bit, we will begin with Schaunard. Oh! Schaunard!" shouted the painter.

"Eh? What is it?" muttered that one, who seemed to be swimming in the peace of sweet drunkenness.

"There is nothing more to drink here and how thirsty we all are."

"Oh yes," agreed Schaunard, "these bottles are so small."

"Well," resumed Marcel, "Rudolph thinks we ought to spend the night, but we must go out foraging before all the shops are closed. . . ."

"My grocer lives at the corner," said Rudolph. "Schaunard, you must go. Buy two bottles of rum for me."

"Oh yes, oh yes, oh yes!" chanted Schaunard as he made a mistake and took instead of his own overcoat that of Colline, who was cutting pictures on the table cloth with his knife.

"That's one," said Marcel when Schaunard had left. "Let's try Colline, he will be difficult. Oh, I have it. I say, Colline," and he struck the philosopher hard.

"What? . . . What? . . . What? . . ."

"Schaunard has just gone and by mistake has taken your nut-brown overcoat." Colline looked around him and, sure enough, perceived in the place where his things were Schaunard's little checked cloak. A sudden idea crossed his mind and agitated him. Colline, as was his habit, had visited the bookshops that day and bought for fifteen sous a Finnish grammar and a short novel by Monsieur Nisard entitled *The Milkmaid's Funeral*. To these two purchases were added seven or eight volumes of deep philosophy which he always carried with him in order to have a storehouse for arguments in case a philosophical discussion should arise. The thought of having his library in the hands of Schaunard put him in a cold sweat.

"The villain!" Colline complained; "why did he take my overcoat?"

"By mistake."

"But my books. . . he might hurt them."

"Don't worry, he won't read them," Rudolph reassured him.

"Yes, I know that; but he is capable of lighting his pipe with . . ."

"If you are worried you can catch up with him," Rudolph interrupted, "he just now left; you will find him at the door."

"To be sure, I will catch him," Colline responded as he put on his hat, the rim of which was so wide that tea for ten could easily be served on it.

"There are two," Marcel told Rudolph; "you are free, I am leaving, and I will tell the janitor not to open the door if anyone knocks."

"Good night, and thanks!" Rudolph replied.

As he had just taken his friend to the door Rudolph heard on the stairway a prolonged meowing to which his red cat responded with another, trying at the same time with a certain subtlety to slip through the half open door. "Poor Romeo," said Rudolph, "here is his Juliet who calls; well, go on," and he opened the door for the enamoured animal which only needed one leap on the stairway to be wrapped in the paws of his lover.

Alone with his mistress, who standing before a mirror was curling her hair in a charmingly provocative manner, Rudolph went to Mimi and took her in his arms. Then, as a musician who before commencing to play, tries a series of chords to assure himself of the tone of the instrument, Rudolph seated the young Mimi on his knees and placed on her shoulder a long and resounding kiss, which created a sudden vibration in the body of that creature of the spring.

The instrument was in tune.

MADEMOISELLE MIMI

"MY friend, Rudolph, what could have happened to change you so? Must I believe the rumours that I hear, and can this unhappiness puncture your robust philosophy to this extent? How can I, historian ordinary of your Bohemian days, bristling so with shouts of laughter, how can I recount in a sad enough tone the sorry adventure which puts to rout your ever present gaiety and suddenly puts an end to the flow of your nonsense? Oh Rudolph, my friend, I understand that your sorrow is great but there, it isn't worth drowning oneself for indeed. Now I beg you to forget the past as quickly as possible. Above all, flee from the solitude peopled with ghosts which make your regrets last forever. Flee from the silence where the echoes of memories will still be full of your past joys and sorrows. Courageously throw to the four winds of forgetfulness the name that you loved so much and throw with it all that is yet left to you of her who bore it. Knots of hair bitten by lips mad with desire; the Venetian glass bottle, where yet remains a bit of perfume, which at this moment would be worse for you to breathe than all the poisons of the world. Throw in the fire the flowers, the flowers of gauze, of silk, and of velvet, the white jasmine; the anemones stained with the blood of Adonis, the blue forgetmenots, and all those charming bouquets which she made in those far off days of your short happiness. Then, I loved her too, I loved your Mimi and I saw no danger in your loving her. But follow my advice; throw into the fire the ribbons, the jolly ribbons, rose, blue and yellow, with which she made collars to provoke attention; throw away the laces and the bonnets, the veils and chiffons in which she arrayed herself to make mathematical love to Monsieur Caesar, Monsieur Jerome, Monsieur Charles or any other gallant of the moment, when you waited her at your window trembling under the wintry blasts and frost; into the fire, Rudolph, and without pity all that belonged to her and all that yet could remind you of her; into the fire with the love letters. Stop, here indeed is one and you have wept over it like a fountain, my poor unfortunate friend!

" 'Since you have not come home I am going to my aunt's; I am taking all the money I find here, to take a carriage.—Lucile.'

"And that evening, you didn't dine, Rudolph, do you remember? And you came to my house and let off fireworks of jokes which bespoke the quietness of your mind. For you thought that Mimi was at her aunt's and if I had told you she was with Monsieur Caesar or with a comedian from Montparnasse you would have certainly wanted to cut my throat. Throw into the fire this other note too, which holds all the laconic love of the other:

" 'I am going to order some slippers. You must absolutely get some money that I can get them day after tomorrow.'

"Ah, my friend, those slippers have indeed danced a quadrille when you were not the partner. Into the flames with all the souvenirs, throw their ashes to the winds.

"But first, O Rudolph, for humanity's sake and for the glory of the *Scarf of Iris* and of *Castor*, assume the reins of good taste which you let go during your selfish suffering, and if you do not, dreadful things may happen for which you will be responsible. We might return to a leg of mutton sleeve, to pantaloons, and a day might usher in a style in hats which would upset the universe and arouse the wrath of heaven."

And now is the moment to recount our friend Rudolph's love affair with Mademoiselle Lucile, nicknamed Mademoiselle Mimi. Rudolph was about twenty-four years old when his heart was suddenly attacked by this passion which had a great influence on his life. At the time when he met Mimi, Rudolph led that casual and odd existence which we have tried to describe in the foregoing chapters of this book. He was assuredly one of the gayest endurers of misery in the Bohemian world. And during a day when he had dined badly but spoken cleverly, more proudly did he walk the streets, which often failed to find a home for him, more proudly did he feel under his black suit, which cried for mercy from every seam, than an emperor beneath his purple robes. In the group which Rudolph frequented, a fairly common attitude for several young men was to consider love as a bit of luxury, an excuse for jesting. Gustave Colline, who had had relations for ages with a garment maker, whom he rendered deformed in body and spirit by having her copy the manuscripts of his philosophical works by day and night, pretended that love was a kind of purge, good to be taken at every new season in order to free one from moods. In the midst of all these false sceptics, Rudolph was the only one who dared to speak with some reverence of love; and when one had the bad fortune to let him get on this subject, he had to listen for an hour to philippics on the joy of being loved, the blue of a restful lake, song of the breeze, concert of stars, etc., etc. This mania had been termed the "Harmonica" by Schaunard. Marcel made an amusing remark on this subject too, when alluding to Rudolph's sentimental and Germanic monologues as well as to his precocious baldness he called him: bald forgetmenot. The real truth of the matter was this: Rudolph then seriously believed that he had finished with all the pleasures of youth and love; he proudly sang the "De Profundis" over his heart which he thought dead when it was only inert, but ready to awake, and be receptive to joy and more than ever tender towards all the dear annoyances which he hoped for no longer and which today filled him with despair. "You wanted it, O Rudolph, and we won't pity you, for this ill which you suffer is one desired most, especially if it is known that one is cured for ever."

Now Rudolph met young Mimi whom he had known formerly when she was the mistress of one of his friends. And he made her his. At first there was a great to-do among Rudolph's friends when they learned of his marriage; but as Mademoiselle Mimi was very prepossessing, not at all proud, and endured without headaches pipe smoke and literary conversations, they became used to her and treated her like a friend. Mimi was a delightful woman and had a temperament which especially fitted in with Rudolph's plastic and poetic sympathies. She was twenty-two years old; she was small, delicate, arch. Her face seemed the rough outline of an aristocratic countenance; but her features, of a certain delicacy and so sweetly illuminated by the depths of her clear blue eyes, took on in certain moments of ennui and ill temper a suggestion of almost wild brutality which a physiologist would perhaps call a sign of a deep selfishness or a great insensibility. But more often it was a charming head with a fresh young smile, with tender glances or full of a lordly flirtatiousness. Her youthful blood ran hot and quick in her veins, and coloured with rose tints the skin, transparent in its camellian whiteness. This unhealthy beauty seduced Rudolph and he often spent many hours of the night crowning with kisses the pale forehead of his sleeping mistress, whose soft and wearied eyes sparkled half closed under the curtain of her magnificent brown hair.

But what contributed more than anything to make Rudolph madly in love with Mademoiselle Mimi were her hands, which, in spite of housework, she knew how to keep whiter than the hands of the goddess of Sloth. In addition, her hands were slight, so small, so soft for lips' caresses, these hands of a child, between which Rudolph had placed his heart, once again in flower, these white hands of Mademoiselle Mimi were soon to scratch the poet's heart with their pink nails.

By the close of a month Rudolph began to perceive that he had married a tempest and that his mistress had a great failing. She was neighbourly, as they say, and spent a great part of her time with the mistresses of the quarter, whose acquaintance she had made. The result soon was that Rudolph was worried when he saw the acquaintances contracted by his mistress. The changing wealth of some of her new friends aroused a forest of ambitions in the spirit of Mademoiselle Mimi, who had until that time only modest desires and was contented with necessities which Rudolph obtained as best he could for her. Mimi began to dream of silk, velvet and lace. And in spite of Rudolph's protests, she went on visiting these women who were united to persuade her to break with the Bohemian who could not even give her one hundred fifty francs to buy a cloth dress.

"Pretty as you are," her advisers said to her, "you can easily find a better situation. You need only search." And Mademoiselle Mimi began to look around. Witness of her many goings out, stupidly explained, Rudolph entered on the pathetic path of suspicion. But when he thought he was on the track of some proof of faithlessness, he unmercifully tied a bandage about his eyes that he might see nothing. Moreover, in spite of what he knew, he adored Mimi. He had for her that jealous love, fantastic, quarrelsome and bizarre that the young woman did not understand, because she then only felt for Rudolph that indulgent attachment which is the result of habit. And in addition half of her heart had already been spent during her first love and the other half was still filled with memories of that first lover.

Eight months passed like this, good days alternating with bad. During this period, Rudolph was twenty times on the verge of separating from Mademoiselle Mimi, who subjected him to all the stupid cruelties of a woman who doesn't love. To tell the truth, this life had become a hell for both of them. But Rudolph was accustomed to these daily battles and feared nothing as much as seeing this state of things stop, because he felt that with it would cease forever these youthful passions and disturbances which he had not experienced for so long a time. And then, if everything must be said, there were hours when Mademoiselle Mimi knew how to make Rudolph forget all the lacerations which covered his heart. There were moments when she brought to his knees like a child under the charm of her blue glance, this poet to whom she had brought back his lost poem, this young man to whom she had given back youth, and who, thanks to her, was on love's equator. Two or three times a month in the middle of their stormy quarrels, Rudolph and Mimi would pause, by common consent, in the fresh oasis of a night of lovemaking and quiet talk. Then Rudolph took the smiling and vivacious head of his love between his arms, and during whole hours he would let himself go and would talk to her in that admirable and absurd language which passion improvises for its high moment. Mimi listened, calm at first, rather astonished than affected, but in the end Rudolph's enthusiastic eloquence, now tender, now gay, now sad, won her little by little. She could feel this love melt the icy indifference which engulfed her heart; contagious fevers began to move her, and she threw herself on Rudolph's neck saying with kisses what she could not put into words. And daybreak came upon them so, embracing one another, eyes together, hands entwined, while their moist and burning mouths still murmured the immortal word

> Which through five thousand years
> Are borne each night upon the lips of lovers.

But the next day, the most silly pretext provoked a quarrel and the overpowering love fled again for a long time.

At the end, finally, Rudolph realized that if he didn't watch out, Mademoiselle Mimi's white hands would have led him on a road to an abyss where his future would be gone, and with it his youth. One moment, austere reason appealed to him more strongly than love, and he was convinced by fine reasoning, supported by proofs, that his mistress didn't love him. He went so far as to say to himself that the hours of love she granted him were only a whim of feeling similar to the feeling which married women evince for their husbands when they have a passion for a new cashmere shawl or a new dress, or when their lover is far away. It reminds one of the proverb: when there is no white bread, one takes brown. In short Rudolph could forgive his mistress for everything but not loving him. He at last took definite action and announced to Mademoiselle Mimi that she would have to look for another lover. Mimi began to laugh and boast. Finally, seeing that Rudolph was firm in his resolution and received her with great calm when she returned home after a night and day spent elsewhere, she began to be agitated a bit because of this firmness to which she wasn't accustomed. Then she was agreeable for two or three days. But her lover did not rescind what he had said and limited himself to asking if she had found anyone.

"I haven't even searched," she replied.

But she had searched, and even before Rudolph had advised her to do so. In two weeks she had made two trials. One of her friends had helped her and first had procured for her the acquaintance of a young fellow who had extended before Mimi's eyes a horizon of Indian shawls and rosewood furniture. But Mimi's own opinion was that this young schoolboy who was so strong at algebra, was no great shakes at lovemaking; and as Mimi did not go in for training people, she left this novice at love, with his shawls still roaming over Tibetan prairies and his rosewood furniture still growing in the forests of the new world.

The schoolboy was not long in being replaced by a Breton gentleman with whom Mimi had rapidly become infatuated, and she didn't have to beg long to become a countess.

In spite of the denials of his mistress, Rudolph got wind of this intrigue. He wished to know exactly where he stood, and one morning, after a night when Mademoiselle Mimi had not come back at all, he hurried to the place where he suspected her of being and where he could leisurely bury in the depths of his heart one of those proofs in which he had to believe whether or not. With her eyes smouldering with sensuous pleasure, he saw Mademoiselle Mimi leave the mansion where she had been ennobled, hanging on the arm of her new lord and master, who, it must be said, seemed much less proud of his new conquest than that handsome Greek farmer, Paris, was after his abduction of the beautiful Helen.

Mademoiselle Mimi seemed a trifle surprised to see her lover approaching. She went up to him and for five minutes they chatted very quietly together. Then they separated, each to go his own way. The break had come.

Rudolph returned home and spent the day wrapping into packages all that belonged to his mistress. During the day which followed the break with his mistress, several of his friends visited him and he told them all that had happened. Everyone congratulated him for it as if it were a great fortune. "I will help you, my poet," one of these said to him, the one who had been most often the witness of the pain Mademoiselle Mimi had made Rudolph endure, "I will help you to take back your heart from the hands of that bad person. And in time you will be healed and quite ready for another Mimi, for the green roads of Aulnay and of Fontenay-aux-Roses."

Rudolph swore that he was through forever with regrets and despair. He allowed himself to be led to the ball Malbille where his tattered clothes were a poor witness for the *Scarf of Iris* which had procured for him his entrance to this fine garden of elegance and pleasure. There Rudolph again met friends with whom he began to drink. He told his sorrow to them in a rich style of an unheard-of oddness and for an hour he was bubbling over with life and spirits.

"Alas! alas!" sighed the artist Marcel when he heard his friend's lips rain a flood of mockery, "Rudolph is too gay, much too gay."

"He is charming!" replied a young woman to whom Rudolph had just offered a bouquet; "and even though he were dressed much worse I should willingly compromise myself to dance with him, should he ask me." Two seconds later, Rudolph, who had heard, was at her feet, folding his invitation in a speech radiant of musk and all the asadulcis of a gallantry worthy of Richelieu at his best. The girl remained dumbfounded before a language starred with overpowering adjectives and chosen phrases and so elegant that the tip of Rudolph's shoes blushed for him who had never before been such an old Sèvres gentleman. The invitation was accepted.

Rudolph was as ignorant of the first principles of the dance as he was of the rule of three. But he was moved by extraordinary boldness, and did not hesitate at all to start out; he even improvised a dance unknown to all past dance forms. It was a dance which he named the dance of regrets and sighs, the originality of which won an incredible success. The three thousand gas burners in vain put out their tongues as if to make fun of him; Rudolph continued, and without mercy sang in his partner's face reams of entirely uncensored songs.

"Alas," sighed Marcel, "it is incredible; Rudolph reminds me of a drunken man who skates on broken glasses."

"In the meantime he has found a proud woman," commented another, as he saw Rudolph fleeing with his dancing partner.

"You aren't saying good-bye," Marcel shouted to him. Rudolph came to the artist and gave him his hand. That hand was cold and damp as a watery rock.

Rudolph's companion was a strong daughter of Normandy, a nature rich and full, whose original simplicity had at once been made aristocratic by the refinements of Parisian luxury and an indolent life. She was called something like Madame Seraphine, and was for the nonce the mistress of a Rheumatism, peer of France, who gave her fifty louis a month, which she shared with a gentleman behind a counter, who gave her only blows. Rudolph had pleased her and she hoped he would give her nothing as she led him home with her.

"Lucile," she said to her chamber maid, "I am not at home to anyone." And she retired into her room but returned at the end of five minutes reclothed in a special costume. She found Rudolph still and silent, for since his entrance, in spite of himself, he had been buried in depths racked with silent sobs.

"You don't look at me now, you don't speak," Seraphine was astonished.

"Come," Rudolph said to himself as he raised his head, "I'll look at her, but for art's sake only."

"And what a spectacle appeared before his eyes!"

As Raoul says in *The Huguenots*.

Seraphine was wonderfully beautiful. Her fine figure, cleverly displayed at its full value by the cut of her clothes, appeared most provocative under the partial transparency of her material. All the urgent fever of desire was renewed in Rudolph's blood. A warm mist rose to his brain. He watched Seraphine for other reasons than aesthetic pleasure, and he took the hands of the beautiful girl in his. They were superb hands and one would have said they had been sculptured by makers of the purest Greek statues. Rudolph felt her remarkable hands tremble in his; and less and less a critic of art, he drew Seraphine to him; her face already was tinged with that flush which is the dawn of desire.

"This creature is a real instrument for pleasure, a true Stradiva-rius of love, on whom I would gladly play an air," thought Ru-dolph, hearing very distinctly the beautiful person's heart beat its quick measures.

At this moment there was a sudden and sharp pull of the doorbell at the apartment.

"Lucile, Lucile," cried Seraphine to the maid, "don't open,—say that I have not yet returned."

At the name of Lucile, pronounced twice, Rudolph got up. "I cannot bother you in the slightest, Madame," he said. "Fur-

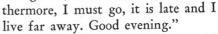

thermore, I must go, it is late and I live far away. Good evening."

"What! you are going away?" Seraphine cried, as she redoubled the brightness of her glances. "Why, oh why do you leave? I am free, you can stay."

"Impossible," Rudolph replied. "I expect one of my parents, who is com-ing from the land of fire, and he would disinherit me if he didn't find me at home to receive him. Good eve-ning, Madame."

And he left in haste. The servant went to make a light for him. Inadvertently Rudolph raised his eyes to hers. She was a young pale woman with a slow step; her very pale face made a pleasing contrast with her black, naturally wavy hair, and her blue eyes seemed like two sick stars.

"Ghost!" Rudolph recoiled from her who bore the name and face of his mistress. "Go away! What do you want of me?"

And he descended the stairway in haste.

"Madame," said the chambermaid as she re-entered the room, "that young man is crazy."

"Call him foolish rather," responded Seraphine, exasperated. "Oh," she added, "that will teach me to be good. If that imbecile of a Leon had only the wit to come now!" Leon was the gentle-man whose love brought a horsewhip.

Rudolph ran home without taking a breath. As he went upstairs he found the red cat which uttered plaintive meows. It had been two nights that he had called in vain for his faithless lover, an angora Manon Lescaut, fled in gallant company over the neighbouring roofs— "Poor beast," said Rudolph, "so some-one has deceived you too; your Mimi has characteristics like mine. Enough! Let's console ourselves. You see, my poor beast, women's hearts and tabbies' are abysms which men and toms can never fathom." When he entered his room, although he was extremely hot, Rudolph felt as if a cloak of ice had fallen on his shoulders. It was the cold of loneliness, of that loneliness at night which nothing comes to dispel. He lit his candle and then saw the ruined room. The furniture showed empty drawers, and from floor to ceiling an immense sadness filled this little room, which seemed to Rudolph larger than a desert. As he paced, he stum-bled over the packages of objects belonging to Mademoiselle Mimi and it was with a start of joy that he realized that she had not yet come for them, as she had said she would do in the morn-ing. Rudolph felt the moment of reaction coming on in spite of all his struggles, and he foresaw that in a horrible night he would expiate all the bitter joy of the evening. But, he hoped that his body, breaking with weariness, would go to sleep be-fore the awakening of his griefs which had been buried in his heart.

He approached the bed, drew the curtains and saw that it had not been disturbed for two days. Before the two pillows placed side by side, under one of which still lay half hidden the trim-ming of a woman's cap, Rudolph felt his heart bound in the invincible vise of that withering sorrow which cannot burst. He fell at the foot of the bed, put his forehead in his hands, and after having thrown a glance around the desolate room, he mourned:

"O little Mimi, joy of my house, is it really true that you are gone, that I have sent you away, and that I shall never see you again? O heavens! O sweet brown head which has slept in this spot for so long, will you never return to sleep there again? O whimsical voice whose caresses made me delirious, and whose angers charmed me, will I never hear you again? O little white hands, have you really had my last kiss?" And Rudolph in a wild rage buried his head in the covers still filled with the perfume of his love's hair. From the depths of this alcove he seemed to see departing the ghost of beautiful nights which he had spent with his young mistres. He heard resound clear and true in the midst of the night silence Mademoiselle Mimi's jolly laugh, and he remembered that delightful and contagious gaiety with which she had known how to make him so many times forget all the difficulties and hardships of their chancy life. During all that night he reviewed the eight months which he had just lived with this young woman who perhaps had never loved him, but whose tender lies could give back to Rudolph's heart its youth and early strength.

The whitening dawn surprised him at the moment, when overcome by fatigue, he had just closed his eyes, reddened with tears shed during the night. Gloomy and terrible vigil, and more than one such the most scoffing and sceptical among us could find in the depths of his past.

In the morning when his friends came in, they were startled when they saw Rudolph. His face was ravaged by all the anguish which had assailed him during his vigil on the Mount of Olives of love.

"Here," said Marcel, "I was sure of it; yesterday's gaiety has reacted on his heart. This can't go on this way."

And in concert with two or three comrades, he began a series of indiscreet revelations about Mademoiselle Mimi, each word of which buried itself like a thorn in Rudolph's heart. His friends proved to him that at all times his mistress had deceived him like a simpleton, at home and away, and that this creature, pale as the angel of consumption, was a mine of evil feelings and wicked instincts.

And one after the other took turns in the task that they had undertaken, whose end was to lead Rudolph to the point where embittered love would turn to hate; but this end was only half attained. The poet's despair changed to anger. He hurled himself in rage on the packages which he had made the day before; he put to one side all the objects which his mistress owned when she came to him, and he planned to keep all that he had given her during their union, that is, the larger part, and it included the toilet articles to which Mademoiselle Mimi clung with all the fibres of her vanity, which had become insatiable in the end.

Mademoiselle Mimi came the next day to fetch her things. Rudolph was at home and alone. It took all the strength of his pride to keep him from throwing himself around his mistress' neck. He received her in a manner full of silent injury and Mademoiselle Mimi answered him by cold and sharp insults that would have made the weakest and most timid put out their claws. In the face of the scorn with which his mistress whipped him with headstrong insolence, Rudolph's wrath broke forth fierce and devastating; one minute, Mimi, white with fear, wondered if she were going to be allowed to get out of his hands alive. At the cries which she uttered, neighbours came and tore her out of Rudolph's room. Two days later a friend of Mimi's came to ask Rudolph if he would return the things he still had.

"No," he replied. And he made his mistress' messenger talk to him. This young woman told him that young Mimi was in a very unhappy state and that she would be without a roof to cover her.

"And her lover, about whom she was so mad?"

"Oh," Amelie responded, "the lover in question never had the slightest intention to make her his mistress. He has had one for ever so long and he seemed little interested in Mimi, who is in my care and bothers me a great deal."

"Let her take care of herself," said Rudolph, "she wanted to; it doesn't interest me." And he said some sweet nothings to Mademoiselle Amelie and persuaded her that she was the most beautiful woman in the world.

Amelie told Mimi about her interview with Rudolph.

"What did he say? What did he do?" asked Mimi. "Did he mention me?"

"Not at all; you are already forgotten, my dear; Rudolph has a new mistress, and he has bought her a fine outfit, for he has received a lot of money and he too is dressed like a prince. He is most agreeable, that young man, and said delightful things to me."

"I know what that means," thought Mimi.

Every day Mademoiselle Amelie went to see Rudolph for one excuse or another; and, however he tried, he could not keep from talking to her about Mimi.

"She is very gay," replied the friend, "and gives no impression of being worried over her situation. Moreover, she is confident she can return to you whenever she likes without making any previous advance and for the sole reason of maddening your friends."

"That's all right," said Rudolph, "let her come and we shall see."

And he again began to court Amelie, who parted to tell all to Mimi and to assure her that Rudolph was very smitten with her.

"He kissed my hand and neck again," she told her; "look, it is all red. He wants to escort me to the ball tomorrow."

"My dear friend," Mimi was a bit annoyed. "I see what you are trying to do,—you are trying to make me believe that Rudolph is in love with you and that he thinks of me no more. But you waste your time both with him and with me."

The fact was that Rudolph was only agreeable to Amelie to get her there often and to have the chance of talking to her about his mistress. With a Machiavellianism which had perhaps an end Amelie, perceiving perfectly that Rudoph continued to love Mimi, and that the latter was not far from going back to him, managed by some cleverly invented reports to avoid everything that could bring the two lovers together.

The morning she was to go to the ball Amelie went to ask Rudolph if the party was still on.

"Yes," he replied, "I don't want to lose the chance of being beau to the most beautiful creature of modern times."

Amelie adopted the coquettish attitude she used the evening of her only appearance in a suburban theatre, in a fourth-rate role of soubrette, as she promised she would be ready for the evening.

"By the way," continued Rudolph, "tell Mademoiselle Mimi

that if she wishes to be faithless to her lover and to spend a night with me, I will give back all her things."

Amelie performed this commission for Rudolph and gave to his words a meaning very different from that he meant to convey.

"Your Rudolph is an unworthy man," she informed Mimi; "his proposal is infamous. He wishes to make you lower yourself by this move to the rank of the most wicked people; and if you go to him, not only will he not give you back your things, but he will make you a laughing stock to all his friends; it is a plan arranged among them all."

"I won't go," said Mimi;—and as she watched Amelie laying out her clothes, she asked her if she were going to the ball.

"Yes," the other replied.

"With Rudolph?"

"Yes, he is to come twenty steps from the house to fetch me this evening."

"I hope you have fun," said Mimi; and when she saw the time for the meeting approaching she ran in great haste to Mademoiselle Amelie's lover and warned him that the latter was in the very act of betraying him with her former lover. The gentleman, jealous as a tiger and rough as a cudgel, appeared at Mademoiselle Amelie's and informed her that he thought it a good plan if she spent the evening with him.

At eight o'clock Mimi flew to the place where Rudolph was to meet Amelie. She perceived her lover who walked up and down in the attitude of a man who is waiting. She passed beside him twice without daring to accost him. Rudolph was very chic that evening and the violent sorrows to which he had been prey for a week gave his face great character. Mimi was strangely moved. Finally, she decided to speak to him. Rudolph received her without anger and inquired for her health, after which he was informed of the reason of her appearance; all this in a soft voice from which she tried to repress a note of tenderness.

"I've come to give you bad news; Mademoiselle Amelie can't go to the ball with you; her lover keeps her."

"Then I shall go to the ball alone."

At this point Mimi pretended to stumble and caught herself on Rudolph's shoulder. He took her arm and proposed to accompany her to her home.

"No," said Mimi, "I live with Amelie; and as she has her lover I cannot return until he has departed."

"Listen," the poet then said to her, "I sent a proposal to you before through Mademoiselle Amelie; has she given it to you?"

"Yes," said Mimi, "in terms which even after what has happened I would put no faith. No, Rudolph, I cannot think, in spite of all you have to reproach me with, that you would think me so heartless as to accept an exchange like that."

"You didn't understand me, or you have been misinformed. What was said still stands," said Rudolph; "it is nine o'clock, you have three hours still to reflect in. My key will be in my door until midnight. Good evening, farewell, or till we meet again."

"Farewell," said Mimi in a trembling voice.

And they left each other. . . . Rudolph went home and threw himself still dressed on his bed. At eleven-thirty Mademoiselle Mimi entered the room.

"I have come seeking your hospitality," she said, "Amelie's lover is still there and I cannot go in."

They talked until three in the morning. An explanatory conversation where from time to time an informal style took the places of the formality of their official discussion.

At four o'clock the candle burned out. Rudolph wished to light a new one.

"No," said Mimi, "it isn't worth the trouble; it is time to go to sleep." And five minutes later her pretty brown head had refound its place on the pillow; and in a voice full of feeling she begged for Rudolph's lips on her small white hands with the blue veins, whose pearly paleness vied with the whiteness of the bed linen. Rudolph did not light a candle.

The next morning Rudolph got up first; and showing Mimi several packages, he said to her very gently:

"Here is all that belongs to you,—you can take it away; I shall keep my word."

"Oh!" said Mimi, "I am very tired, you see, and I cannot

carry all those big packages at one time. I prefer to return." And after she had dressed she took only a collar and a pair of cuffs. "I will take what remains . . . little by little," she added smilingly.

"See here," said Rudolph, "take all or nothing, but this is the end."

"Let it be the beginning, on the contrary, and let it last above everything," said young Mimi, kissing Rudolph. After lunching together, they set out for the country. Passing through the Luxembourg, Rudolph met a great poet who had always received him with a charming grace. For propriety's sake, Rudolph pretended not to see him. But the poet wouldn't let him; and as he passed signalled to him in a friendly way and gave his young friend a charming smile.

"Who is that gentleman?" Mimi asked. Rudolph told her a name which made her blush with pleasure and pride.

"Oh," said Rudolph, "this meeting with the poet who has sung so well of love is a good omen and presages happiness in our reconciliation."

"I love you," said Mimi, clasping his hand although they were in midst of a crowd.

"Alas," thought Rudolph, "which is better, to let one's self be deceived constantly in order to believe or never believe for fear of being always deceived?"

DONEC GRATUS

W E have told how the artist Marcel came to know Mademoiselle Musette. United one morning by the machinations of Chance, who is the mayor of the thirteenth district, they had decided to unite,—just as very often happens without having their hearts in it. But one evening after a violent quarrel, when they had resolved to leave each other at once, they perceived that their hands, which were clasped in farewell, were no longer willing to separate. Almost without their knowing it, what was a whim had become love. They admitted it to each other half smilingly.

"This thing that has happened to us is very serious," said Marcel. "How the devil has it happened?"

"Oh!" Musette replied, "we are very stupid; we didn't take enough precautions."

"What's wrong?" asked Rudolph, now Marcel's neighbour, who had just come in.

"It is this," replied the latter as he bowed to Musette, "that Mademoiselle and I have just made a charming discovery. We are in love. It must have happened while we were sleeping."

"Oh! Oh! While you were sleeping, I shouldn't think so," said Rudolph. "But what proof have you that you are in love? Perhaps you are magnifying the danger."

"My word!" replied Marcel. "We cannot bear each other."

"And we cannot leave each other," added Musette.

"Then, my children, your situation is plain. You wanted to play to the limit and you have both lost. It's the same thing with Mimi and me. Presently there will be two calendars about which we will argue day and night. It is by such a system as this that marriages are made everlasting. Join one yes with a no, and you obtain a union similar to that of Philemon and Baucis. Your private life will be the same as mine; and if Schaunard and Phemie come to live in this building as they have threatened

to do, our trio of nests will make a very happy community."

At this moment Gustave Colline entered. He was informed of the accident which had just happened to Marcel and Musette.

"Well, philosopher, what do you think of it?" Marcel asked.

Colline scratched the felt hat which served as a roof for him and murmured: "I was sure of it in advance. Love is an instrument of chance. Meddle and smart for it. It isn't good for a man to live alone."

That evening when he returned home Rudolph said to Mimi: "There is news. Musette is mad about Marcel and no longer wishes to leave him."

"Poor girl," responded Mimi. "She who has such a good appetite."

"And for his part, Marcel is taken up with Musette. He adores her thirty-six karats' worth, as that joker Colline would say."

"Poor fellow," pitied Mimi, "he who is so jealous!"

"That's true," agreed Rudolph, "he and I are pupils of Othello."

Some time later, to the households of Rudolph and Marcel was joined that of Schaunard; the musician moved into the house with Phemie Teinturiere. Beginning with that day, all the other neighbours in the house slept upon a volcano, and, at the end of their quarter, unanimously gave notice to the proprietor.

Few days actually went by without a storm bursting in one of the households. Often it was Mimi and Rudolph, who, no longer having the strength to speak, explained themselves to each other with the aid of any missiles which were at hand. Most often it was Schaunard who made certain observations to the gloomy Phemie with the end of his cane. As for Marcel and Musette, their arguments were carried on in the privacy of their own house; they at least took the precaution of closing their doors and windows.

If by any chance harmony reigned in the establishments the other tenants were no less victims of this passing peace. The thinness of the partitions allowed to penetrate to them all the secrets of the Bohemian homes and initiated them in spite of themselves into all their mysteries. So, more than one neighbour preferred the "casus belli" to the ratifications of the peace treaties.

To tell the truth, it was a very odd existence that was led there during six months. The most loyal devotion was practised without favouritism in this group where everything belonged to everybody and good or bad fortune was shared by all alike.

During the month there were certain days of splendour, when not one went on the street without wearing gloves—days of gaiety—when they dined the whole day. There were others when they almost had to go down to the courtyard without shoes—days of lent—when, after not lunching in common, they did not dine together, or indeed they were forced by economic reasons to face one of those meals when plates and utensils took a holiday, as Mademoiselle Mimi termed it.

But the amazing thing was that in this association where there were three young and pretty women, no evidence of discord rose between the men; they were often brought to their knees by the most futile whims of their mistresses, but not one of them would have hesitated a minute between mistress and friend.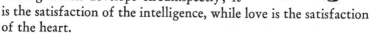

Love thrives especially on spontaneity; it is an improvisation. Friendship, on the contrary, is built up so to speak; it is a feeling which develops circumspectly; it is the satisfaction of the intelligence, while love is the satisfaction of the heart.

The Bohemians had known each other for six years. This long period had been spent in a daily intimacy without its affecting the highly developed individuality of each, and they had established among them an agreement in ideas, a harmony which they would never have found elsewhere. They had habits which were peculiar to them, a secret language to which strangers would not have known how to find the key. Those who did not know them well called their freedom of conduct cynicism. However, it was only frankness. Spirits that were restive under any duty imposed, they hated all falseness and distrusted common things. Accused of exaggerated vanities, they replied by listing proudly the program of their ambition; and having a knowledge of their worth, they did not abuse each other.

During all the years of following the same ways together, and though often rivals through necessity, they had never ceased being friends and had, without being aware of it, avoided all conceit every time that someone had tried to raise it in order to cause dissension among them. Moreover, they judged each other exactly for what each was worth; and pride, which is the counter irritant for envy, kept them from all the petty jealousy of their crafts.

However, after six months of living together, an epidemic of divorce suddenly broke out in every establishment.

Schaunard started it. One day, he perceived that Phemie Teinturiere had one knee better made than the other; and, as in matters of sculpture he was an extreme purist, he sent Phemie away giving her as a souvenir the cane with which he made so many observations to her. Then he went to live with a relative who offered him free lodgings.

Two weeks later, Mimi left Rudolph to ride in the carriages of young viscount Paul, the former pupil of Carolus Barbemuche, who had promised her dresses of the colour of the sun.

After Mimi, it was Musette who gained her freedom and entered with great clatter the haunts of aristocracy which she had given up to live with Marcel. This separation had taken place without a quarrel, without agitation, without premeditation. Born of a whim which had turned into love, this liaison was broken by another fancy.

One evening during the carnival, at the mask ball at the Opera, which she had attended with Marcel, Musette had as her partner in a square dance a young man who at other times had flirted with her. They recognized each other, and while dancing exchanged a few words. Without intending to, perhaps, while she told the young man about her present life, she let escape a regret for her past. When they came to the end of the quadrille, Musette made a mistake, and, instead of giving her hand to Marcel who was her escort, she took the hand of her partner opposite her who led her away and disappeared with her in the crowd.

Marcel looked for her, rather upset. At the end of an hour he found her on the young man's arm. She was leaving the café of the Opera, her mouth full of refrains. When she saw Marcel, who had stationed himself, arms crossed, in a corner, she made a sign of farewell to him, while she said: "I am coming back."

"That is to say, do not wait for me," Marcel translated. He was jealous, but he was logical and knew Musette; so he did not wait for her; he went home with a heavy heart for all that, but with a light stomach. He looked in a cupboard to see if there were any remains to eat; he found a piece of granite-like bread and a skeleton of red herring.

"I would not protest against truffles," he thought. "At least Musette will have supper." And after having wiped his eyes with a corner of his handkerchief under the pretext of drying them, he went to bed.

Two days later Musette woke up in a boudoir hung in rose. A blue coupé waited her at the door; and all the fairies of fashion dancing attendance brought to her feet their wonders. Musette was ravishing, and her youth seemed to be rejuvenated again in the midst of this frame of elegancies. Then she began her former mode of living, went to all the festivities and regained her celebrity. Everyone spoke of her, in the Exchange corridors and even in the parliamentary refreshment rooms. As for her new lover, Monsieur Alexis, he was a charming young man. Often he complained to Musette that he found her a bit light and a bit impatient when he talked to her of his love; then Musette would smile at him, tap him on the hand and say:

"What do you wish, my dear? I have stayed six months with a man who fed me on salad and soup without butter, who dressed me in an Indian cotton dress and took me very often to the Odeon because he had no money. As love costs nothing and as I was mad about this monster, we have expended it particularly. There remains now for me nothing but some crumbs. Gather them up, and I shan't hinder you. In addition, I haven't tricked you; and if ribbons didn't cost so much, I would still be with my artist. As for my heart, since I am wearing a corset which cost eighty francs, I cannot hear it making a loud racket, and I am quite afraid that I forgot it in one of Marcel's drawers."

The breakup of the three Bohemian establishments was the occasion of a celebration in the house where they had lived. To show his pleasure, the proprietor gave a great dinner and the lodgers put lights in their windows.

Rudolph and Marcel had gone to live together; they had each taken an idol whose names they didn't even know exactly. Sometimes they happened to speak, one of Musette, the other of Mimi; then they were busy for an evening. They reminded each other of their former life, of the songs of Musette and of Mimi, and the white nights, and the lazy mornings and the dinners they had in their dreams. One by one they went over in those duets of memories every hour that had passed; and they generally finished by telling each other that after all they were happy to find themselves together again, feet on the mantels poking the December fire, smoking their pipes, and having in the other the excuse for chatting, for telling aloud to each other what they would say to themselves when they were alone; that they had loved much these beings who had left, taking away the brightness of their youth, and that perhaps they loved them still.

One evening while crossing the boulevard, Marcel perceived at a short distance from him a young woman who while getting out of her carriage displayed a bit of her white stocking which had a very special charm; even the coachman devoured with his eyes this charming tip.

"Heavens," said Marcel, "that's a pretty leg; I have a strong desire to offer it my arm; let's see . . . how can I accost her? This is a task. . . . It is rather new."

"Pardon, Madame," he said as he approached the unkown, the whole of whose face he couldn't see, "you wouldn't by any chance have found my handkerchief."

"Yes, Monsieur," the young woman replied; "here it is." And she placed in Marcel's hand a handkerchief which she had in hers.

The artist stepped back overcome with astonishment.

But suddenly a shout of laughter full in his face made him recover; at this joyous fanfare he recognized his former love.

It was Mademoiselle Musette.

"Ah," she teased, "Monsieur Marcel is chasing adventures. How do you like this one, eh? She doesn't lack gaiety."

"I can bear her," Marcel responded.

"Where are you bound in this section so late?" Musette questioned.

"I am going to this monument," replied the artist pointing to a little theatre where he was admitted free.

"For love of art?"

"No, for love of Laura. Stop," thought Marcel, "that's a pun, I will sell it to Colline; he is making a collection."

"Who is Laura?" continued Musette, whose looks were interrogation points.

Marcel continued his mean joking.

"She is a wraith I am following, who plays ingénue parts in this small place." And he stroked an ideal jabot.

"You are certainly witty this evening," Musette said.

"And you very curious," Marcel replied.

"Don't talk so loud, —everyone can hear you; we shall be taken for lovers who are quarrelling."

"It wouldn't be the first time that that had happened," Marcel said.

Musette was provoked by this sentence to reply at once: "And perhaps it won't be the last, eh?"

The thought was plain; it whistled like a bullet in Marcel's ear.

"Splendours of the heavens," he remarked as he gazed at the stars, "you are witnesses that it isn't I who have fired the first shot. Quick my armour!"

Counting from that moment, the firing began. It was only a question of finding a proper hyphen to join these two fancies which had just awakened so gaily.

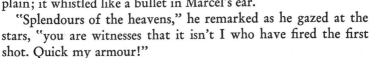

While walking along, Musette looked at Marcel, and Marcel looked at Musette. They didn't speak to each other; but their eyes, plenipotentiaries of the heart, often met each other. After a quarter of an hour of diplomacy this congress of glances had quietly arranged the matter. Only its ratification remained.

The conversation which had been interrupted was renewed.

"Honestly," Musette asked Marcel, "where were you going just now?"

"I told you I was going to see Laura."

"Is she pretty?"

"Her mouth is a nest of smiles."

"That's an old story," said Musette.

"But you," asked Marcel, "whence were you coming on the wings of this hackney coach?"

"I have just accompanied Alexis to the railroad as he was leaving for a visit to his family."

"What kind of man is this Alexis?"

In her turn, Musette made a ravishing portrait of her real lover. As they walked along Marcel and Musette continued right on the boulevard this comedy of the "revenez-y" of love. With the same naïveté, now tender, now joking, they remade, verse by verse, that immortal ode where Horace and Lydia boast with so much grace of the charms of their new loves and finish by adding a postscript to their old loves. As they came to the end of a street, a rather large night patrol appeared suddenly.

Musette managed a slightly frightened attitude and leaning against Marcel's arm, said to him:

"Oh, dear me, look, there is a troop coming; there must be going to be another revolution. Let us save ourselves,—I am terribly afraid; take me home."

"But where are we going?" asked Marcel.

"To my place," said Musette, "you can see how pretty it is. I shall give you supper, and we shall talk politics."

"No," said Marcel, who thought of Monsieur Alexis; "I will not go home with you in spite of supper. I don't like to drink my wine in other persons' glasses."

Musette remained silent before this refusal. Then, through the mist of her memories, she perceived the starved interior of the poor artist, for Marcel had not become a millionaire; then Musette had an idea, and profiting by the meeting with another patrol, she displayed new terror.

"They are going to fight," she shouted; "I shall never dare to go home. Marcel, my friend, take me to one of my friends who must live in your quarter."

As they crossed the Pont Neuf, Musette burst out laughing.

"What's wrong?" asked Marcel.

"Nothing," said Musette; "I remember that my friend has given up housekeeping and lives near the Batignolles."

Seeing Marcel and Musette come in arm in arm, Rudolph was not astonished. "These love affairs which are badly buried," he said,—"they always rise again like this."

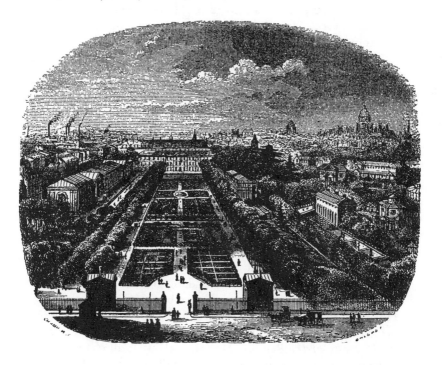

THE CROSSING OF THE RED SEA

FOR five or six years Marcel had been working on this famous canvas which he swore was to represent the Crossing of the Red Sea; and for five or six years this colour masterpiece had been refused obstinately by the jury. In fact, by reason of going and returning from the artist's studio to the Museum and from the Museum to the studio the picture knew the way so well that if it had been put on wheels it could have gone alone to the Louvre. Marcel, who had done it over ten times and touched it up from top to bottom, laid to a personal enmity of the members of the jury the ostracism which excluded it annually from the Salon Carré; and in his dejected moments he had composed in honour of the Cerberuses of the Institute a small dictionary of injuries with illustrations which had a sharp ferocity. This collection, now become famous, had obtained in the studios and at the school of fine arts the popular success which was attached to the immortal complaint of Jean Belin, artist ordinary to the Grand Sultan of the Turks;—all the daubers of Paris had a copy of it in their memories.

For a long time Marcel was not discouraged by the obstinate refusals which he encountered at each exposition. He was comfortably fixed in his opinion that his picture was even in its least details the counterpart awaited by the Marriage of Cana, that enormous masterpiece, whose overpowering splendour the dust of three centuries has not been able to dim. So each year at the time of the Salon, Marcel sent his picture to be examined by the jury. However, to confuse the examiners and to lure them from the principle of exclusion which they seemed to have adopted toward the *Crossing of the Red Sea,* Marcel, without at all changing the general composition, modified some detail and changed the title of the picture.

Thus at one time it came before the jury under the name of the *Crossing of the Rubicon;* but Pharaoh, poorly disguised under Caesar's mantle, was recognized and buried with all the honours which were due him.

The following year Marcel threw over one of the drafts of his canvas a white blanket simulating snow, stationed a fir tree in the corner, and, dressing an Egyptian as a grenadier in the imperial guard, baptized his picture *Crossing of the Beresina.*

The jury, who had that day polished its spectacles on the cuffs of its Prize Day suits, was not at all a dupe of this new ruse. It recognized perfectly the obstinate canvas, particularly a great devil of a particoloured horse which pranced at the edge of a wave of the Red Sea. This horse's robe was used by Marcel for all his colour trials, and in his intimate speech he called it a synoptic picture of the fine tones because he reproduced with their play of light and shade all the most varied combinations of colour. But one other time, insensitive to this detail, the jury didn't have enough black balls to reject the *Crossing of the Beresina.*

"Very well," said Marcel, "I expected it. Next year I shall send it again under the title of *Crossing of the Panoramas.*"

"They will certainly be caught . . . caught . . . caught . . . caught," chanted Schaunard, the musician, to a new tune of his invention, a terrible tune, rumbling like a scale of thunder bolts, the accompaniment of which was feared by all the neighbouring pianos.

"How can they refuse that without having all the vermillion of the Red Sea mount to their faces and cover them with shame?" murmured Marcel as he contemplated his picture. "When one considers what there is in it, one hundred écus of colour and one million of genius, without counting my lovely youth become as bald as my felt hat. A serious work which opens new horizons to the knowledge of glaze. But they haven't seen it for the last time; till my dying day I will send my picture. I wish to have it engraved on their memories."

"It's the surest way of ever getting it engraved," said Gustave Colline in a plaintive tone; and to himself he added: "It is very pretty, it is, very pretty . . . I will tell it in the meetings."

Marcel continued his imprecations, which Schaunard continued to set to music.

"Ah, they don't want to receive me," Marcel said. "Oh, the

government pays them, gives them lodgings and the cross, for the sole end of refusing me once a year, the first of March, a large canvas on an easel. I see their idea clearly, I see it very distinctly; they hope to have me break my brushes. Perhaps they hope, by refusing my Red Sea, to drive me to hurling myself out of the window from despair. But they don't know the human heart if they count on my being tricked by this clumsy ruse. From now on I shan't await the time for the Salon. Counting from today my work becomes the sword of Damocles, eternally suspended over their heads. Now I shall have it sent once a week

to the home of each one of them, to the bosom of their families, to the very heart of their private life. It will bother their domestic joys, it will make them find the wine sour, the roast burned, and their wives bitter. They will become crazy very soon, and they will have to wear a strait-jacket to go to the Institute the days of the sitting. That idea makes me laugh."

Some days later when Marcel had already forgotten his frightful plans for vengeance against his persecutors, he received a call from Father Medicis. So the club called a Jew named Salomon, who, at this period, was very well known by all artistic and literary Bohemia. Father Medicis did business in all kinds of bric-a-brac. He sold complete house-furnishings for twelve francs up to one thousand écus. He bought everything and knew how to sell it again for profit. The exchange bank of Monsieur Proudhon is indeed a small thing compared with the system used by Medicis, who possessed a genius for bargaining that even the cleverest of his religion had not yet equalled at that time. His shop, located at the Place du Carrousel, was a magic place where anything that could be desired could be found. All the products of Nature, all creations of art, everything which comes from the entrails of the earth and from human genius, Medicis made a part of his business. His commerce touched everything, absolutely everything which exists,—he even dealt in the Ideal. Medicis bought ideas to exploit them himself or to resell them. Known by all the literary folk and all the artists, intimate with the palette and with the writing desk, he was the Asmodée of the arts. He sold cigars in return for a literary supplement, slippers for a sonnet, fresh fish for jokes; he talked by the hour with writers employed to write in their papers the scandals of the day; he procured seats in the parliamentary halls, and invitations for certain parties; he provided lodgings by the night, week, or month for wandering daubers who paid him with copies of the old masters in the Louvre. Behind the scenes there were no mysteries for him. He made the theatres buy plays; he obtained certain favours. He had in his head a model almanac of twenty-five thousand addresses, and knew the address, the name and the secrets of every celebrity, even the obscure one.

Some pages copied from the confusion of his bookkeeping can, better than the most detailed explanations, give an idea of the universality of his business:

20 March, 184. . . .

—Sold to M. L . . . ., antiquarian, the compass which Archimedes used during the siege of Syracuse, 75 francs.

—Bought from M. V . . . ., journalist, the complete works, uncut, of M . . . ., member of the Academy, ten francs.

—Sold to the same, a critical article on the complete works of M . . . ., member of the Academy, thirty francs.

—Sold to M . . . ., Member of the Academy, a literary supplement of twelve columns about his complete works, two hundred fifty francs.

—Bought from M. R . . . ., man of letters, a critical appreciation of the complete works of M . . . ., of the French Academy, 10 francs, in addition to 50 pounds of coal and 2 kilos of coffee.

—Sold to M . . . ., a porcelain vase belonging to Madame Du Barry, 18 francs.

—Bought from the little D . . . ., her hair, 15 francs.

—Bought from M. B . . . ., a batch of articles on manners and the three last faults in spelling made by M., the prefect of the Seine, 6 francs; more than one pair of Neapolitan shoes.

—Sold to Mlle. O . . . ., a blonde wig, 120 francs.

—Bought from M. M . . . ., historical painter, a series of gay designs, 25 francs.

—Indicated to M. Ferdinand the hour when Madame the Baroness R....de P....goes to mass.— To the same, rented for a day the little mezzanine apartment of the Faubourg Montmartre, the whole 30 francs.

—Sold to M. Isidore, his portrait as Apollo, 30 francs.

—Sold to Mlle. R...., a pair of lobsters and 6 pairs of gloves, 36 francs. (Received 2 fr. 75)

—For the same, procured a six months credit from Mme...., millinery. (Charge to be decided)

—Procured for Mme....milliner, the patronage of Mme. R.... Received for this, 3 metres of velvet and 6 yards of lace.

—Bought from M. R...., literary man, a credit of 120 francs on the newspaper...., actually in bankruptcy, 5 francs; more than 2 pounds of Moravian tobacco.

—Sold to M. Ferdinand, two love letters, 12 francs.

—Bought from M. J...., artist, the portrait of M. Isidore as Apollo, 6 francs.

—Bought from M...., 65 kilos of his work entitled: Submarine Revolutions. 15 francs.

—Rented to Mme. la Comtesse de G...., a Saxony service, 20 francs.

—Bought from M...., journalist, 52 lines in his Courier de Paris, 100 francs, also a decoration for a fireplace.

—Sold to Mme. O...., and Co., 52 lines in the Courier de Paris de M....,300 francs in addition 2 fireplace decorations.

—To Mlle. S....G...., rented a bed and a coupé for a day (nothing).—(See the account of Mlle. S....G...., Journal, Pages 26, 27)

—Bought from M. Gustave C...., a memoir on the flax industry, 50 francs; also a rare edition of the works of Flavius Josephus.

—To Mlle. S....G...., sold a modern furnishing, 5,000 fr.

—For the same, paid a note at the pharmacist's, 75 francs.

—Id, Paid a note at the milkman's, 3 fr. 85.

Etc., etc., etc.,

It can be seen from these notes over what a large scale the operations of the Jew Medicis extended. In spite of the slightly illicit notes of his infinitely eclectic commerce, he had never been disturbed by anyone.

When he called on the Bohemians with that air of intelligence which distinguished him, the Jew had divined it was at an auspicious moment. In fact, the four friends were gathered together in council, and, under the urgence of a ferocious appetite, were discussing the serious question of bread and meat. It was Sunday! The end of the month. A day fatal and so sinister.

Consequently the entrance of Medicis was greeted with a joyful chorus; for it was known that the Jew was too careful of his time to waste it in polite calls; his presence always announced some business deal.

"Good evening, gentlemen," said the Jew, "how are you?"

"Colline," said Rudolph, stretched out on his bed and contemplating the beauties of the horizontal line, "you be the host, offer a chair to our guest; a guest is sacred. I salute you in Abraham," added the poet.

Colline went to fetch a chair which had the elasticity of bronze and put it near the Jew, saying to him in a friendly voice:

"Suppose for the nonce that you are Cinna, and take this chair."

Medicis sat down in the chair, and was about to complain of its hardness when he remembered that he himself had once exchanged it with Colline for a profession of faith sold to a deputy who had no talent for improvising. As he sat down his pockets jingled with the sound of silver and that melodious symphony threw the four Bohemians into a revery full of delights.

"Let's hear the song now," Rudolph whispered to Marcel, "the accompaniment seems nice."

"Monsieur Marcel," Medicis began, "I come simply to make your fortune. That is to say I have come to offer you a grand chance to enter the artistic world. Art, you know well, Monsieur Marcel, is a desert way whose glory is the oasis."

"Father Medicis," said Marcel, wild with impatience, "in the name of fifty percent, your revered patron, be brief."

"Yes," said Colline, "brief as King Pepin who was a sire concise as you, for you must be, circumcise, son of Jacob!"

"Ouh, ouh, ouh!" shouted the Bohemians, looking to see if the floor would not open to swallow up the philosopher.

But Colline was not devoured that time.

"This is the thing." Medicis resumed, "A rich amateur who is starting a gallery destined to be taken all over Europe has ordered me to procure for him a series of remarkable works. I come to offer you your admittance in this museum. In a word, I have come to buy your *Crossing of the Red Sea*.

"Ready money?" asked Marcel.

"Ready money," responded the Jew as he made resound the orchestra of his purse.

"Are you satisfied?" asked Colline.

"Decidedly," said Rudolph, who was raging, "it will be necessary to get a choke pear to stop the foolish outbursts of that rascal there. Brigand, don't you see that he is talking of écus? Is there then nothing sacred to you, atheist?"

Colline got up on a chest and took the pose of Harpocrates, god of silence.

"Go on, Medicis," said Marcel, bringing out his picture. "I wish to give you the honour of naming the price of this picture which is without price." Then the Jew put on the table fifty écus in fine new money.

"And the rest?" asked Marcel, "that's only the advance payment."

"Monsieur Marcel," said Medicis, "you well know that my first word is also my last. I will add nothing; reflect: fifty écus, that makes one hundred fifty francs. That's a real price, that is!"

"A small price," replied the artist, "for nothing but the robe of my Pharaoh it took fifty écus of cobalt. At least pay the piper, equalize the piles, round off the figures, and I will call you Leon X, Leon X bis."

"Here is my last word," resumed Medicis; " I won't add a sou more but I offer dinner to everyone, wines chosen to your taste, and with dessert I pay in gold."

"Nobody says anything?" shouted Colline, giving three blows of his fist on the table. "Sold."

"Let's go," said Marcel, "agreed."

"I will take the picture tomorrow," said the Jew. "Let's go, gentlemen, the table is laid."

The four friends descended the stairway singing the chorus of the Huguenots: "A table, a table!"

Medicis treated the Bohemians in a most palatial fashion. He offered them a host of things which till that moment had remained completely unknown to them. At this dinner lobster ceased to be a myth for Schaunard and at this time he developed for that amphibian a passion which was to rise to the point of delirium.

The four friends left this splendid feast drunk as on a day of grape-gathering. This drunkenness even failed to have deplorable results for Marcel who, when he passed the shop of his tailor, at two in the morning, wished to wake up his creditor to give him on account the one hundred fifty francs which he had just received. A remnant of reason, which still remained in Colline's mind, restrained the artist on the edge of this precipice.

A week after this celebration, Marcel learned in what gallery his picture had been hung. Walking along the faubourg Saint-Honoré, he stopped in the midst of a group who seemed to be studying curiously the placing of a signboard above a shop. This signboard was nothing other than Marcel's picture sold by Medicis to an edibles merchant. Only the *Crossing of the Red Sea* had undergone yet one more modification and bore a new title. A steamboat had been added and it was called: *In the Harbor of Marseilles*. A flattering ovation was given by the curious onlookers when they saw the picture. So Marcel went home thrilled by his triumph, and murmured to himself: "The voice of the people is the voice of God."

THE TOILET OF THE GRACES

MADEMOISELLE MIMI, who was in the habit of sleeping the whole morning, awoke one morning on the stroke of ten, and seemed very astonished not to see Rudolph beside her or even in the room. The evening previous, before she had gone to sleep she had seen him at his desk, arranging to spend the night on an extra-literary labour which had just been ordered and in whose accomplishment the young Mimi was particularly interested. In fact, with the proceeds of his labour, the poet had given his friend reason to hope that he would buy her a certain spring dress, a remnant for which she had one day seen in the Deux Magots, a store for fine novelties, at whose altar Mimi's vanity led her often to make frequent devotions. Now that the work in question was begun, Mimi enthusiastically busied herself about his progress. Often she went to Rudolph while he was writing, and, leaning her head over his shoulder, she spoke to him seriously:

"Well, is my dress advancing?"

"It now has one sleeve. Be calm," Rudolph replied.

One night having heard Rudolph snap his fingers, a habit which indicated ordinarily that he was pleased with his work, Mimi sat up suddenly in bed, and putting her brown head out between the curtains, she cried:

"Do you mean to say that my dress is done?"

"There," Rudolph responded, showing her four large sheets covered with closely written lines, "I have just accomplished the waist."

"What joy!" said Mimi, "there only remains the skirt. How many pages like that are necessary to make the skirt?"

"That depends; but as you aren't big, with about ten pages of fifty lines of thirty-three letters each we could have a suitable skirt."

"I am not big, that's true," Mimi said solemnly; "but for lack of material it must not have the air of weeping; dresses are worn very full and I should like lovely pleats to make a grand rustling."

And Mimi went back to sleep happy.

As she had been imprudent enough to tell her friends, Mademoiselles Musette and Phemie, about the beautiful dress which Rudolph was in the act of making for her, the two young people were not slow to inform Messieurs Marcel and Schaunard of their friend's generosity to his mistress; and these confidences had been followed by no slight provocations that the others should imitate the example of the poet.

"That is to say," added Mademoiselle Musette, pulling Marcel's moustaches, "that is to say, if it goes on a week like this I shall be forced to borrow your trousers to go out."

"A reliable house owes me eleven francs," Marcel replied; "if I recover this money I will devote it to buying you a fig leaf in the current fashion."

"And what about me?" Phemie questioned Schaunard. "My wrapper is falling into pieces."

Schaunard then took three sous from his pocket and gave them to his mistress. "Here is the wherewithal to buy needle and thread. Repair your blue wrapper,—that will instruct you as well as amuse you—*utile dulci.*"

However, in a meeting held most secretly, Marcel and Schaunard acknowledged to Rudolph that each was forced to satisfy the legitimate vanity of his mistress.

"These poor girls," Rudolph had said, "a nothing adorns them, but still it is essential that they have this nothing. For some time the fine arts and literature have been doing well; we are earning as much as messengers."

"It is true that I can't complain," interrupted Marcel; "the fine arts are behaving like a charm; one would think it was the reign of Leo X."

"In fact," Rudolph said, "Musette told me that you have been leaving in the morning and only returning at night for a week. Is it really true that you have work?"

"My dear, a grand job, which Medicis got for me. I am doing some portraits in the Ave Maria barracks,—eighteen grenadiers who have demanded their pictures for six francs, one after the other, the likeness guaranteed, as a watch is, for one year. I hope to have the whole regiment. It is certainly my plan to deck out Musette when Medicis pays me, for it is with him that I dealt and not with my models."

"As for me," Schaunard spoke disparagingly, "without having any evidence, I have two hundred francs which are sleeping."

"Heavens, wake them up," admonished Rudolph.

"In two or three days I plan to draw them out," replied Schaunard. "When I leave the bank I shall not disguise the fact that I plan to give free course to some of my passions. Particularly there is at the junk dealer's on this side a nankeen suit and a hunting horn which have taken my eye for a long time; I will certainly do homage to them."

"But," Rudolph and Marcel talked at the same time, "from where do you hope to draw this enormous sum?"

"Listen, gentlemen," Schaunard assumed a solemn air as he sat down between his two friends. "It isn't necessary to pretend to either one of you that before being members of the Institute and taxpayers we have still not enough rye bread to eat and the daily loaf is hard to eke out. From another angle,—we are not alone; as heaven has made us sensitive, each of us has chosen another, to whom he has offered the privilege of partaking of his lot."

"Preceded by an herring," interposed Marcel.

"But," Schaunard went on, "even while living with the strictest economy, when one has nothing it is difficult to put any aside, especially if one always has an appetite greater than his plate."

"What are you driving at?" demanded Rudolph.

"At this," Schaunard resumed, "that in the present situation we would be wrong—any one of us—to turn up our noses at a chance to put a figure before the zero which indicates our social goods, whenever the chance offers, even if it is outside the realm of our art."

"Well," asked Marcel, "which one of us do you accuse of this? Great painter that I will be one day, have I not consented to devote my brushes to the pictorial reproduction of French warriors who pay me with their pocket money? It seems to me that I do not fear to descend the ladder of my future greatness."

"And I," Rudolph went on, "do you not know that for two weeks I have been composing a didactic poem, *Medical-Surgical-Dentist*, for a famous dentist who endows my inspiration at the rate of fifteen sous for a dozen alexandrines, a bit dearer than oysters, eh? Furthermore, I do not blush about it,—rather than see my muse standing with arms crossed, I gladly would have put the *Parisian conducteur* into novel form for him. When one has a lyre . . . what the devil! It is to be used. . . . And then Mimi is degraded by her boots."

"Then," resumed Schaunard, "you will not hold it against me when you know the source of the stream of gold whose overflow I am awaiting."

This is the story of Schaunard's two hundred francs.

About two weeks before, he had gone to a music editor who had promised to find for him among his clients either piano lessons or tuning jobs. "Gracious heavens!" ejaculated the editor when he saw him enter, "you come at a happy moment, for just today I have been asked to name a pianist. He is an Englishman; I think that he will pay you well. . . . Are you really good?"

Schaunard thought that a modest front would prejudice him in the eyes of his editor. A musician and especially a pianist, modest, indeed that is a rare occurrence! So Schaunard responded with much bravado: "I am of the first grade; if I had only one lung, long hair and a black suit, I would truly be as well known as the sun, and instead of asking me eight hundred francs to have my score of the *Death of the Young Girl* printed, you would have gone on your knees to offer me three thousand upon a silver platter.

"It is a fact," the artist went on, "that since my ten fingers have been forced to ten years of practice on the five octaves, I play very nicely on the ivory keys and the sharps."

The person to whom Schaunard was sent was an Englishman named Monsieur Birn'n. The musician was first received by a lackey in blue who presented him to a lackey in green, who passed him on to a lackey in black who led him into a drawing-room where he found himself in the presence of an islander doubled up in a splenetic position which made him resemble Hamlet thinking on our insignificance. Schaunard started to explain the reason for his appearance there when piercing cries were heard which interrupted him. This frightful noise which hurt his ears was uttered by a parrot resting on his perch on the balcony of the floor below.

"O that beast, that beast!" moaned the Englishman, bounding up from his chair, "he will kill me."

And at that same minute the winged one began to run through his repertory, much more extensive than that of ordinary poll parrots; and Schaunard stood confounded when he heard the animal, encouraged by a feminine voice, began to recite the first lines of the story of Theramene with the accent of the Conservatory.

This parrot was a favourite of an actress popular—in her boudoir. She was one of these women who, no one knows why or how, are priced very extravagantly on the turf of chivalry, and whose name is inscribed upon the menus of gentlemen's suppers where they act as living dessert. In our time it places one as a Christian to be seen with one of these pagans, who often are only antique from the point of view of their birthday. When they are pretty, the evil is not great after all; the most one risks is of having to sleep on straw for having placed them on rosewood. But when their beauty is bought by the ounce at the beauty specialists and does not resist three drops of water poured on a dainty handkerchief, when their wit is contained in a vaudeville couplet, and their talent in the palm of a clacker's hand, it is difficult to explain how distinguished people, often with a good name, intelligence, and a suit that is in style, let themselves be carried away, through love for the commonplace, to raise from the most vulgar and shallow whim, such creatures from among whom their Frontin would not like to take his Lisette.

The actress in question belonged to this class of ephemeral beauties. She was called Dolores and she said she was Spanish, although she was born in that Parisian Andalusia, called the rue Coquenard. Although it is not ten minutes from the rue Coquenard to the rue de Provence, it had taken her seven or eight years to make the journey. Her prosperity had increased in proportion to her personal decadence. The day when she had her first false tooth, she had a horse, and two horses, the day when she got her second tooth. Actually she had a great following, lived in a veritable Louvre, was the centre of the walks on Longchamps days and gave parties to which everyone came. All Paris for these women? That is to say that group of lazy courtiers of everything silly and every scandal; all Paris, player of cards and jokes, the pretendants to wit and brawn; killers of their time and

of that of others; writers who try to be men of letters to use the feathers which nature has put on their backs; debauched gallants; gentleman gamblers, knights of mysterious orders, all of gloved Bohemia, coming from nobody knows where and returning there; all the women famous and infamous, all the daughters of Eve who formerly sold the maternal fruit in a basket and who retail it now in boudoirs; all the corrupt, from swaddling clothes to  shrouds which one finds on the first pictures with Golconda on the forehead and Thibet on the shoulders, and for whom bloom the first spring violets and the first adolescent loves. All that world which the chroniclers call all Paris was received at Mademoiselle Dolores', the mistress of the parrot we have just mentioned.

That bird, whose oratorical powers had made him famous in every section, had become little by little the terror of his nearest neighbours. Exposed on the balcony, he used his perch for a tribune where he held forth from morn till night with endless speeches. Since some newspapermen, intimate with his mistress, had taught him certain parliamentary specialties, the flying bird had developed surprising strength on the question of sugars. He knew by heart the repertory of the actress and spoke it in such a way as to be able to double for her should she be indisposed. Furthermore, as she was polyglot in her affections and received callers from every corner of the earth, the parrot spoke every tongue and sometimes indulged in each idiom in blasphemy which would have made the sailors to whom Vert-vert owed his advanced education blush. The society of this bird, which could be instructive and agreeable for ten minutes, became a real punishment when it was prolonged. The neighbours had complained several times but the actress had insolently overlooked their complaints. Two or three lodgers, honest fathers of families, irritated by the lax manners to which the indiscretions of the parrot gave insight, had even given notice to the proprietor, whom the actress had known how to get around.

The Englishman, whose place we have just seen Schaunard enter, had kept his patience for three months.

One day he disguised his rage, which had just burst forth, under a grand state costume; and, just as he was presented to Queen Victoria at one of her levees at Windsor, he had himself announced to Mademoiselle Dolores.

When she saw him enter, she thought at first that it was Hoffman in his costume of Lord Spleen; and wanting to be gracious to her comrade, she offered him luncheon. The Englishman responded solemnly in a French that he had learned from a Spanish refugee in twenty-five lessons:

"I accept your invitation on condition that we eat that bird . . . that horrible," and he pointed to the parrot, which had already smelled an Islander and had greeted him by humming "God Save the King."

Dolores, sure that her English neighbour had come to make fun of her, was inclined to be irritated when he added: "Since I am very rich I shall offer a certain price for the animal."

Dolores replied that she clung to her bird and that she would not like to see it pass into another's hands.

"Oh, I don't want to get it into my hands," replied the Englishman, "it is under my feet," and he showed her the points of his shoes.

Dolores trembled with rage and perhaps was going to fly into a passion when she noticed on the Englishman's finger a ring whose diamond represented probably two thousand five hundred francs in rent. This discovery fell like a shower on her anger. She reflected that it was possibly imprudent to get angry with a man who had fifty thousand francs on his little finger.

"Well, sir," she said, "since this poor Coco bothers you, I shall put him in the back, in such a place that you won't be able to hear him."

The Englishman limited himself to a motion of satisfaction.

"However," he added showing his shoes, "I would have much preferred. . . ."

"Have no fear," Dolores went on, "where I will put him it will be impossible to bother my lord."

"Oh, I am not nobility . . . I am only a gentleman."

Just as Monsieur Birn'n was preparing to leave, after having saluted her with a modest bow, Dolores, who never neglected her own interests at any time, took a small package left on the table and said to the Englishman:

"Monsieur, this evening at the theatre they are giving me a benefit production, and I am to appear in three plays. Will you permit me to offer you some tickets for a box? The price of the seats has been only slightly increased."

And she put about ten box coupons in the Islander's hands.

"After I have so promptly shown myself agreeable to him," she thought to herself, "if he is a man of breeding he cannot refuse me; and if he sees me act in my rose costume, who knows? Between neighbours!—The diamond which he wears on his finger is the advance guard of a million. My word, but he is ugly, he is very sad, but that will give me a chance to go to London without being seasick."

The Englishman took the tickets and had her explain a second time the use to which they were designed; then he asked the price.

"The boxes are sixty francs and there are ten of them. . . . But it isn't pressing," Dolores added as she saw the Britisher about to take out his pocketbook, "I hope that as a neighbour you will from time to time do me the honour of calling."

Monsieur Birn'n replied: "I don't like to do business at all by the quarter," as he put a thousand franc note upon the table and slipped the tickets for the boxes in his pocket.

"I shall give you the change," said Dolores as she opened a little drawer where she kept her money.

"Oh, no indeed," said the Englishman, "that's a tip for a drink," and he left, leaving Dolores outraged by the suggestion.

"A tip," she cried when she was alone. "What a creature! I shall return his money."

But this rudeness of her neighbour had only scratched her pride; meditation calmed her for she thought that after all twenty louis bonus made a nice killing, and that on other occasions she had borne impertinence for less.

"Oh pshaw!" she told herself, "one cannot be so proud. No one has seen me, and today is the end of my laundress' month. After all, that man speaks the language so poorly that perhaps he thought he was giving me a compliment." And Dolores gaily pocketed her twenty louis.

But that evening after the play she went home raging. Monsieur Birn'n had not used the tickets at all, and the ten boxes remained empty.

Besides, when she came on the stage at twelve-thirty the unhappy beneficiary read on the countenances of her friends in the lobby the joy they felt over the hall's being so poorly filled.

She even heard one of her actress friends say to another, pointing to the fine unoccupied boxes:

"That poor Dolores has sold only one stage box."

"The boxes are hardly filled."

"The orchestra is empty."

"Heavens, her name on the advertisement produces the effect of an airpump in the hall."

"Yes, what an idea—to raise the price of the seats!"

"A fine benefit. It seems to me that the receipts could be put in a money box or in the toe of a stocking."

"Ah! There is her famous cock costume in red velvet."

"She has the appearance of a school of crayfish."

"How did you come out in your last benefit?" one of the actresses asked her companion.

"Packed, my dear, it was like a first night; the stools were worth a louis; but I have only used six francs; my dressmaker has gotten the rest. If I weren't so afraid of chilblains I should go to St. Petersburg."

"What! You are not yet thirty and you already dream of going to Russia?"

"What are you talking about!" the other replied, and then added: "And when is your benefit? Soon?"

"In two weeks. I already have one thousand écus' worth of tickets taken—without counting my Saint Cyrians."

"There, all the orchestra is leaving."

"Dolores is singing."

Dolores, actually as purple as her costume, trilled her song of sour grapes. As she achieved it not without great difficulty, at her feet fell two bouquets, tossed by her two good actress friends, who moved to the edge of their corner box shouting "Bravo, Dolores!"

One can easily imagine the rage of the latter. When she got home, although it was the middle of the night, she opened her window and woke up Coco, who woke up the honest Monsieur Birn'n who had gone to sleep relying on Dolores' pledged word.

Beginning with that day war was declared between the actress and the Englishman; war to the end, without rest or truce, in which the combatants did not hesitate at any expense. The parrot, educated accordingly, had pursued the study of the English language and all day long heaped insults on his neighbour in the sharpest falsetto. In truth, it was unbearable. Dolores herself suffered, but she hoped from one day to another that Monsieur Birn'n would give notice; it was on that she pinned her pride. The Islander on his side had thought of all sorts of means wherewith to avenge himself. He had in the beginning formed a school for tambourines in his drawing room; but the commissioner of the police intervened. Monsieur Birn'n, more and more ingenious, had then established a pistol shooting gallery where his servants shot fifty cartons a day. The commissioner intervened again, and showed him an article of the city code which forbade the use of firearms in houses. Monsieur Birn'n stopped it, but a week later Mademoiselle Dolores perceived that it rained in her apartment. The proprietor made a call on Monsieur Birn'n whom he found taking sea baths in his drawing room. This very large room had had its walls recovered with metal sheets; every door had been walled up; and in this improvised harbour had been mixed a hundred pailfulls of water with fifty hundredweight of salt. It was a real invasion of the Ocean. Nothing was lacking, not even the fish. It was approached through an opening cut into the upper panel of the middle door and Monsieur Birn'n bathed there daily. After some time one could smell the sea in the neighbourhood, and Mademoiselle Dolores had an inch of water in her bedroom.

The proprietor was furious and threatened to serve Monsieur Birn'n with a warrant to leave on account of the ravages made on his property.

"Didn't I have the right," asked the Englishman, "to bathe at home?"

"No, sir."

"If I didn't have the right, very well," the Englishman was full of respect for the law of the country where he lived. "That's too bad. I was very much amused." And that same evening he gave orders to have the ocean rolled away. He was just in time; there was already a bank of oysters on the floor. But Monsieur Birn'n had not given up the struggle, and looked for a legal way to carry on the strange war which was the talk of all idle Paris; for the adventure had been spread about in all the theatre lobbies and other public places. Dolores felt it a point of honour to come out of this battle triumphant, on the outcome of which bets were being made.

It was then that Monsieur Birn'n had thought of the piano. And it wasn't such a bad idea; the most unpleasant of instruments was forcibly to fight against the most unpleasant of winged creatures. When this bright idea had come to him, he hastened to carry it out. He rented a piano and he sought for a pianist. The pianist, it will be recalled, was our friend Schaunard. The Englishman recounted to him in a friendly way his grievances against his neighbour's parrot and all that he had done heretofore in his endeavour to force the actress to capitulate.

"But, my lord," advised Schaunard, "there is a way to rid yourself of this beast, it is parsley. Every chemist is willing to testify that this savoury plant is prussic acid for animals; spread chopped up parsley on your draperies, have them shaken out the window on Coco's cage; he will die assuredly as if he had been invited to dine by Pope Alexander VI."

"I have thought of that, but the animal is guarded," replied the Britisher; "the piano is surer."

Schaunard looked at the Englishman and at first did not understand.

"This is what I have planned," the Englishman went on. "The comedienne and her beast sleep until noon. Follow my reasoning closely. . . ."

"Go on," said Schaunard, "I am walking on your heels."

"I plan to interrupt their sleep. The law of this country permits me to have music from morning to night. Do you understand what I expect from you?"

"But," remonstrated Schaunard, "it wouldn't be so bad for the comedienne if she heard me playing the piano all day, and for nothing too. I am of the first rank and if I only had a bad lung. . . ."

"No, no!" interrupted the Englishman. "I didn't say you were to play fine music. It will be necessary for you only to strum on your instrument. Like this," added the Englishman, running up a scale; "and always, always the same thing without mercy, M. Musician, always the scale. I know a little about medicine; the same thing makes one crazy. They will become mad beneath us; it is upon that that I count. Well, sir, begin at once; I shall pay you well."

"And there you have it," said Schaunard, who had told all these details which have just been given, "that is the job which I have had for two weeks. A scale, nothing else, from seven in the morning until evening. It certainly isn't exactly serious art. But what more do you expect, my children? The Englishman pays me for my racket two hundred francs a month. One would be one's own hangman to refuse such a windfall. I have accepted, and in two or three days I am going to the bank to collect my first month's pay."

As a result of these mutual confidences the three friends agreed to take advantage of the common possession of funds by  giving their mistresses the spring equipment which each in her vanity had longed for for so long. It was agreed, moreover, that whoever got his money first would wait for the others, that the possessions might be had at the same time and that Mademoiselles Mimi, Musette and Phemie could enjoy together the pleasure of getting a new skin, as Schaunard described it.

Two or three days after this council, Rudolph led, as his poem Osanore had been paid for,—it weighed eighty francs. Two days later Marcel had extracted from Medicis the price of ten corporal's portraits at six francs.

Marcel and Rudolph had the greatest difficulty in the world hiding their fortune.

"It seems to me that I sweat gold," complained the poet.

"It is so with me," agreed Marcel. "If Schaunard is much longer it will be impossible for me to continue this role of anonymous Crœsus."

But the next day the Bohemians saw Schaunard coming home resplendently clothed in a gold nankeen jacket.

"Oh! My God," cried Phemie, overcome at the sight of her lover so elegantly clad, "where did you find that suit?"

"I found it among my papers," responded the musician, signifying to his two friends to follow him. "I have got it," he told them when they were alone. "Here are the piles," and he stacked up a handful of gold.

"Well," cried Marcel, "let's be off! Let's pillage the stores! How happy Musette will be!"

"How happy Mimi will be!" added Rudolph. "Let's go. Are you coming, Schaunard?"

"Let me think," replied the musician. "If we give these women of a thousand whims stylish things, perhaps we shall be very foolish. Think of it. When they resemble the pictures in the *Scarf of Iris,* aren't you afraid that these splendours will exert a lamentable influence on their character? And is it becoming in men like us to behave toward women as if we were decrepit and wrinkled Mondors? It isn't that I hesitate to sacrifice fourteen or eighteen francs to buy Phemie a dress, but I tremble for the time when she has a new hat, lest she will no longer wish to speak to me! A flower in her hair is so becoming to her! What do you think about it, philosopher?" interrupted Schaunard, calling to Colline, who had appeared a few minutes before.

"Ingratitude is the daughter of kindness," replied the philosopher.

"On the other hand," Schaunard continued, "when your mistresses are well dressed, what sort of a figure will you make at their side in your dilapidated outfits? You will have the appearance of being their chambermaids. It isn't for myself that I say this," interrupted Schaunard, as he squared his shoulders in his nankeen suit, "for, thank God, I can go everywhere now."

However, in spite of the spirit of opposition which Schaunard evinced, it was agreed upon again that the next day all the shops of the neighbourhood be pillaged for the benefit of the ladies.

And the next morning at the same hour when we saw, at the beginning of this chapter, Mademoiselle Mimi waking up so astonished by Rudolph's absence, the poet and his two friends were mounting the stairs of the hotel, accompanied by a clerk from the Deux Magots and by a dressmaker who was carrying some samples. Schaunard, who had bought the famous trumpet, was marching in front playing the overture to the *Caravan.*

Musette and Phemie, called by Mimi who lived on the mezzanine floor, at the news that hats and dresses were being brought to them, descended the stairway with the speed of an avalanche. When they saw all these poor glories ranged before them, the three women just escaped going crazy with delight. Mimi was overcome by a fit of hilarity and jumped about like a goat, waving a little barége scarf. Musette had thrown herself around Marcel's neck, while she held in each hand a little green slipper which she beat against each other like cymbals. Phemie looked at Schaunard and sobbed. All that she could say was:

"Ah, my Alexander, my Alexander!"

"There is no danger that she will refuse the gifts of Artaxerxes," murmured the philosophic Colline.

After the first fever of joy had passed, when the choices were made and the invoices paid, Rudolph announced to the three women that they were to plan to try their new costumes the next morning. "We shall go to the country," he said.

"What a fine plan," triumphed Musette. "It isn't the first time that I have bought, cut, sewed and worn a dress in one day. And in addition we have the night. We shall be ready, eh, ladies?"

"We'll be ready!" Mimi and Phemie shouted together.

They started to work at once and for sixteen hours they put up neither scissors nor needle.

The next morning was the first day of May. The Easter bells had rung in the resurrection of spring some days before, and from all sides it came eager and joyous. She was coming, as the German song goes, light as the young lover who plants May under his beloved's window. She painted the heavens blue, the trees green and all things in bright colours. She wakened the languid sun which slept reclining on a bed of fogs, his head resting on great clouds of snow which served as a pillow, and cried to him: "Ha ha, Friend, it's time and here I am! Quick at your job. Put on without further delay your lovely suit of new beautiful rays and show yourself at once on your balcony to announce my coming."

Whereupon, the sun had really taken himself to the country and was taking a walk proud and pompous as a lord of the court. The swallows, returned from their Eastern pilgrimage, filled the air with their flight; the hawthorn whitened the thickets, the violet filled with sweetness the grass of the woods where already could be seen all the birds leaving their nests with notebooks of romances under their wings. It really was spring, the true spring of poets and lovers, and not the spring foretold by the almanac,—an ugly spring with a red nose, claws for fingers, which makes the poor still shiver in the corner of his hut where the last cinders of his last faggot have long since been extinguished. The soft breezes swept through the translucent air and spread abroad in the city the first smells of the surrounding country. The clear and warm rays of the sun knocked on the window panes. To the sick they said: "Open, we are health!" And in the garret of the young girl standing before her mirror, that innocent first love of the very innocent, they said: "Open, beautiful, that we may brighten your beauty! We are the messengers of fine weather; you can now put on your linen dress, your straw hat and your coquettish laced boots; here in the woods where one dances are carpets of beautiful new flowers, and the violins are waking up for the Sunday ball. Good-day, beautiful!"

As the Angelus sounded in the nearest church, the three struggling coquettes who had not taken the trouble to sleep for hours, were already before their mirrors, giving a last glance to their new toilet.

They were all three charming, similarly dressed, and reflecting in their faces the same satisfaction, evidence of the realization of a long held desire.

Musette was especially shining with beauty.

"I have never been so happy," she said to Marcel; "it seems to me that the good God has put into this moment all the happiness of my whole life, and I am afraid that there remains nothing more for me! Ah, pshaw, when it is all gone still there will be more. We have the recipe to make it," she added gaily, embracing Marcel.

As for Phemie, one thing bothered her. "I love the greenness and the little birds," she said, "but in the country one doesn't see anyone, and no one can see my pretty hat and my beautiful dress. If we could only go to the country by way of the boulevards."

At eight in the morning the whole street was aroused by the fanfare of Schaunard's trumpet, which gave the signal to leave. All the neighbours were at their windows to watch the Bohemians depart. Colline, who was at the celebration, closed the march, carrying the ladies' umbrellas. An hour later all the gay band had scattered in the fields of Fontenay-aux-Roses.

When they returned to their house that evening very late, Colline, who during the day had served as treasurer, declared that they had forgotten to spend six francs and he placed them on the table.

"What can we do with them?" Marcel inquired.

"Perhaps we might pay the rent!" suggested Schaunard.

FRANCINE'S MUFF

O F the true Bohemians who lived in Bohemia, at one time I knew one—a boy named Jacques D. . . . ; he was a sculptor and gave promise of some day doing great work. But misery did not give him time to carry out his promise. He died of exhaustion in the month of March, 1844, in bed number fourteen, the Sainte-Victoire ward, at the Saint-Louis hospital.

I knew Jacques at the hospital where I myself was detained by a long sickness. Jacques had, as I said above, the makings of a great artist and furthermore he didn't boast of it. During the two months that I lived near him, during which time he knew that he was being rocked in the arms of death, I did not hear him complain once, nor did he give himself over to the lamentations which make a misunderstood artist so ridiculous. He died without posing, as a horrible grimace from his death agony proved. This death reminds me, too, of one of the most horrible scenes that I have ever witnessed in this caravanserai of human sorrow. His father, informed of the event, had come to fetch the body and for a long time haggled over giving thirty-six francs demanded by the hospital. He had bargained also over the church service fee with such insistence that he succeeded in having it reduced six francs. When they were putting the corpse in the coffin the nurse took off the hospital sheet and asked one of the deceased's friends, who was there, for something with which to pay for the shroud. The poor fellow, who hadn't a sou, looked for Jacques' father who appeared in a terrific temper, demanding when they would cease bothering him.

The student nurse who was present at this horrible discussion glanced at the corpse and made this sweet and simple remark:

—"Oh! Sir, he cannot be buried like that, that poor boy; it is so cold; at least give him a shirt so that he will not appear completely naked before the good God."

The father gave the friend five francs to buy a shirt but he suggested to him to go to an old-clothes dealer on the rue Grange-aux-Belles, where linen was sold cheap.—"It will cost less," he added.

This cruelty of Jacques' father was explained to me later; he was furious that his son had taken up the career of art and his wrath was not appeased even before his coffin.

But I am very far from Mademoiselle Francine and her muff. I will return. Mademoiselle Francine was Jacques' first and only mistress; he was not yet old when he died, for he was hardly twenty-three years of age at the time when his father wished to have him buried completely naked. This love story had been told to me by Jacques himself when he was number fourteen and I was number sixteen in the Saint Victoire ward,—such an ugly place in which to die.

Ah, wait, my reader, before beginning this story, which might be beautiful if I could tell it as it was told to me by my friend Jacques, let me smoke a pipe in the old clay pipe that he gave me the day when the doctor had forbidden him its use. However, during the night, when the nurse was sleeping, my friend Jacques borrowed his pipe from me and demanded a bit of tobacco.—It is so dull during a whole night in the large wards when one cannot sleep and when one is suffering!

"Only one or two puffs," he would say to me and I let him have it. Sister Sainte-Geneviève never gave any evidence of smelling the smoke when she made her rounds.—Ah! Good Sister, how kind you were and how beautiful you were, too, when you came to sprinkle us with holy water! We could see you coming from afar, walking slowly under the dark archways, draped in your white veils, which fell in the lovely folds my friend Jacques admired so much. Ah! Kind Sister, you were the Beatrice of that Inferno; so gentle were your consolations that we always complained that we might have you comfort us. If my friend Jacques had not died, that day when it was snowing, he would have modelled for you a sweet little virgin to place in your cell, kind Sister Sainte-Geneviève.

FIRST READER.—Well, what of the muff? For myself I don't see any muff.

SECOND READER.—And Mademoiselle Francine? Where is she?

FIRST READER.—This story isn't one bit happy.

SECOND READER.—We wish to hear the end.

I beg your pardon, gentlemen, it was my friend Jacques' pipe which made me disgress so. But indeed, I have never sworn absolutely to make you laugh. It isn't always gay in Bohemia.

Jacques and Francine had met each other in a house in the rue La Tour-d'Auvergne, where they had moved simultaneously in the spring.

The artist and the young girl remained a week without establishing a neighbourly acquaintanceship, which is almost always necessary when one lives on the same floor. However, without having exchanged one single word each already knew something about the other. Francine learned that her neighbour was a poor devil of an artist and Jacques knew that his neighbour was a little dressmaker who had run away from her family to escape the unpleasant treatment of a stepmother. She performed miracles of economy in order to make both ends meet, as they say; and, as she had never known pleasure, she never once desired it.

This is the way they succeeded in breaking through the barrier of the partition wall between their two rooms. One evening during April, Jacques came home absolutely exhausted, as he hadn't eaten since morning and he was profoundly discouraged by one of those vague moods which have no exact cause. Such moods to which those unhappy ones who live alone are especially liable may seize one completely at any hour as a kind of apoplexy of the heart. Jacques, who felt smothered in his narrow room, opened the window to get some air. The evening was beautiful and the setting sun spread his pensive magical charm over the hills of Montmartre. Jacques remained thoughtful at his casement window, listening to the winged choir which chanted its spring songs in the evening calm; this served to increase his sadness. When he saw fly before him a croaking raven he thought of the time when the ravens brought bread to Elijah, the pious hermit, and he reflected that crows now were not so charitable. Then, not being able to bear it longer he closed his window and drew the curtain; as he had nothing with which to buy oil for his lamp, he lit a resin candle which he had brought with him from a trip in the Grande Chartreuse; and growing sadder by degrees, he filled his pipe.

"It's fortunate that I still have enough tobacco to hide the pistol," he murmured, as he began to smoke. Indeed he must have been very sad that evening, my friend Jacques, since he had to think of hiding the pistol. It was his last resource in grave crises and it generally succeeded. And this is what he did. Jacques smoked tobacco upon which he sprinkled several drops of laudanum and he smoked until the cloud of smoke which came from his pipe had become sufficiently thick to hide from him all the objects which were in his small room, and particularly a pistol hung on the wall. It was a matter of about ten pipes. When the pistol had become completely invisible it almost always happened that the smoke and the laudanum combined put Jacques to sleep, and it happened as often that his despondency left him on the threshold of his dreams. But that evening although he used all his tobacco, and the pistol was perfectly hidden, Jacques was still wretchedly unhappy.

That same evening on the contrary, Mademoiselle Francine was very happy when she came home, and her happiness was as much without reason as was Jacques' unhappiness. It was one of those blessings which fall from heaven, showered by the kind God upon good hearts. Mademoiselle Francine was in a lovely humour and was humming as she mounted the stairway. Just as she was opening her door a puff of wind entered through the open window in the hall, and abruptly extinguished her candle.

"Dear me, how annoying!" exclaimed the young girl. "Now I shall have to retrace my steps down these six flights."

But when she noticed a light under Jacques' doorway, a lazy instinct strengthened by a feeling of curiosity led her to ask from the artist a light. It is a service that is daily rendered between neighbours and was not at all compromising. She gave two small raps on Jacques' door; he opened it, a bit surprised by this late visit. But hardly had she taken a step into the room when the smoke which filled it suddenly overcame her; and before being able to utter a word she fell unconscious upon a chair and let fall to the ground her candle and key. It was midnight, everyone was sleeping in the house. Jacques didn't consider it proper to call for help as he was afraid he might embarrass his neighbour. Consequently he limited himself to opening the window in order to let a little bit of air come in; after he had sprinkled some drops of water on the young girl's face, he saw her open her eyes and gradually come to herself. When, at the end of five minutes, she had entirely regained consciousness, Francine explained the reason she had come to the artist and she apologized at length for what had happened.

"Now that I have recovered," she added, "I can return to my room."

He had already opened the door of the room when she realized that she had forgotten not only her candle but also the key to her room.

"How crazy I am," she said, picking up her candle of resin, "I have come here to get a light and I am leaving without it."

But at the same moment the draft, established in the room between the door and the window which had remained open, suddenly put out the flame and both young people were in darkness.

"You will think that I have done it on purpose," said Francine. "Pardon me, sir, all the trouble I have caused you, and be good enough to make a light that I may find my key."

"Certainly, Mademoiselle," responded Jacques, groping for some matches. He found them very quickly. But an odd thought crossed his mind, and he put the matches in his pocket, saying as he did so;—"What a bore! Mademoiselle, here is another difficulty. I haven't one single match here. I used the last one when I came home." (I hope that this unblushing fabrication is successful! he thought to himself.)

"There, there," said Francine, "I can certainly go into my room without a candle: indeed the room is not so large that I will get lost. But I must have my key; I beg you, sir, help me to find it, it must be on the floor."

"We shall search, Mademoiselle," said Jacques.—And there were the two of them hunting in the darkness for the lost article. But as if they had been moved by the same instinct it happened during their searching that their hands, which groped in the same place came into contact ten times a minute. And one was as unskilful as the other; they did not find the key.

"The moon, which is hidden by the clouds, will shine full in my room," said Jacques. "Let us wait a little, in a minute it will lighten our searches."

So while waiting for the rising of the moon, they began to talk. A chat in the midst of shadows in a little room, during a spring night, a talk which, at first light and inconsequential, ends in a chapter of confidence,—you know where that will lead. . . . The words become little by little confused, more and more reticent; the voices are low, the words are alternated with sighs— the hands which have been joined finish the thought, which from the heart mounts to the lips, and—search for the conclusion in your memories, oh young people. Remember, young man, remember, young woman, you who walk today hand in hand, how you had never seen each other two days ago.

At last the moon was uncovered and its clear light flooded the room; Mademoiselle Francine ceased to dream and uttered a little cry.

"What's wrong?" Jacques asked her, taking his arms from around her body.

"Nothing," murmured Francine. "I thought I heard someone knock. And without letting Jacques see, she shoved the key which she had just discovered under a chest of drawers.

She did not want him to find it.

.   .   .   .

FIRST READER—I certainly will not let my daughter get hold of this story.

SECOND READER—Up till now I have not yet seen one single hair of Mademoiselle Francine's muff; and as for that young girl, I don't even know how she looks,—whether she is a blonde or a brunette.

Patience, oh readers, patience, I promise you a muff, and I will give it to you in the end as my friend Jacques did to his poor friend Francine, who had become his mistress, as I have suggested by the dotted line which you see above. She was blonde, Francine was, blonde and gay; that isn't a frequent combination. She had never known love until she was twenty; but a vague feeling advised her at that time to put it off no longer if she wished to know it.

She met Jacques and loved him. The liaison lasted six months. They united in the springtime and they separated in the fall. She was tubercular,—she knew it,—and her friend Jacques knew it too. Two weeks after they had met, Jacques was informed of this by one of his friends who was a doctor.—"She will die with the falling of the leaves," the latter had said.

Francine heard this confidence and showed her despair as she chatted with her friend.

"What do the yellow leaves matter?" she said to him, revealing all her love in a smile. "What does autumn matter? This is summer now and the leaves are green. We must take advantage of it, my friend. . . . When you see me ready to take leave of my life, you will take me in your arms and kissing me you will forbid me to go. I am obedient, you know, and I shall stay."

And this charming person spent five wretched months of a Bohemian life with a song and a smile on her lips. As for Jacques, he let himself be deceived. His friend often said to him: "Francine is getting worse, she needs care." Then Jacques knocked on every door of Paris in order to borrow enough to carry out the doctor's orders; but Francine would not listen and she threw the medicines out of the window. At night when she was overcome by coughing, she left the room that Jacques might not hear her.

One day when they had both gone to the country, Jacques perceived a tree whose foliage was becoming yellow. He sadly looked at Francine who was walking slowly and meditatively. Francine saw Jacques become pale, and she guessed the reason for it.

"You are wrong," she said to him as she kissed him, "it is only July; it is three months until October; if we love each other night and day, as we do, we will double the time that we have to spend together. And moreover if I feel worse when the leaves are yellow we shall go to stay in a pine woods;—there the leaves are always green."

. . . .

When October came, Francine was forced to stay in bed. A friend of Jacques cared for her. . . . The little room where they were living was situated at the very top of the house and gave upon a courtyard where a tree was growing. Each day this tree shed a few more of its leaves. Jacques had put a curtain in the window to hide it from the sick girl but Francine demanded that it be taken away.

"Oh, my dear," she said to Jacques, "I will give you a hundred more kisses than that tree has leaves" . . . and then she added:—"I am going to be a great deal better soon. . . . I am going to go out soon; but as it will be winter, and, as I do not want to have red hands, you must buy me a muff." During all her illness this muff was her only dream.

The day before All Saints Day, since she noted that Jacques was more disconsolate than ever she wished to cheer him. In order to prove to him that she was better, she got up.

The doctor came in at the same moment and he forcibly sent her back to bed.

"Jacques," he whispered to the artist, "you must have courage! everything is over. Francine is going to die."

Jacques burst into tears.

"You can give her everything she asks for now," the doctor went on. "There is no longer any hope."

Francine divined what the doctor was saying to her lover.

"Do not listen to him," she cried holding her arms out to Jacques. "Do not listen to him,—he is lying. We will go out

together tomorrow,—All Saints Day. It will be cold, go buy
me a muff. . . . I beg you, I am so afraid of getting chilblains
this winter."

Jacques was going to leave with his friend but Francine kept
the doctor with her. "Go look for my muff," she told Jacques;
"find a beautiful one so that it will last a long time."

And when she was alone she said to the doctor:

"Oh! doctor, I am going to die and I know it. . . . But before leaving me give me something which will give me strength
for one night I beg you; make me beautiful for one more night
and let me die afterwards, if the good God does not wish that
I live any longer."

As the doctor consoled her the best he could a breeze came
into the room and dropped upon the invalid's bed a yellow leaf
from the tree in the little courtyard.

Francine opened the curtain and saw that the tree was completely despoiled of its leaves.—"That's the last," she said as she
put the leaf under her pillow.

"You won't die until tomorrow," the doctor said to her. "You
have one more night."

"Ah! what joy!" said the young girl. . . . "A winter night
. . . it will be a long one."

Jacques returned; he brought a muff.

"It is very pretty," said Francine; "I shall wear it to go out."

She spent the night with Jacques.

The next day, All Saints Day, at the midday Angelus, she was
overcome with agony and all her body began to tremble.

"My hands are cold," she murmured. "Give me my muff."
And she buried her poor hands in the fur. . . .

"It's all over," the doctor told Jacques. "You may embrace
her."

Jacques placed his lips on those of his love. At the last moment when they wished to take her muff from her, she clutched
it in her hands.

"No, no," she said; "leave it to me . . . it is winter; it is
cold. . . . Ah! my poor Jacques . . . my poor Jacques . . .
What is going to become of you? Ah! Ah! my God!"

And the next morning Jacques was alone.

First Reader.—I said truly that this wasn't a happy story. "What do you want, reader? One can't laugh all the time."

It was the morning of All Saints Day, Francine had just died.

Two men were watching at the bedside; the one who remained standing, was the doctor; the other, kneeling beside the bed, clung with his lips to the dead girl's hands and seemed to wish to bind them there in a despairing kiss. It was Jacques, Francine's lover. For more than six hours he had been buried in an unconscious grief. A hand organ which passed beneath the window had just aroused him.

This organ was playing a tune which Francine had been in the habit of singing every morning when she awoke.

One of those unreasonable hopes which could only arise after great despair crossed Jacques' mind. He went back a month in the past, to the time when Francine was still dying; he forgot the present moment, and imagined a moment when the dead girl was only asleep and that she was going to wake up soon, and begin to sing her morning song.

But the sounds of the organ had not yet died away before Jacques had already returned to reality. Francine's mouth was closed forever to song, and the smile, which her last thought had brought to it was effaced from her lips when death began to come.

"Courage, Jacques," said the doctor, who was the sculptor's friend.

Jacques got up and said as he looked at the doctor, "It is finished, is it not? There is no longer any hope?"

Without answering this sad question the friend closed the curtains of the bed and returning to the sculptor he took his hand.

"Francine is dead—." he said, "We had to expect it. God knows that we have done what we could to save her. She was a fine girl, Jacques, who loved you a great deal, more, and differently than you loved her; for her love was only made of love, while yours was an alloy. Francine is dead . . . but everything is not over; we must now think of attending to the necessary details for her burial—we must do this together, and, during our absence we will ask the neighbour to watch here."

Jacques permitted himself to be led away by his friend. All day they were busy going to the Mayor's office, taking care of the details for the funeral, going to the cemetery. As Jacques had no money at all, the doctor pawned his watch, a ring, and several suits of clothes to defray the expenses of the funeral, which was set for the next day.

They returned home very late in the evening; the neighbour forced Jacques to eat a bit.

"Yes," he said, "I need something; I am cold and I have need of gaining a little strength for I have work to do tonight."

The neighbour and the doctor did not understand what he meant.

Jacques sat down at the table and took several mouthfuls so quickly that he almost choked, then he asked for something to drink. But as he lifted the glass to his mouth, Jacques let it fall to the floor. The glass, which was broken, aroused in the artist's mind a memory which awakened for the moment an overwhelming sorrow. The day when Francine had come to his room for the first time, the young girl, who was at that time suffering, felt ill, and Jacques had given her a little sip of water in this glass. When they were living together they made it a love token.

In his rare moments of richness, the artist bought for his friend one or two bottles of a bracing wine whose use was prescribed for him, and it was in this glass that Francine drank the wine which changed her love to a charming gaiety.

Jacques remained for more than a half hour looking at the broken pieces of this fragile and dear souvenir without saying anything, and it seemed that his heart, too, had just been broken, and that he felt its pieces cutting his breast. When he came to himself, he gathered up the bits of glass and placed them in a drawer. Then he begged the neighbour to find him two candles and to have the janitor fetch him a bucket of water.

"Do not go away," he said to the doctor, who hadn't dreamed of it, "I will need you in a minute."

The water and the candles were brought; the two friends remained alone.

"What are you going to do?" the doctor asked when he saw Jacques who, after he had poured the water into a wooden bowl, was throwing into it equal handfuls of fine plaster.

"Do you not guess what I am going to do?" asked the artist, "I am going to mould Francine's head, and as I would lack the courage to do it if I were alone, you must not leave me."

Jacques went at once to pull aside the bed curtains and took away the cloth which had been thrown over the dead girl's face. Jacques' hand began to tremble and a muffled sob mounted to his lips.

"Bring the candles," he said to his friend, "and hold the bowl for me."

One of the lights was placed at the head of the bed in such a way as to throw all its light on the consumptive's face; the other light was placed at the foot of the bed. By the aid of a brush dipped in olive oil, the artist moistened her brows, her lashes and hair, which he arranged just as Francine was in the habit of doing.

"I do this that she will not suffer when we remove the cast," Jacques murmured to himself.

These precautions taken, and after he had placed the dead girl's head in a nice position, Jacques began to pour the plaster over the mold until the mixture had attained the necessary thickness. At the end of a quarter of an hour the operation was finished and was completely successful.

By a strange chance, a change had come over Francine's face. The blood, which had not had time to become entirely cold and warmed doubtless by the heat of the plaster, had flowed toward the upper portion of her head, and a blush of transparent rose gradually mingled with the dead white of her forehead and cheeks. Her eyelids, which had been raised when the mould was removed, permitted the quiet blue of her eyes to be seen, whose glance seemed to reveal vague intelligence; and her lips half-open in a dawning smile seemed to leave, forgotten in the last farewell, this last word, which could only be heard with the heart.

Who dares affirm that the mind ceases absolutely when the body becomes insensible? Who can say that the passions are extinguished and die at once with the last heart beat which they have aroused? Could not the soul sometimes remain a willing captive in a body already dressed for the tomb, and, from the depth of its fleshy prison, spy upon for a moment the regrets and the tears? Those who go away have so many reasons to distrust those who stay!

At the moment when Jacques thought of preserving her features by the means of art, who knows what happened? A thought of another life had come perhaps to waken Francine in the first sleep of her eternal rest. Or had she remembered that he whom she had just left was an artist at the same time as a lover; that he was one and the other because he could not be one without the other; that for him love was the soul of art, and that if he had loved her so much it was because she had known how to be for him a woman and a mistress, a feeling clothed in a body. And then perhaps Francine wishing to leave to Jacques a human face which was to become for him an ideal incarnate, had known, dead, already cold, how to reclothe once more her face with all the radiance of love and all the grace of youth;—she brought an object of art to life.

And perhaps the poor girl had thought truly; for there exists among real artists some strange Pygmalions who, contrary to the other one, would like to change into marble their living Galateas.

Before the calmness of that face, where agony no longer showed any traces, no one would have been able to believe in the long suffering which had prefaced her death. Francine seemed to continue her love dream; and seeing her so, one would have said that she had died of beauty.

The doctor, overcome by fatigue, slept in a corner.

As for Jacques, he was again overcome by his doubts. His illusioned spirit persisted in believing that she, whom he had so much loved, was going to wake up; and, as some nervous jerkings, brought about by the recent action of the plaster, disturbed at intervals the immobility of the body, this pretense of life encouraged Jacques in his happy illusion which lasted until morning, until the moment when an officer came to confirm the death and to authorize the burial.

Moreover, if all the folly of despair was needed to doubt the death of this beautiful creature, to believe in it, all the infallibility of science was required.

While a neighbour was dressing Francine in her shroud, Jacques had been taken into another room where he found some of his friends who had come to follow the funeral. The Bohemians abstained from, when they were face to face with Jacques, whom they loved like a brother, all those commiserations which only serve to aggravate the sorrow. Without saying any of those words so difficult to find, and so painful to listen to, one by one they silently wrung their friend's hand.

"This death is a great misfortune for Jacques," one of them said.

"Yes," responded the painter Lazare, a bizarre wit, who had learned how to overcome at an early time all his youthful rebellions by opposing to them the immobility of an adopted position, and in whom the artist had succeeded in killing the man,—"yes; an unhappiness which he has voluntarily brought into his life. Since he came to know Francine, Jacques has certainly changed."

"She has made him happy," said another.

"Happy!" responded Lazare, "what do you call happiness? How can you call this passion happiness, which puts a man in the state which Jacques is in at the present moment? Let him be shown a work of art—he would not look at it; and to see his mistress once more I am sure that he would walk over a Titian or a Raphael. My mistress is immortal for me, and will never deceive me. She lives in the Louvre and her name is Mona Lisa."

At the moment when Lazare was uttering his theories on art and passion they were informed that it was time to leave for the church.

After some low prayers, the procession started for the cemetery. . . . As it was All Souls' Day an immense crowd thronged
the sad sanctuary. A great many people turned around to look
at Jacques, who marched with head uncovered behind the hearse.

"Poor boy!" one said, "it is doubtless his mother."

"It is his father," said another.

"It is his sister," another said.

Come hither to study the expressions of sorrow, on this
memorable feast day which is celebrated once a year under the
November mist, one alone, a poet, when he saw Jacques passing
by, divined that he was following the corpse of his mistress.

When they had arrived near the grave reserved for them,
the Bohemians with head bare arranged themselves around it.
Jacques stood at the edge, his friend the doctor held his arm.

The grave-diggers were in a hurry, and wished to get it over
very quickly.

"There is no sermon to be said," one of them said, "let us
begin! So much the better. Houp! comrade! Let us get through
with it! !"

And the coffin, when it was taken from the carriage, was
tied with cord and lowered into the grave. The man removed
the cords and got out of the grave; then with the aid of one of
his comrades he took a spade and began to throw in the earth.
The grave was soon filled. A little wooden cross was planted
on it.

The doctor heard Jacques let escape this selfish cry in the
midst of his sobs:

"Oh my youth! It is you that is being buried!"

Jacques was a member of a society called *The Drinkers of
Water*, which seemed to have been founded with the idea of imi-
tating that famous club of the rue des Quatre-Vents, of which
mention is made in the fine novel of *The Grand Homme de
Province*. Only there existed a great difference between the
heroes of that club and the *Drinkers of Water*, who, like all
imitators, had exaggerated the principle which they wished to
apply. The difference can be shown by this fact alone, that, in
the book of M. de Balzac, the members of the club had finished
by attaining the end which they set for themselves, and showed

that every system is a good one which is successful; while after several years of existence the society of the *Drinkers of Water* had been naturally dissolved by the death of every member without any one name's being left engraved on a work which can testify to their existence.

During his liaison with Francine Jacques had less and less to do with the society of the *Drinkers of Water*. The needs of living had forced the artist to violate certain of the conditions signed and solemnly sworn to by the *Drinkers of Water*, the day when the society had been established.

Constantly exalted on the stilts of an absurd pride, these young people had established as a sovereign principle, in their association, that they would never come down from the high peaks of art, that is to say, that in spite of mortal misery, not one of them was willing to make any concession to necessity. So, the poet Melthior would never have consented to give up what he called his lyre to write a commercial prospectus or a profession of faith. That was all right for the poet Rudolph, who was fit for nothing and good at everything, who never let a hundred sou piece pass before him without drawing it to him, no matter how. The painter Lazare, proud wearer of rags, would never have wished to soil his brushes to make a portrait of a tailor holding a parrot upon his fingers, as our friend the painter Marcel had once done in exchange for his famous suit called Methuselah, which the hand of each of his mistresses had decorated with darns. All the time that he had lived in the communion of ideas with the *Drinkers of Water*, the sculptor Jacques had submitted to the tyranny of this rule; but while he knew Francine, he did not wish to subject the poor child, already ill, to the regime which he had accepted during his solitude. Jacques was, above all, upright and loyal. He went to the president of the society, the exclusive Lazare, and told him that from that time on he would accept all work which could be productive for him.

"My dear man," Lazare responded to him, "your declaration of love was your resignation as an artist. We will remain your friends if you like, but we will no longer be your colleagues. Carry on your trade as you like; to me you are no longer a sculptor, you are a plaster worker. It is true that you can drink wine, but we will continue to drink our water and to eat our bread of resignation,—we remain artists."

In spite of what Lazare said, Jacques remained an artist. But in order to keep Francine with him, he indulged in productive labour, whenever occasion permitted. Thus he worked for a long time in the studio of the decorator Romagnesi. Clever at execution, original in invention, Jacques could have, without abandoning serious art, acquired a great reputation in those special compositions, which have become the principal features in the business of luxuries. But Jacques was lazy, like all true artists, and in love, after the fashion of poets. His youth had awakened late, but it flamed; and, with a premonition of her near end, he wished to exhaust it completely between Francine's arms. So it often happened that good opportunities for work knocked at his door without Jacques' wishing to respond,  because he would have had to inconvenience himself, and as he found himself too comfortable dreaming in the glow of his friend's eyes.

When Francine died, the sculptor went to see his former friends the *Drinkers* but Lazare's spirit still dominated the group, where each one of the members was being petrified by the selfishness of art. Jacques did not find there what he was searching for; his despair was not at all understood, as they wished to calm him by reasoning. Realizing this lack of sympathy, Jacques preferred to hide his sorrow rather than to have it exposed to their discussion. So he broke completely with the *Drinkers of Water* and went to live alone.

Five or six days after Francine's burial, Jacques visited a marble cutter in the Montparnasse cemetery and offered to make the following bargain with him: The marble worker would furnish a frame for Francine's tomb, which Jacques would design; moreover, the marble worker would give the artist a piece of white marble on condition that Jacques would put three months of his time at the disposal of the marble worker, whether as stone cutter or as sculptor. The dealer in tomb stones at that period had several special orders; he visited Jacques' studio, and when he noted several of the jobs he had commenced, he got proof that chance which had brought Jacques to him had brought him good fortune too. A week later Francine's tomb had a frame, in the midst of which the wooden cross had been replaced by a stone cross with the name engraved on it.

Jacques fortunately had bargained with an honest man who understood that one hundred kilograms of wrought iron and three square feet of Pyrenean marble could not pay for three months of Jacques' labour, whose talents had won for him several thousand écus. He offered the artist a partnership, giving him an interest, but Jacques would not consent. The lack of variety in the subject matter was not pleasing to his inventive nature; moreover, he had what he wanted, a large piece of marble, out of which he wished to produce a masterpiece which he planned for Francine's tomb.

At the beginning of spring, Jacques' situation became better; his friend the doctor introduced him to a great foreign gentleman who had just settled at Paris and was having built a magnificent hotel, in one of the most beautiful sections. Several famous artists had been engaged to create the luxury for this small palace. He ordered from Jacques a fireplace for the drawing room. It still seems to me on looking at Jacques' cartoons that it was a charming thing. The entire winter poem was revealed in this marble which was to serve as a frame for the flames. Jacques' studio, being too small, he asked and obtained a space in the yet uninhabited hotel to execute his commission. They even advanced him a sufficiently large sum on the price arranged for this work. Jacques began to pay back his friend the doctor the money which the latter had loaned him when Francine had died.

Then he went to the cemetery to hide under a blanket of flowers the earth under which his mistress was sleeping. But spring had come before Jacques, and upon the young girl's tomb a thousand flowers had chanced to grow with the green grass.

The artist did not have the courage to pull them up for he thought that these flowers contained something of his friend. As the gardener asked him what he was going to do with the roses and the pansies he had brought, Jacques ordered him to plant them on a grave newly made nearby, a tomb of a poor person without any monument or any sign except a piece of wood stuck in the earth, and surmounted by a crown of imitation flowers. A pitiful offering out of the grief of a poor person. Jacques departed from the cemetery in a quite different frame of mind than he had entered it. He looked with joyful curiosity at the beautiful spring sunlight, the same which had so often crowned Francine's hair when she ran over the meadows, plucking the wheat with her white hands. A whole crowd of lovely thoughts made Jacques' heart sing. When he passed before a little cabaret on one of the outer boulevards, he was reminded of a day when, surprised by a storm, he had entered it with Francine and had dined there. Jacques went in and had dinner at the same table. The dessert was brought to him in an engraved saucer; he

recognized the saucer and remembered that Francine had stayed a half hour working out the rebus which was painted on it; and he remembered too a song which Francine had sung, being in a charming mood from a small violet wine which did not cost very much and which contained more gaiety than raisins. But this group of gentle memories wakened his love without renewing his sorrow. Subject to the superstition like all poets and dreamers, Jacques imagined that it was Francine who hearing him walk just now near her, had sent him this bouquet of charming memories from her coffin and he did not wish to dampen them with a single tear. He left the café with a slow foot, head up, his eye bright and heart beating, with almost a smile on his lips, murmuring as he walked this refrain from Francine's song:

> Love is roaming in my neighbourhood—
> I must keep my door ajar.

This refrain on Jacques' lips was still a memory, but, it was now a song too; and perhaps without knowing it, that evening Jacques took the first step on the road of change which leads from sadness to melancholy and from there to forgetfulness. Alas! Although in spite of what one wishes and in spite of what one does, the eternal and proper law of progress so arranges it.

In the same way as the flowers, which born perhaps from Francine's body had grown upon the tomb, some elements of youth had blossomed in Jacques' heart, where the memories of an old love awakened vague desires toward new love. Moreover, Jacques was of that race of artists and poets who make passion an instrument for their art and poetry. His spirit had not activity which was not put into motion by the forces of his heart. With Jacques, invention was actually the child of feeling and he put a bit of himself into the very smallest things which he made. He perceived that his memories were no longer enough for him and that like the grindstone which works on itself when it has no grain, his heart was wearing out for lack of exercise. Work no longer had any charm for him; his invention formerly feverish and spontaneous no longer came except from patient effort; Jacques was discontented and almost envied the life of his former friends, the *Drinkers of Water*.

He tried to distract himself, he held his hand out to pleasure. He created for himself new liaisons. He went to visit the poet Rudolph, whom he had met in a café and each developed great sympathy for the other. Jacques had explained to him his difficulties; it did not take Rudolph a long time to understand the reason for them.

"My friend," he said to him, "I understand;—" and tapping him on his chest above his heart, he added: "Quickly, quickly you must light the fire there. Arouse without delay a little passion and ideas will return to you."

"Ah!" said Jacques, "I love Francine too well."

"That will not keep you from loving her always. You will kiss her upon the lips of another."

"Oh," said Jacques, "if only I could meet a woman who resembled her!"—and sunk in thought, he left Rudolph.

.   .   .   .

Six weeks later Jacques had regained all his spirit, aroused by the charming glances of a pretty girl who was called Marie, whose beauty reminded him a little of that of poor Francine. One couldn't find anyone prettier really than this sweet Marie, who would be eighteen years old in six weeks,—as she never failed to say. Her love for Jacques was born in the moonlight, in the garden at an outdoor ball, to the sound of a harsh violin, a consumptive bass viol, and a clarinet which whistled like a blackbird. Jacques had met her one evening when he was walking solemnly around the space reserved for dancing. When they saw him passing in his gloomy and eternally black suit buttoned up to his chin, the jolly and pretty habitués of the place, who knew the artist by sight, said to each other, "Why does this undertaker come here? Is there somebody to bury?" Jacques always walked alone, making his heart bleed inwardly from the thorns of memory, the keenness of which the orchestra aroused when they played a gay dance which rang in the artist's ears sad as a De Profundis. It was in the midst of this revery that he perceived Marie, who watched him from a corner and laughed foolishly when she saw his sombre countenance. Jacques raised his eyes as he heard, three steps away from him, this shout of laughter from under a rose hat. He went up to the young girl and said something to her, to which she responded; he offered her his arm to make a round of the garden, she accepted. He said to her that he found her as pretty as an angel. She made him repeat it twice; he stole for her some green apples, which were hanging to the trees in the garden, she devoured them with delight, laughing with her deep voice, which seemed to be the flourish of her constant gaiety. Jacques thought of the Bible and believed that no one could despair with any woman and still less with those who loved apples. He made another turn in the garden with the rose hat and it was thus that, having arrived alone at the ball, he did not leave it the same way.

However, Jacques had not forgotten Francine. Remembering the words of Rudolph, he kissed her every day when he kissed Marie's lips, and he worked in secret on the figure which he wished to place upon the dead girl's tomb.

One day when he had received some money, Jacques bought a dress for Marie, a black dress. The girl was very happy, only she thought that black was not very suitable for summer, but Jacques said to her that he loved black a great deal and that she would give him much pleasure if she would wear this dress every day. Marie obeyed him.

One Saturday, Jacques said to the young girl,—"Come early tomorrow, we are going to the country."

"What joy!" said Marie, "I will bring you a surprise, you will see; tomorrow the sun will shine."

Marie spent the night at home making a new dress, which she had bought with her savings, a pretty pink dress. And Sunday she appeared at Jacques' studio clothed in her stylish purchase.

The artist received her coldly, almost brutally.

"I believed to give you pleasure in giving myself this present of a new dress!" said Marie, who could not explain Jacques' coldness.

"We will not go to the country," he responded, "you can go away,—I must work."

Marie went home, her heart heavy. On the way, she met a young man who knew Jacques' story and had courted her at one time.

"Well, Mademoiselle Marie, you are no longer wearing mourning?"

"Mourning," asked Marie, "and for whom?"

"What! didn't you know? You should certainly have known; that black dress which Jacques gave you. . . ."

"Well?" asked Marie.

"Well, it was mourning. Jacques made you wear mourning for Francine."

From that day Jacques never saw Marie again.

This rupture made him unhappy. His unhappy days returned; he had no more work and fell into a frightful state of despondency and knowing no longer what was going to happen to him

he begged his friend the doctor to have him placed in a hospital.
The doctor saw at the first glance that this admission would not
be difficult to obtain. Jacques, who was not ignorant of his
condition, was on the road to join Francine.

He was placed in the Saint-Louis hospital.

As he could still work and walk, Jacques begged the director
of the hospital to give him a little room for which they had no
use that he might go to work. They gave him a room and he had
his stool brought, his chisel and some clay. During the first two
weeks he worked on the figure which he planned for Francine's

tomb. It was a large angel with outspread wings. This figure,
which was Francine's portrait, was not entirely finished, for
Jacques could no longer mount the ladder, and soon he could not
leave his bed.

One day the nurse's notebook fell into his hands, and Jacques,
seeing the medicine which was ordered for him, understood that
his case was fatal; he wrote to his family and had sister Sainte-
Genevieve called, who surrounded him with all her tender care.—
"Sister," Jacques said to her, "up there, there is in the room
which you loaned me, a little plaster cast. This statuette, which
represents an angel, was planned for a tomb, but I haven't the
time to carry it out in marble. Furthermore, I have a beautiful
piece of marble, white veined with pink for it, and last, Sister,

I am giving you my little statuette to put in the community chapel."

Jacques died a few days later. As the funeral took place the same day as the opening of the Salon, the *Drinkers of Water* did not attend.—"Art before everything," Lazare had said.

Jacques' family was not rich, and the artist had no special grave.

He was buried somewhere.

MUSETTE'S WHIMS

PERHAPS it will be remembered how one day Marcel, the artist, sold his famous canvas of *The Crossing of the Red Sea* to the Jew Medicis, to be used as a signboard for a grocer's shop. The day after the sale, which had been followed by a sumptuous supper offered by the Jew to the Bohemians, as a part of the payment, Marcel, Schaunard, Colline and Rudolph wakened very late in the morning. Still stupefied from their drunkenness of the day before, none of them remembered at first what had happened; and as the midday Angelus sounded from a neighbouring church, they all looked at each other with wan smiles.

"There's the bell with its pious notes calling humanity to the refectory," Marcel remarked.

"That's true," Rudolph agreed, "it is the solemn hour when honest people are going into the dining room."

"Then we must study how to become honest people," murmured Colline, for whom every day was the feast of Saint Appetite.

"Oh! Bottles of my nurse's milk. Ah! Four meals of my childhood, what has become of you?" sighed Schaunard. "What has become of you?" he repeated in a voice full of dreamy and seductive melancholy.

"To think that there is at this time in Paris more than one hundred thousand cutlets on the grill," Marcel remarked.

"And as many beefsteaks," added Rudolph.

As an ironical chorus, while the four friends laid before each other the dreadful daily problem of lunch, the waiters in the house restaurant shouted at the top of their lungs the clients' orders.

"They will never be quiet, those brigands," said Marcel, "Each word produces the effect upon me of a blow of a pickax hollowing out my stomach."

"The wind is in the north," Colline remarked solemnly, and pointed out a weathervane revolving on a neighbouring roof, "We shall not lunch today, the elements are against it."

"Why so?" asked Marcel.

"It's an atmospherical observation I made," the philosopher went on; "the wind in the North almost always indicates abstinence, just as wind in the South ordinarily brings joy and good cheer. It is what philosophy calls news from above."

On an empty stomach Gustave Colline indulged in mad jests.

At this point Schaunard, who had just sunk one of his arms in the abysm, which served as his pocket, drew it back, uttering an anguished cry. "Help! There is someone in my greatcoat," Schaunard groaned as he tried to disengage his hand, caught in the claws of a live lobster.

To the cry which he had just uttered, suddenly another cry responded. It was Marcel who, as he instinctively put his hand in his pocket, had just discovered an America of which he no longer dreamed; that is to say, the one hundred fifty francs which the Jew Medicis had given him the day before in payment for *The Crossing of the Red Sea!*

Then the Bohemians remembered all at once.

"Cheer, Gentlemen!" Marcel placed on the table a pile of écus, among which gleamed five or six new louis.

"They seem alive," Colline said.

"What a pretty voice," said Schaunard as he made the gold pieces sing.

"How pretty they are, those medals," added Rudolph; "you could call them pieces of sun. If I were king, I would not have any other money, and I would have it stamped with the effigy of my mistress."

"When you think that there is a country where it is as common as stones," said Schaunard. "In earlier days, the Americans gave four for two sous. I had one old relative who made a visit to America; he was buried in the stomachs of the savages. It was very unfortunate for the family."

"But I say!" Marcel looked at the lobster which began to walk around the room, "where does that animal come from?"

"I recall," said Schaunard, "that yesterday I took a turn in

Medicis' kitchen; believe it or not, this reptile fell in my pocket accidentally. Those beasts are nearsighted. Since I have it," he added, "I intend to keep it, I will tame it and paint it red. It will be very jolly. I am lonesome since Phemie left,—it will be company for me."

"Gentlemen," Colline announced, "look, I beg you, the vane has turned to the south; we shall lunch."

"I think so," said Marcel, as he picked up a gold piece, "here is one of them which we will have cooked and served with a lot of sauce."

They proceeded to discuss the menu solemnly and lengthily. Each item was the occasion of a discussion adopted by a majority vote. The omelet soufflé, suggested by Schaunard, was carefully defeated; likewise the white wines, against which Marcel aligned himself in an extempore speech which brought out in relief his knowledge of wine.—"Wine's first duty is to be red," the artist affirmed; "don't speak to me of your white wines."

"Well," Schaunard suggested, "what about champagne?"

"Ah, pshaw! A fine cider! An epileptic liquorice water! I would give all the cellars of Epernay and of A1 for a small cask of Burgundy. In addition we have no shopgirls to seduce, nor any vaudeville show to give. I vote against champagne."

When the menu was finally adopted, Schaunard and Colline departed to a restaurant in the neighbourhood to order the repast.

"If we might build a fire!" suggested Marcel.

"Indeed," said Rudolph, "we wouldn't be averse to it. The thermometer has invited us to for a long time; let's have a fire. The chimney will be surprised." And he hastened to the stairway and told Colline to have some wood brought up.

Some moments later, Schaunard and Colline returned, followed by a coal man laden with a large bundle of firewood.

As Marcel felt in a drawer for a few useless papers to light his fire, he chanced on a letter whose writing made him tremble. He began to read it, hiding it from his friends as he did so.

It was a pencil note, written sometime ago by Musette during the time she was living with Marcel, dated back a year to the day. It only contained these few words:

My Dear Friend,

Don't worry about me, I shall return soon. I have gone out to walk a bit to warm myself. It is freezing in the room and the coal seller has gone to sleep. I broke the last two legs of the chair, but it didn't burn long enough to cook an egg. Besides the wind comes in through the floor as if it were his own home and blows me bad advice which would irritate you if I listened to it. I prefer to go out for a while, I will look at the stores in the quarter. They say that there is some velvet at ten francs a metre. It is incredible, I must see it. I will be back for dinner. Musette.

"Poor girl," Marcel murmured, folding the letter in his pocket. And he stayed thoughtful a moment, his head between his hands.

At this time, the Bohemians had been for a long period in a bereaved state, with the exception of Colline only, whose lover had always remained invisible and anonymous.

Phemie even, that agreeable companion of Schaunard, had met a simple soul who had offered her his heart, furniture in walnut, and a ring of his hair, red hair. However, two weeks after he had given them to her, Phemie's lover had wanted to take back his heart and his furniture, because he perceived when he looked at his mistress' hands, that she was wearing a hair ring but it was black; and he dared suspect her of unfaithfulness.

But Phemie hadn't ceased to be virtuous; only as several times her friends had teased her on account of the ring with the red hair, she had had it dyed black. The gentleman was so happy that he bought a silk dress for Phemie. It was her first. The day when she wore it for the first time, the poor child said: "Now I can die."

As for Musette, she had again become almost an official personage. It had been three or four months since Marcel had run into her. For Mimi, Rudolph had not heard her mentioned, except by himself when alone.

"Ah look!" Rudolph suddenly shouted, when he saw Marcel crouched and dreaming in a corner of the fireplace. "This fire doesn't want to burn."

"Here you are, here you are," said the artist, as he lit the wood which began to burn and sparkle.

While the friends developed their appetite by making preparations for the repast, Marcel again isolated himself in the corner and mused over certain memories of Musette which the letter, he had chanced to find, had aroused in him. Suddenly he remembered the address of a woman who was an intimate friend of his old passion.

"Ah, I have it!" he cried loud enough to be heard. "I know where to find her."

"To find what?" asked Rudolph. "What are you going to do now?" he asked as he saw the artist starting to write.

"Nothing—an important letter which I forgot. I'll be with you in a moment," Marcel added, and he wrote as follows:

My Dear Child,

I have money in my desk, this withering fortune came as suddenly as a stroke of apoplexy. There is a large dinner simmering on the fire, lots of wine, and we have a fire, my dear, just like any new rich citizen. It ought to be seen, as you said before. Come spend a while with us, you will find Rudolph, Colline and Schaunard here; you could sing some songs for us with dessert—there is dessert.—While we are at it, we will probably continue to eat for a week. So have no fear of  coming too late. It has been such a long time since I heard you laugh! Rudolph will compose some madrigals for you, and we will drink all kinds of toasts to our dead loves, free to revive them. Between persons like us . . . the last kiss is never the last. Ah! If it hadn't been so cold the last year, perhaps you wouldn't have left me. You have deceived me for a log of wood, and because you were afraid of having red hands; you have done well, I do not bear a grudge against you for this any more than for other times; but come warm yourself while there is wood to burn. I kiss you as often as you like.   Marcel.

Having finished that letter, Marcel wrote another to Madame Sidonie, Musette's friend, asking her to have the other letter forwarded to the person addressed. Then he went to find the janitor to have him deliver the letters. As he was paying him for the errand in advance, the janitor noticed a piece of gold money shining in the painter's hands; so before starting on his mission he apprised the proprietor of the fact, since Marcel was late with his rents.

"Mossieu," he said completely out of breath, "the artisse on the sixth floor has money! You know, that big fellow who laughed in my face when I carried his order to leave."

"Yes," said the proprietor, "the one who had the nerve to borrow money from me to pay me back on account. He has been asked to leave."

"Yes, Monsieur. But today he is lined with money, its gleam hurt my eyes just now. He is giving a party. It is a propitious moment . . ."

"Yes, indeed," said the proprietor, "I will go myself at once."

Madame Sidonie, who was at home when Marcel's letter was brought to her, sent her maid immediately with the letter addressed to Musette.

The latter was living at the time in a charming apartment in the Chaussée-d'Antin. When Marcel's letter was brought she was to entertain that same evening, with a large formal dinner.

"A miracle has happened," Musette cried, as she began to laugh uproariously.

"What's the matter now?" a handsome young man stiff as a statue asked.

"It's an invitation for dinner," the young woman replied. "Well, well! How that fits in!"

"It fits in very badly," the young man responded.

"Why so?" asked Musette.

"What! . . . Would you consider going to this dinner?"

"I believe indeed that I am thinking of it . . . you do as you like."

"But my dear, it isn't suitable at all . . . Go another time."

"Ah! that's a fine idea! Another time! It is an old acquaintance who has invited me to dinner, Marcel, and it is extraordinary enough that I may see him face to face! Another time! But serious dinners in that house are as infrequent as eclipses!"

"What! You are breaking your word to me to go see that

person," said the young man, "and it was to me that you gave it! . . ."

"To whom did you want me to give it then? To the Grand Turk? This man has nothing to do with that."

"Well, that's being remarkably frank."

"You know perfectly well that I don't behave like other people," Musette replied.

"But what will you think of me if I let you go, knowing where you are going? Think of it, Musette, from my point of view, from yours, it is very unconventional. You will have to excuse yourself to this young man. . . ."

"My dear Monsieur Maurice," Mademoiselle Musette used a very firm tone, "you knew me well before you took me; you knew that I was full of whims, and that there isn't a person alive who can boast of making me give up one of them."

"Ask me anything you want" . . . said Maurice . . . "But that! . . . It's folly . . . folly."

"Maurice, I will go to Marcel's; I am going there," she added as she put on her hat. "You can leave me if you like; but it is stronger than I; he is the best man in the world, and the only one I have ever loved. If his heart were made of gold he would have had it melted to make rings for me. Poor boy!" she said as she showed him the letter . . . "you see while he has a bit of fire he invites me to come and get warm. Ah! If I weren't so lazy and if there weren't velvets and silks in the stores!!! I was very happy with him; he knew how to make me suffer, and it is he who gave me my name, Musette, on account of my songs. At any rate, if I go to him, you can be sure that I will return to you . . . that is if you don't close the door in my face."

"You could not tell me more directly that you do not love me," responded the young man.

"Stop it, dear Maurice, you are too intelligent to indulge in a serious discussion about this. You keep me in the same way men keep a beautiful horse in a stable; I love you . . . because I love luxury, the excitement of parties, everything which clatters and all that glistens; let us not talk of feeling—that would be silly and useless."

"At least let me accompany you."

"But you wouldn't be amused at all," Musette replied, "and you would keep us from enjoying ourselves. Then, remember that he is going to kiss me, this fellow, naturally."

"Musette," asked Maurice, "do you often find persons as accommodating as I?"

"Monsieur Viscount," responded Musette, "one day as I was riding in a carriage along the Champs Élysées with Lord ——, I met Marcel and his friend Rudolph, who were walking, both very poorly dressed, bedraggled like shepherd dogs, and smoking their pipes. It had been three months since I had seen Marcel and it seemed as if my heart were going to jump through the carriage door. I had the carriage stop, and for an half hour I chatted with Marcel before all of Paris, which was passing by my carriage. Marcel gave me some Nanterre cakes and a bunch of violets costing a sou, which I put in my belt. When he left me, Lord —— wanted to call him back to invite him to dine with us. I kissed him for the thought. And that's my nature, my dear Monsieur Maurice; if it doesn't please you, you must say so at once. I am going to take my slippers and my boudoir cap."

"Indeed, it's a good thing to be poor sometimes!" mused the Viscount Maurice with an air of envious sadness.

"Oh! no," said Musette, "if Marcel were rich, I would never have left him."

"Go along then," said the young man, as he clasped her hand. "You put on your new dress," he added; "it is marvellously becoming."

"Indeed, that's true," said Musette, "it must have been a premonition I had this morning. Marcel will have the first look at it. Adieu! I am going to eat a little of the blessed bread of gaiety."

That day Musette had on a ravishing outfit; never had a more seductive garment clothed the poem of her youth and beauty. Furthermore, Musette instinctively possessed the appearance of elegance. When she came into the world the first thing she looked for must have been a mirror so that she could arrange her swaddling clothes; and before being baptized she had already committed the sin of flirting. At the time when her situation was the most humble, when she was still reduced to printed cotton dresses, to little hats with pom-poms on them, to shoes of goatskin, she was charming in this simple and humble working-girl's outfit. These pretty girls, half bees, half grasshoppers, who sing as they work all the week long, only ask God for a bit of sunshine on Sunday, make love from their hearts generally, and sometimes throw themselves out the window. It is a race which has now disappeared, thanks to the new generation of young people; a generation corrupted and corrupting, but above all, absurdly vain, stupid and cynical. For the pleasure of making bad paradoxes, they have teased these poor girls about their hands which were marked by the holy scars of work, and for which they can't earn very soon enough to buy almond cream. Little by little they have succeeded in inoculating them with their vanity and their foolishness, and it is then that the working girl disappeared. Then the gay woman appeared. A hybrid breed, impudent creatures, moderate beauties, half skin, half cosmetics, whose boudoir is a counter where they retail pieces of their heart, as one would sell chunks of roast beef. Most of these girls, who dishonour pleasure and are the shame of modern chivalry, haven't the intelligence of the animals whose feathers they wear on their hats. If they happen by any chance to have, with no admixture of love or even fancy, a vulgar desire, it is for the benefit of some common clown whom the foolish crowd surrounds and pays tribute to in the public dance halls, and whom the newspapers, pursuers of everything ridiculous, celebrate by their publicity. Although she was forced to live in this world, Musette never had any of its habits or its tastes; she did not have the grasping servility, common to these creatures, who only know how to read a ready reckoner and to write in figures. She was an intelligent and spiritual girl, having in her veins some of Manon's drops of blood; and she rebelled at everything imposed on her; she never had been able to learn how to resist a whim, whatever might be the consequences.

Marcel was truly the only man whom she had loved. At least he was the only one for whom she had really suffered. And it took all the concentration of her instincts, which attracted her to everything which gleams and sparkles, to make her leave him. She was twenty years old; and in her case luxury was almost a question of health. She could give it up for a while, but never 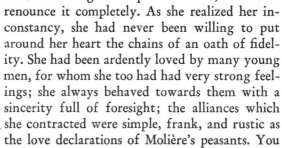 renounce it completely. As she realized her inconstancy, she had never been willing to put around her heart the chains of an oath of fidelity. She had been ardently loved by many young men, for whom she too had had very strong feelings; she always behaved towards them with a sincerity full of foresight; the alliances which she contracted were simple, frank, and rustic as the love declarations of Molière's peasants. You love me well and I love you too, agreed, let's get married. Ten times, if she had wished, Musette could have found a settled state, what is called a future. But she didn't believe in the future and showed in her conduct the scepticism of Figaro.

"Tomorrow," she used to say sometimes, "that's a folly of the calendar. It is a daily excuse which people have invented not to do their business today. Tomorrow,—perhaps there will be an earthquake. Fortunately, today the earth is solid."

One day, a gentleman with whom she had lived for nearly six months, who had fallen madly in love with her, had seriously suggested marriage to her. Musette burst out laughing at the proposal.

"I, to jeopardise my liberty with a marriage contract! Never," she said.

"But I spend my days fearing that I will lose you."

"You would lose me sooner if I were your wife," responded

Musette. "Don't mention it again. I am not free, furthermore," she added, doubtless thinking of Marcel.

Thus she spent her youth, her spirits blown by all the winds of the unforeseen, giving a great deal of happiness, and almost making herself happy. The Viscount Maurice, with whom she lived at the moment had great difficulty to conform to this uncontrollable creature, insane about liberty; and after he saw her depart for Marcel's he waited for her in a state of burning and jealous impatience.

"Will she stay there?" the young man asked himself the entire evening, thus burying this question mark in his heart.

"That poor Maurice," Musette said on her side, "he finds this a bit sudden. Ah! bah! one must shape one's youth."

Then, her attention turned quickly to other channels and she thought of Marcel, whither she was going; and passing in review the memories which the former adorer's name aroused she asked herself by what miracle he had had a tablecloth laid. She reread as she went the letter which the artist had written her, and could not help but be a little saddened. But that didn't last but a moment. Musette thought rightly that this was less than ever an occasion for sadness, and as at the moment a great wind had come up, she cried:

"It is certainly funny, if I didn't wish to go to Marcel's, the wind would blow me there." And she hastened on her way, happy as a bird that is flying back to its first nest.

Suddenly it began to snow very hard. Musette looked about to find a carriage. She didn't see one. As she happened to be at the moment in the same street where her friend Madame Sidonie lived, the person who had Marcel's letter sent to her, Musette decided to stop there for a moment to wait for the weather to improve so that she could continue on her way.

When Musette entered Madame Sidonie's, she found many people there. A game of lansquenet had been going on for three days.

"Don't disturb yourselves," said Musette, "I am only coming in and going right out."

"Did you receive Marcel's letter?" Madame Sidonie whispered in her ear.

"Yes," Musette answered. "Thanks! I am going to his house now. He invited me to dinner. Do you wish to come with me? You would be most amused.

"Oh! no, I cannot," Sidonie pointed to the table in play, "and my bet?"

"There are six louis," the banker who held the cards said very loudly.

"I double it," announced Madame Sidonie.

"I'm not proud, I draw two at a double raise," responded the banker, who already had passed several times. "King and an ace. I am done for!" He continued as he put his cards down, "all the kings are dead . . ."

"You aren't talking politics," observed a journalist.

"And the ace is the enemy of my family," remarked the banker who again turned up a king . . . "Long live the king!" he shouted. "My little Sidonie, give me two louis."

"Keep them in your memory." Sidonie was furious at having lost.

"That makes five hundred francs that you owe me, little one," the banker said. "You will owe me a thousand. I pass the hand."

Sidonie and Musette talked together in undertones. The party went on.

Almost at the same minute the Bohemians were sitting down at the table. During the whole dinner Marcel seemed nervous. Each time a noise of steps was heard they saw him jump.

"What's wrong?" Rudolph asked. "One would think that you expect someone. Aren't we enough?"

But at the look the artist threw him, the poet understood his friend's preoccupation.

"That's true," he thought to himself, "we aren't all here. Marcel's glance suggested Musette; Rudolph's look meant Mimi."

"We lack women," Schaunard said suddenly.

"Confound it!" growled Colline, "will you be quiet with your libidinous thoughts? It was agreed that we wouldn't speak of love—it would turn the sauces."

And the friends began to drink the fullest of bumpers, while outside the snow continued to fall and in the chimney the wood burned bright, sending up fireworks of sparks.

At the moment when Rudolph was humming very noisily the refrain of a song which he had just found in the bottom of his glass, there were several raps on the door.

At this noise, like a diver who, touching with his foot the depths of the water then returns to the surface, Marcel, overcome in the beginning of drunkenness, got up quickly from his chair and hastened to open the door.

It wasn't Musette.

A gentleman appeared on the threshold. He held in his hand a little piece of paper. His exterior seemed pleasant enough, but his dressing gown was very badly made.

"I find you in happy circumstances," he said, as he saw the table, in whose centre there appeared an enormous leg of mutton.

"The proprietor!" exclaimed Rudolph; "let us pay him the respects due him." And he began to beat a salute on his plate with his knife and fork.

Colline offered him his chair, and Marcel remarked:

"There, Schaunard, a white glass for the gentleman. You arrive just in time," the artist told the proprietor. "We were just drinking a toast to the building. My friend over there, Monsieur Colline, was saying some very impressive things. Since you are here, he will go over them again in your honour. Repeat a little, Colline."

"Pardon, gentlemen," said the proprietor, "I do not want to bother you." And he unfolded the little piece of paper he held in his hand.

"What is that document?" Marcel asked.

The proprietor, who had cast an inquisitive glance around the room, perceived the gold and silver which lay on the mantelpiece.

"It is the order to leave," he said quickly, "I have already had the honour of having it presented to you."

"So you did," said Marcel, "my faithful memory brings back that event perfectly; it was a Friday, October eighth, at a quarter past twelve—very well."

"It is marked with my signature," said the proprietor, "and if it doesn't disturb you. . . ."

"Sir," said Marcel, "I was just considering visiting you. For a long time I have had many things to talk to you about."

"I am completely at your orders."

"Then give me the pleasure of refreshing yourself," Marcel went on forcing him to drink a glass of wine. "Monsieur," resumed the artist, "recently you sent me a little document . . . with a picture of a woman holding a scale. The message was signed Godard."

"That is my bailiff," responded the proprietor.

"He had a dreadful handwriting," remarked Marcel. "My friend, who knows every tongue," he went on, pointing to Colline, "my friend was very glad to translate for me this dispatch whose carriage cost five francs. . . ."

"It was an order to leave," the proprietor interrupted, "just a precautionary measure . . . that is the custom."

"A notice, so that was it," Marcel went on. "I wanted to see you to have a talk about that deed, as I would like to have it changed into a lease. This house pleases me, the stairway is clean, the street is very gay; and then family reasons, a thousand things make me attached to these walls."

"But," said the proprietor in unfolding his order to leave, "there is the last term's rent to be paid."

"I will pay it, sir; such is my dear wish."

During this time the proprietor's eyes never left the fireplace where the money was; and the magnetic quality of his glance, full of desire, was such that the pieces seemed to move and to advance toward him. "I am happy to arrive at a moment when, without its bothering you, we can end this small account," he said as he held the paper out to Marcel who, not being able to ward off the attack, turned it again and began over again with his creditor the scene of Don Juan with M. Dimanche.

"You have, I think, some property in the provinces?" he asked.

"Oh!" the proprietor answered, "very little; a small house in Burgundy, a farm, very little, unproductive . . . the tenants don't pay . . . So," he added still holding out the note, "this little reimbursement comes in wonderfully. It is sixty francs, as you know."

"Sixty, yes," Marcel said as he went to the chimneyplace

where he took three gold pieces. "We say sixty," and he put three louis on the table at some distance from the proprietor.

"At last!" the latter murmured as his countenance cleared suddenly, and he put the notice carefully on the table.

Schaunard, Colline and Rudolph watched the proceedings with disquiet.

"Forsooth! Monsieur," Marcel addressed him, "since you are a Burgundian you will not refuse to say two words to a compatriot." And making the cork pop from a bottle of Vieux-Macon, he poured a full glass for the proprietor.

"Ah! perfect," the latter sighed . . . "I have never drunk better."

"It is from my uncle who lives there and who sends me occasional hampers now and again."

The proprietor rose and stretched his arm towards the money in front of him, when Marcel interrupted him again.

"You won't refuse to pledge me once more," he said as he poured out more wine to drink and forced the creditor to clink glasses with him and with the three other Bohemians.

The proprietor did not dare refuse. He drank again, put down his glass, and got ready again to pick up his money when Marcel burst forth:

"See here, Monsieur, I've just had an idea. I am quite rich at the moment. My uncle from Burgundy has supplemented my pension. I am afraid of squandering away this money. You know, youth is foolish. . . If it doesn't bother you I will pay one quarter's rent in advance." And, taking sixty more francs in écus, he added them to the louis which were on the table.

"I shall then give you a receipt for the current quarter, which is not yet due," said the proprietor. "I have some blanks in my pocket," he added as he pulled out his bill folder. "I shall fill it in and date it forward. How charming this tenant is," he added to himself in an undertone, covering as he did so the one hundred francs with his eyes.

Before this transaction, the three Bohemians, who didn't understand in the least Marcel's diplomacy, remained speechless.

"But this chimney smokes, and that is most annoying."

"Why haven't you warned me? I would have had the chimney maker come," said the proprietor, who didn't want to be behindhand in fair dealings. "Tomorrow I will have the workmen come." And, having finished filling out the second receipt, he clipped it to the first, shoved both towards Marcel, and again reached out for the pile of money. "You can't know how op-

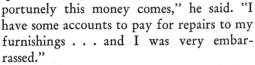

portunely this money comes," he said. "I have some accounts to pay for repairs to my furnishings . . . and I was very embarrassed."

"I regret having made you wait a little," Marcel replied.

"Oh! I wasn't in trouble . . . Gentlemen . . . I have the honour . . ." And his hand went out again . . .

"Oh! Oh! I beg," Marcel went on, "we haven't yet finished. You know the proverb; when the bottle is open . . ." And he filled the proprietor's glass once more.

"One must drink . . ."

"That's right," the latter said, as he seated himself again for politeness' sake.

This time, from a wink which Marcel sent to them, the Bohemians understood his objective.

Meantime the proprietor began to leer in an extraordinary way. He rocked on his chair, made some risqué remarks, and promised Marcel, who asked him for some repairs for his rooms, fabulous improvements.

"Forward the heavy artillery!" the artist whispered to Rudolph, indicating a bottle of rum.

After the first liqueur glass full, the proprietor sang a coarse song which made Schaunard blush.

After the second glass he recounted his marital misfortunes;

and as his wife was called Helena, he compared himself to
Menelaus.

After the third glass, he became philosophical, and uttered
such epigrams as these:

Life is a river.

Fortune doesn't bring happiness.

Man is mortal.

Ah! but love is grand!

And adopting Schaunard as a confidant, he told him about
his secret affair with a young girl whom he had surrounded
with walnut furniture and who was named Euphemie. And he
gave such a detailed description of this young creature, with
simple affections, thᵣt Schaunard began to be moved by a strange
suspicion which became a certainty when the proprietor showed
him a letter, which he took from his bill fold.

"Oh! Heavens!" Schaunard cried as he perceived the signature. "Cruel woman! you drive a dagger in my heart."

"What's up?" demanded the Bohemians, who were agitated
by this strange speech.

"Look," said Schaunard, "this letter is from Phemie; see that
blot which serves as a signature;" and he passed around the
letter from his former mistress; she began with these words:

"My big louf-louf!"

"It is I who am her big louf-louf," affirmed the proprietor,
as he tried to get up, without any success.

"Very well!" remarked Marcel, who was watching him, "he
has cast anchor."

"Phemie! Cruel Phemie!" muttered Schaunard, "You hurt
me indeed."

"I have furnished a little apartment on the mezzanine for
her, number twelve, rue Coquenard," said the proprietor. "It
is pretty, pretty. But it costs me a great deal . . . but true
love has no price, and then I have twenty thousand francs in
rent. . . . She asks me for money," he added as he picked up
the letter. "Poor dearie! . . . I will give her that; that will
please her," and he stretched out his hand toward the money

put out by Marcel. "What! What!" In his astonishment he tapped on the table, "But where is it?"

The money had disappeared.

"It is unthinkable for a decent man to lend himself to such questionable behaviour," Marcel said. "My conscience, morals, forbid me to give the money for my rent into the hands of this old debauchee. I won't pay my rent at all. But my conscience will at least rest without any pangs. What manners! A man as bald as that!"

Meantime the proprietor managed to slide down to the floor and held a very loud senseless conversation with the bottles.

As he had been absent for two hours, his wife, now worried about him, sent the servant to look for him. He uttered great cries when he saw him. "What have you done to my master?" he asked the Bohemians.

"Nothing," replied Marcel; "he came up just now to ask for his rent; as we had no money to pay him, we asked him to give us some time."

"But he is drunk," objected the servant.

"The greatest part of that drunkenness," Rudolph replied, "came before he arrived here. He told us that he had gone to look over his cellar."

"And he had so little sense," Colline added, "that he wanted to leave us our receipts without any money."

"Give them to his wife," the painter added, as he returned the receipts. "We are honest men and we do not wish to take advantage of his condition."

"O my God! What will Madame say?" moaned the servant, as he dragged the proprietor out, since he could not longer stand on his feet.

"At last!" sighed Marcel.

"He will return tomorrow," Rudolph said. "He has seen money."

"When he returns," rejoined the artist, "I will threaten to tell his wife of his relations with young Phemie and he will extend our time."

As soon as the proprietor got out, the four friends began to drink and smoke again. Only Marcel had preserved a suggestion of sense in his drunkenness. From time to time, at the slightest sound of steps he heard in the hallway, he ran to the door. But those who were ascending always stopped at lower floors; then the artist went slowly to seat himself at the corner of his fire. Midnight sounded, and Musette had never come.

"Well," thought Marcel, "perhaps she wasn't even at home when the letter was delivered to her. She will find it this evening when she returns and will come tomorrow, there will still be a fire. It is impossible for her not to come. We must wait till tomorrow."

And he went to sleep in the corner of the hearth.

At the same moment when Marcel was going to sleep and dreaming of her, Mademoiselle Musette left her friend Madame Sidonie's, where she had stayed until then. Musette wasn't alone. A young man was with her, a carriage was waiting at the door, they both got in, and the carriage started away at a gallop.

The game of lansquenet continued at Madame Sidonie's.

"But where is Musette?" someone suddenly asked.

"And where is little Seraphin?" asked another.

Madame Sidonie began to laugh.

"They have just escaped together," she said. "Ah! that's a strange story. What a peculiar person is that Musette! Imagine . . ."

And she told the group how Musette, after almost getting on bad terms with the Viscount Maurice, had started out for Marcel's, but had stopped for a moment there, by chance, and had met the young Seraphin.

"Ah! I thought there was something afoot indeed," said Sidonie, interrupting her story; "I have been watching them all evening; he isn't clever, that little man. In short," she continued, "they have left together without a word and he, who could overtake them, is smart indeed. Just the same, it is very funny when you think that Musette is mad about her Marcel."

"If she is mad about him, why Seraphin, almost a child? He has never had a mistress," one young man said.

"She wants to teach him how to read," the journalist replied, who was very cross when he lost.

"Just the same," Sidonie resumed, "since she loves Marcel, why Seraphin? That's what amazes me."

"Alas! yes, but why?"

.   .   .   .

For five days without leaving their rooms the Bohemians led the most perfect life in the world. They stayed at the table from morning till evening. A remarkable disorder reigned in the room, which suggested a pantagruelian atmosphere. Upon almost a whole bank of oyster shells was formed an army of bottles of different sizes. The table was laden with leftovers of all kinds and a forest burned in the fireplace.

The sixth day, Colline, who was the master of ceremonies, made out, as he was in the habit of doing every morning, the menu for luncheon, dinner, light refreshments, and supper, and submitted it for his friends' approval, who each initialed it in approval.

But when Colline opened the drawer, which served as a till, to take out the money needed for the days' repasts, he recoiled two steps, and became as pale as Banquo's ghost.

"What's wrong?" the others demanded carelessly.

"There is nothing more than thirty sous," the philosopher replied. "The devil, the devil!" responded the others, "that will mean some change in our menu. However, thirty sous well used! . . . Just the same, we'll have difficulty getting truffles."

Some minutes later the table was set. Three plates could be seen filled with much symmetry:

One plate of herrings;

One plate of potatoes;

One plate of cheese;

In the fireplace smoked two small firebrands as big as your thumb.

Outside it continued to snow.

The four Bohemians seated themselves at the table and solemnly unfolded their napkins.

"It's strange," commented Marcel, "this herring has a taste of pheasant."

"It's due to the manner in which I arranged it," responded Colline; "the herring has not been appreciated."

At this moment a jolly song came up the stairs and knocked on the door. Marcel, who could not keep from trembling, hastened to open.

Musette flung herself around his neck and embraced him for five minutes. Marcel felt her tremble in his arms.

"What's wrong?" he asked her.

"I am cold," Musette replied in a mechanical way, as she approached the fire.

"Ah!" said Marcel, "we have had such a good fire."

"Yes," said Musette, looking over the table full of the remnants of a feast which had lasted five days; "I have come too late."

"Why?" asked Marcel.

"Why?" repeated Musette . . . blushing a little. And she seated herself on Marcel's knees; she kept on trembling and her hands were purple.

"Then you weren't free?" Marcel whispered in her ear.

"I! Not free!" exclaimed the lovely girl. "Oh, Marcel! Were I seated in the midst of the stars, in the paradise of the good God, and were you to make one sign to me, how I should come down to you. I! not free!"

And she began to tremble again.

"There are five chairs here," Rudolph said. "It is an odd number, not to mention the fact that one of them has a ridiculous shape." And knocking the chair against the wall, he threw the pieces into the fire. The fire was quickly revived with bright and happy flames. Then signalling to Colline and Schaunard, the poet took them away with him.

"Where are you going?" asked Marcel.

"We are going to buy some tobacco," they answered.

"To Havana," added Schaunard, nodding knowingly to Marcel, who thanked him with a look.

"Why didn't you come sooner?" he asked Musette again when they were alone.

"That's true, I am a bit late. . . ."

"Five days to cross the Pont Neuf; you must have gone by way of the Pyrenees," Marcel replied.

Musette lowered her head and remained silent.

"Ah! bad girl!" the artist replied sadly, as he tapped lightly on his mistress' breast. "Whom are you holding under there?"

"You know well," the other replied quickly.

"But what have you been doing since I wrote you?"

"Don't ask me." replied Musette quickly, as she kissed him several times. "Ask me nothing! let me warm myself at your side while it is cold. You see I have put on my prettiest frock to come. That poor Maurice, he didn't understand at all when I left to come here; but it was stronger than I. I started on the way . . . The fire is good," she added as she stretched out her little hands to the flames. "I will stay with you until tomorrow. Do you wish it?"

"It will be very cold here," Marcel said, "And we have nothing for dinner. You came too late," he repeated.

"Ah, pshaw!" Musette said. "It will the more resemble old times."

Rudolph, Colline and Schaunard spent twenty-four hours looking for tobacco. When they returned to the house Marcel was alone.

After six days of absence, the Viscount Maurice saw Musette coming in.

He didn't reproach her at all and only asked why she seemed sad.

"I have quarrelled with Marcel," she said. "We parted unpleasantly."

"And still," wondered Maurice, "who knows? You will go back to him again."

"What do you expect?" asked Musette. "I need to breathe the atmosphere of that life from time to time. My crazy life is like a song; each of my love affairs is a stanza, but Marcel is the chorus."

MIMI WEARS A FEATHER

"Oh, no, no, no, you are no longer Lisette. Oh, no, no, no, you are no longer Mimi.

"Today you are Madame the Viscountess; day after tomorrow you will be perhaps Madame the Duchess, for you have put your feet on the ladder of fame; the door of your dreams has finally opened to you after twice knocking, and here you are having just entered victorious and triumphant. I was very sure that you would finish thus one night or another. What must be, must be finally; your white hands were fashioned for ease, and for a long time have insisted on a ring to indicate an aristocratic alliance. At last you have a coat of arms! But we still prefer that one which youth gave to your beauty which, through your blue eyes and your pale face, seemed to provide azure quarters on a field of white. Noble or lowly, no matter, you are always charming; and I recognized you perfectly when you passed the other evening on the street, with rapid and finely shod foot, with a gloved hand helping the wind to raise the ruffles of your new dress a bit so as not to soil it, but more to show your embroidered petticoat and your transparent stockings. You had a hat marvellously stylish, and you appeared to be buried in a profound difficulty over your rich lace veil which hung about your expensive hat. Very serious difficulty, in fact! for it was a question of knowing which was more valuable and would be most profitable for your vanity, to wear the veil lowered or raised. Wearing it lowered you ran the risk of not being recognized by those of your friends whom you would have been likely to meet, and who obviously would have passed near you ten times without guessing that this opulent exterior hid Mademoiselle Mimi. On the other hand, if you wore the veil up, you risked having it go unseen, and then what is the good of wearing it? You have spiritually solved the difficulty in raising and lowering it in turn every ten steps, this superb tissue, woven doubtless in that country of the Arachnes, that is called Flanders, and which alone cost him more than all your old wardrobe. Ah! Mimi . . . Pardon, Ah! . . . Madame the Viscountess! I was indeed right, you knew it, when I told you: Patience, don't despair; the future is full of cashmere shawls, shining jewel boxes, intimate suppers, etc., etc. You would not believe me, doubting one! Well, now my predictions are realized and I am indeed as good as your *Oracle for Women,* I hope, a little wizard in eighteen pages which you bought for five sous from

a bookseller on the Pont Neuf, and which you wore out with your constant interviews. Still again, was I not right in my prophecies, and will you believe me now, if I told you that you won't stay there; if I told you as I listen I already hear rising in the dimness of your future, the stamping and whinnying of horses hitched to a blue coupé driven by a powdered coachman who sets the mounting stool before you and says: Where to, Madame?—Would you believe me again if I told you too that later ah! as late as possible, oh Lord! attaining an ambition which you have long held, you will have a table at the Belleville or Batignolles and you will be courted by old military men and reformed lovers who will come to play lansquenet and baccarat secretly with you? But before coming to this stage when the sun of your youth will have already gone down, believe me, dear child, you will use many yards of silk and velvet; many fortunes doubtless will have been sacrificed to the satisfaction of your whims; indeed flowers will fade on your forehead, and they will fade under your foot; many times you will change your crest. One by one upon your head will gleam the baroness' wreath, the countess' crown, and the jewelled diadem of the marquise; you will take for your motto: Inconstancy. And you will know, depending on whim or necessity, how to satisfy each in his turn or at the same time all your many adorers, who will stand in line in the outer room of your heart, as they stand in line at a theatre where a popular play is being given. Go now, go forward with your mind freed from memories, and filled with ambition; go, the way is beautiful, and we wish it to be soft for your feet for a long time to come; but we hope above all that all this sumptuousness, all these fine clothes, will not too soon become the tomb where you bury your gaiety."

So the painter Marcel spoke to young Mademoiselle Mimi, whom he happened to meet three or four days after her second rupture with the poet Rudolph. Although he had forced himself to modify the jokes he scattered through his horoscope, Mademoiselle Mimi was not at all fooled by Marcel's fine words and understood perfectly that, lacking respect for her new title, he was even making fun of her.

"You are unkind to me, Marcel," said Mimi, "that is wrong; I was very nice to you when I was Rudolph's mistress, but I left him; after all, that's his fault. It is he who sent me away; and yet how did he treat me those last days I spent with him? I have been most unhappy, so there! You have no idea, you haven't, what kind of man Rudolph was, a disposition ruined by anger and jealousy, who was killing me bit by bit. He loved me,—I know that well,—but his love was as dangerous as a firearm and what a life I have led for fifteen months! Ah, believe me, Marcel, I don't wish to appear better than I am, but I have certainly suffered for Rudolph,—furthermore you know it. It isn't suffering which made me leave, no—I swear it,—I was accustomed to it; and then I repeat, it is he who sent me away. He walked with both feet on my pride; he told me that I had no heart if I stayed with him; he told me that he didn't love me any more, that I must take another lover; he even went so far as to show me a young man who would court me, and he, by his challenges, acted as a connecting bond between me and this young man. I went with him as much through spite as through need, for I didn't love him; you know well, you do, that I don't love such young men for they are boring and sentimental as harmonicas. However, what's done is done, and I don't regret it and I would do it again. Now that he is no longer with me and knows that I am happy with another, Rudolph is furious and most unhappy; I know somebody who meets him now; he has red eyes. That doesn't astonish me, I was perfectly sure that it would be like that, and that he would run after me; but you can tell him that he will waste his time, and that this time it is serious and permanent. Has it been long since you saw him, Marcel, and is it true that he is much changed?" asked Mimi in a different tone.

"Very much changed, really," Marcel responded. "Changed enough."

"He is desolate, that is obvious; but what do you want me to do? So much the worse for him! He wished it; it had to come to an end, to the end. Console him . . . won't you?"

"Oh now," Marcel was tranquil, "the biggest need is over. Don't get upset, Mimi!"

"You aren't telling the truth, my dear," Mimi said, as she made a slightly sceptical face; "Rudolph wouldn't console himself that quickly; if you knew in what condition I saw him the day of my departure! It was Friday; I didn't want to spend the night with my new lover for I am superstitious and Friday is an unlucky day."

"You were wrong, Mimi; for love, Friday is a good day; the ancients used to say: *Dies Veneris.*"

"I don't know Latin," said Mimi, as she went on with her story. "So I came back from Paul's; I found Rudolph waiting for me, behaving like a guard in the street. It was late, after midnight, and I was hungry as I had had a poor dinner. I begged Rudolph to look for something for supper. He returned a half hour later; he had searched everywhere to bring back something very good: bread, wine, sardines, cheese and an apple tart. I had gone to bed during his absence and he arranged the table near the bed; I pretended not to look but I saw him well; he was pale as death; he shivered, and moved about in the room like a man who doesn't know what he is doing. In a corner he noticed several packages of my belongings which were on the floor. This sight seemed to make him ill, and he put a parasol

in front of the packages so as to see them no more. When all
was ready, we began to eat; he tried to make me drink, but I
was neither hungry nor thirsty, and my heart was oppressed.
It was cold, for we had nothing out of which to build a fire;
we heard the wind whistling in the chimney. It was very sad.
Rudolph looked at me, he stared; he put his hand in mine, and
I felt his hand tremble, at the same time feverish and icy cold.

" 'This is the funeral supper of our love,' he spoke very low.
I didn't reply but I hadn't the courage to withdraw my hand.

" 'I am sleepy,' I finally told him; 'it is late,—let's go to sleep.'

"Rudolph looked at me; I had put one of his scarves over my
head to keep from getting cold; he took it off without speaking.

" 'Why do you take that off?' I demanded. 'I am cold.'

" 'Oh! Mimi,' he then said, 'I
beg you,—it will cost you nothing,—put on your little striped
bonnet, for tonight.' It was a
boudoir cap of striped brown and
white cotton. Rudolph liked to
see me in this cap, for it recalled
to him some lovely nights and
some fine days as one followed the
other for this was the way we
counted our fine days. Remem-

bering that it was the last time that I would sleep beside him,
I didn't dare refuse to satisfy his whim; I got up and searched
for my striped bonnet which was at the bottom of one of my
packages; inadvertently I forgot to put back the parasol; Rudolph noticed it and hid the packages as he had done before.

" 'Good night,' he said to me. 'Good night,' I responded.

"I thought he was going to kiss me, and I would not have
prevented him but he only took my hand which he raised to his
lips. You know, Marcel, how he liked to kiss my hands. I heard
his teeth chatter, I felt his body cold as marble. He clutched
my hand continuously and he had put his head on my shoulder
which was not slow to become very damp. Rudolph was in a
dreadful way. He chewed the bed covers to keep from crying,
but I could easily hear his heavy sobs, and I felt his tears drop-

ping ever on my shoulder, hot at first and then icy cold. At this moment it took all my courage; and it took a lot, I can tell you. I had only to say one word, I had only to turn my head, my mouth would have met Rudolph's mouth, and we would have made up once more. Ah! for a moment I thought really he was going to die in my arms or at least that he was going crazy,—as he almost did once before, you remember? I was going to yield, I felt it coming on; I was going to give in first, I was going to fold him in my arms, for no one could be so heartless as to remain unmoved in the presence of such sorrow. But I remembered the words which he had said to me the day before: 'You have no heart if you stay with me, for I love you no more.' Ah! In recalling these hard sayings I could have watched Rudolph almost die, and if a kiss from me were the one thing necessary I would have turned away my mouth and I would have let him die. At last overcome by fatigue, I fell half to sleep. I continued to hear Rudolph sobbing and I swear to you, Marcel, the sobbing lasted all night long; and when day came and when I looked at the bed where I had slept for the last time with the lover whom I was going to leave to go to the arms of another, I was incredibly agitated when I saw the ravages which grief had made on Rudolph's face.

"He got up, as I did, without speaking and he was so weak and so exhausted that he almost fell down when he took his first few steps. However, he dressed very quickly and only asked where my things were and when I was leaving. I told him that I didn't know. He went away without saying good-bye, without shaking hands. That's how we have left each other. What a blow for his heart when he came back and didn't find me!"

"I was there when Rudolph returned," said Marcel to Mimi, who was out of breath from having talked so much. "As he took his key from the clerk of the hotel, the latter said to him: 'The little one has gone.'

" 'Ah.' " responded Rudolph," 'that doesn't surprise me, I was expecting it.' " And he went up to his room where I followed him, fearing too, some crisis, but there wasn't any.

" 'As it is too late to rent another room this evening we must put it off until tomorrow morning,' he said to me, 'we shall

go together. Let's dine.' I thought that he wanted to get drunk,
but I was wrong. We dined very soberly in a restaurant where
you used to eat sometimes with him. I requested some Beaune
wine to deaden Rudolph's pain a bit.

" 'That's Mimi's favourite wine,' he told me; 'we have often
drunk it together at this very table. I even remember a day
when she said to me as she held out her empty glass for the third
or fourth time,"Oh fill it again, it puts balm in my heart."—
It was a sufficiently bad pun, don't you think? Much more
worthy of a mistress of a vaudeville star. Ah, she liked to drink,
Mimi did.' On seeing that he was about to lose himself in sentimental bypaths, I talked to him about something else and no
further mention was made of you. He spent the whole evening
with me and seemed as calm as the Mediterranean. What
astonished me most was that his calmness wasn't assumed,—
it was real indifference. At midnight we returned.

" 'You seem surprised at my tranquillity under the circumstances,' he
said to me. 'Let me make a comparison
for you, my dear, and if it is a homely
one it has the merit of being true. My
heart is like a fountain whose plug has
been left open all night; in the morning not one drop of water remains. In
truth, my heart is the same. I wept all
the tears that were left to me last
night. It is strange, for I thought myself more capable of grief, and through
one night of suffering here I am ruined,
perfectly dry, on my word of honour! It is just as I say; and
in this same bed where I just escaped dying last night by the
side of a woman who was no more disturbed than a stone, now
that this woman rests her head upon the pillow of another, I
am going to sleep like a porter who has done a good day's work.'
Comedy, I thought to myself; I shall no sooner have left than
he will begin knocking his head against the walls. However, I
left Rudolph alone and returned to my own room, but I didn't
go to sleep. At three o'clock I thought I heard a noise in Ru-

dolph's room; I went down in great haste, thinking I would find him in the midst of a fever of grief."

"Well?" asked Mimi.

"Well, my dear, Rudolph was sleeping, the bed was not upset, and everything showed that his sleep had been calm and that he was not slow in giving himself up to it."

"That's possible," Mimi admitted; "he was so exhausted from the night before; but the next day?"

"The next day, Rudolph came to waken me early, and we went to rent rooms in another hotel into which we moved the same evening."

"And," Mimi pursued, "what did he do when he left the room which we occupied? What did he say when he left the room where he loved me so much?"

"He packed quietly," replied Marcel, "and when he found in a drawer a pair of lace gloves which you had forgotten, as well as two or three letters also yours. . . ."

"I remember," Mimi used a tone which seemed to suggest: I forgot them purposely that they might serve as a remembrance of me. "What did he do with them?" she added.

"I think I remember that he threw the letters in the fireplace and the gloves out the window; but without any dramatic gesture, without any posing,—quite naturally, as one does when one is getting rid of something useless."

"My dear M. Marcel, I assure you that from the depths of my heart I hope for this hard indifference. But one thing more, very sincerely I do not believe in this rapid cure, and in spite of all you have told me, I am convinced that my poor poet has a broken heart."

"That may be," replied Marcel as he took leave of Mimi, "but, unless I am much deceived, the pieces are still good."

While this colloquy was taking place on the public thorough-fare, his honour the Viscount Paul awaited his new mistress, who was very late indeed. She seemed most distracted to the viscount. He sat down at her knees and recounted to her his favourite romance, to wit: that she was lovely, pale as the moon, sweet as mutton, but that he loved her above all for the beauties of her character.

"Ah!" thought Mimi, as she let down the waves of the brown hair upon the snow of her shoulders; "my lover Rudolph was not so exclusive."

Just as Marcel had reported, Rudolph seemed to be radically cured of his love for Mademoiselle Mimi, and three or four days after his separation from her, the poet was making his reappearance, completely changed. He was dressed with an elegance which must have made him hard to recognize, even in his own mirror. Nothing about him, furthermore, seemed to cause any fear that he intended to hurl himself into the abysses of nothingness, which tale Mademoiselle Mimi had started with all sorts of hypocritical regrets. Rudolph was actually perfectly calm; he listened without moving a muscle, to the reports told him of the new and luxurious life of his mistress, who was pleased to be kept informed about him by a young woman who had remained her confidante and who had occasion to see Rudolph almost every evening.

"Mimi is very happy with the Viscount Paul," the poet was informed; "she seems madly in love with him. Only one thing bothers her,—she worries lest you will not bother her by pursuing her, a course which furthermore would be dangerous for you, for the viscount adores his mistress and for two years has had a room for firearms."

"So! So!" responded Rudolph, "then let her sleep peacefully. I haven't the slightest desire to mix vinegar with the sweetness of her honeymoon. As for her young lover, he can leave his dagger sheathed with perfect safety like Gastibelza, the man with the gun. I certainly don't wish any harm to happen to a man in the days when he still is fortunate enough to cherish some illusions." And as Mimi couldn't fail to be told of the attitude with which her former lover heard all the details, for her part she didn't forget to reply, shrugging her shoulders the while:

"That's good, that's good; some of these days we will see what will happen."

And, more than anyone else, Rudolph himself was most astonished at this sudden indifference of his, which, without going through the customary phase of sadness and melancholy, had advanced some days before to stormy tempests which still bothered him. Forgetfulness, so slow to come, particularly for those disappointed in love, forgetfulness which they beg for so violently and how violently do they repel it when they feel it nearing. This pitiless consolation had suddenly, without his being able to protect himself, invaded Rudolph's heart, and the name of the woman he loved so much could be heard without awakening any echo there. Strange thing, Rudolph, whose memory was powerful enough to recall to his mind the things which had happened in the farthest days of his past, and the beings who had had a part in, or exercised an influence over his most distant past—Rudolph no matter what efforts he made, could not distinctly call to mind after four days of separation the features of this mistress who had just failed to ruin his life between her frail hands. The sweetness of the eyes, in the gleam of which he had so often gone to sleep, he could no longer recover. The tone of that voice even whose anger and whose tender caresses made him delirious he did not remember. One of his poet friends, who had not seen him since his separation, met him one night; Rudolph seemed worried and anxious as he walked up the street taking great steps and twirling his stick.

"So," said the poet extending his hand, "there you are," and he looked at Rudolph curiously.

When he saw that he had a long face, he thought he ought to use a tone of condolence.

"Brace up, have courage, my dear fellow, I know that it is hard, but eventually it must come to that; it may be better now than later; in three months you will be completely cured."

"What are you buzzing about?" asked Rudolph. "I am not sick, my friend."

"Oh! my God!" said the other, "don't try to act brave, heavens! I know the story, and if I didn't I could read it in your countenance."

"Look out, you are making a blunder," warned Rudolph. "I am very tired tonight, that's true; but the reason for this irritation, you have not quite put your finger on."

"Good, but why protect yourself? It's very natural,—one

doesn't break that easily a liaison which has lasted almost two years."

"They all tell me the same thing," Rudolph was irritated. "Well, on my honour, you are mistaken, you and all the others. I am very sad, and it is possible I appear so; but this is why: today I expected my tailor to bring me a new suit, and he didn't come; there you have the reason for my irritation."

"How bad," the other said as he laughed.

"Not bad; good, on the contrary, very good, even excellent. Listen to me and you will see."

"Let me see," said the poet, "I am listening; prove to me how one can reasonably have such an aggrieved air because a tailor fails to keep his word. Go on, go on, I am listening."

"Well, you know well how small causes produce the biggest results. This evening I was to make a very important call which I cannot make because I have no suit. Do you understand?"

"Not at all. You haven't given sufficient reason to justify despair. You are desolate . . . because . . . finally. . . . You are a brute to pose to me. That's my opinion."

"My friend," said Rudolph, "you are most obstinate; there is always reason to be disappointed when one misses some happiness or at least a pleasure, because they are so often lost, and it is wrong to say, speaking of the one or the other, I will catch you the next time. I shall resume: This evening I had an engagement with a young lady; I was to meet her in a house whence I should perhaps have taken her to mine, if that were the shorter way to go to her home, and even if it had been very long. In this house there was a party, but suits are worn at parties; I have no suit, my tailor was to bring me one, he did not bring it to me, I am not going to the party, I shall not meet the young woman, who has perhaps met another; I shall not take her home to my home nor to hers, where she is perhaps being taken by another. Now, as I said before, I am missing happiness or a diversion; therefore, I am sad, so I seem, and it is very natural."

"That may be," said the friend, "with one foot just out of one hell you put the other one in another, you do; but my good friend, when I came across you there in the street you had all the appearance of dancing attendance."

"So I was too,—that's just so."

"But," the other continued, "we are in the same quarter in which your former mistress lives, how can you prove to me that you weren't waiting for her?"

"Although separated from her, certain reasons have forced me to stay in this region; although we are neighbours, we are as far apart as if she were at one pole and I at the other. Furthermore, at the hour, my former mistress is sitting by her fire taking French grammar lessons from his honour Viscount Paul who is trying to make her virtuous by means of orthography. God! how it must irritate her. After all, that's his affair,

now that he is the editor-in-chief of her happiness. Really, you must see, indeed, that your reactions are absurd, and that instead of being on the wornout tracks of my old passion, I am, on the contrary, on the traces of a new one. She is almost my neighbour too and will become a closer one, for I am willing to take all the necessary trouble, and if she is willing to do the rest, we shall not be long in understanding each other."

"Actually," asked the poet, "you are already in love?"

"That's just what I am," Rudolph responded; "my heart is like those lodgings where a new tenant comes in just as the old one leaves. When a love leaves my heart, I put up a signboard for another affair. Furthermore, the place is habitable and in perfect repair."

"Who is this new idol? Where and when did you meet her?"

"Well, this is the way," Rudolph replied, "let's proceed in order. When Mimi left, I decided that I would never again be in love during my life, and I thought that my heart was dead with fatigue, exhaustion, whatever you like. It had beaten so much, so long, so quickly, that I could hope for nothing else. In short, I thought it dead, quite dead, very dead, and I considered interring it, as Monsieur Marlborough did. On this occasion I gave a small funeral dinner to which I invited some friends. The guests were to assume a sad countenance, and the bottles had crêpe tied about their necks."

"You didn't invite me?"

"I'm sorry, but I didn't know the address of the cloud on which you are stopping! One of my friends brought a woman, a young woman recently deserted by her lover too. She heard my story, it was told by one of my friends, a man who plays very well on the violincello of feeling. He spoke to this young widow of the qualities of my heart, this poor shell which we were going to bury, and invited her to drink to its eternal rest. 'Come now,' she said raising her glass, 'on the contrary drink to its health,' and she winked at me, a wink to waken the dead, as someone said, appropriately enough, for she had hardly finished her toast when I felt my heart singing immediately the O *Filii* of the Resurrection. What would you have done in my place?"

"That's a fine question! What is her name?"

"I don't know it yet, I shall ask her name the moment we sign our contract. I know well that I haven't delayed the required time from certain persons' point of view; but there you are, I canvass my own kind, I grant myself dispensation. What I know is that my future lady will bring me for a dower, gaiety, which is the health of the mind, and health which means the joy of the body."

"Is she pretty?"

"Very pretty, especially her colour; one might say that she washes her face in the morning with Watteau's palette."

> She is blonde, my dear, and her vanquishing gaze
> The hearts' four corners set ablaze.

"My witness."

"A blonde? You astonish me."

"Yes, I have had enough ivory and ebony. I am taking to a blonde;" and Rudolph began to sing, skipping as he did:

> We'll sing in a round this air
> If you entreat,
> I love her and she's fair
> As is the wheat.

"Poor Mimi," mourned the friend, "forgotten so quickly!"

This name, mentioned during Rudolph's lightheartedness, gave a sudden turn to the conversation; Rudolph took his friend's arm and told him at length the reasons for his break with Mademoiselle Mimi; the horrors which had attacked him when she left; how desolate he was because he thought she had carried away with her all that remained of his youth, of his passion; and how, two days later, he had realized that he was wrong, realizing that the cockles of his heart, which had been drenched by so many sobs and tears, were beginning to be warm again, to lighten and to explode under the first glance of youth and passion which the first woman he had met had shot

at him. He told him of this sudden and imperious encroachment which forgetfulness had made on him, without his even calling upon it to ameliorate his grief, and how that grief was dead, buried in this forgetfulness.

"Isn't all this a miracle?" he asked the poet, who, knowing by heart and by experience all the dolorous chapters in broken love affairs, replied:

"Oh, no, my friend, it is no more a miracle for you than for the others. What has happened to you has happened to me. The women we love when they become our mistresses cease to be for us their real selves. We see them only through lovers' eyes, we see them with poets' eyes. As an artist throws upon a model imperial purple robes or the starry veil of a sacred virgin, we too always have stores of shining cloaks and pure linen dresses, which we throw over the shoulders of the unintelligent creatures, disagreeable or bad, whatever they are; and when they are so clothed in the costume in which our ideal loves exist in the azure purity of our dreams, we let them assume this disguise; we incarnate the first woman who comes along with our dream and to her we speak our language which she doesn't understand.

"Moreover this creature, at whose feet we live prostrated, herself snatches away the divine veil under which we have hidden her, that we may better see her poor nature and wicked instincts; she puts our hands too over the place of her heart where nothing beats any longer, where perhaps nothing has ever beaten; again, she discards her veil and shows her exhausted eyes, and her pale lips, and her withered features. We tell her to resume her veil and we cry to ourselves: 'You lie! You lie! I love you and you love me too. That white breast enfolds a heart which is very young; I love you and you love me! You are beautiful, you are young! Back of all your meannesses there is love. I love you and you love me.'

"Then at the end, oh! always at the end when, after in vain having put triple bandages on our eyes, we perceive that we ourselves are the dupes of our own errors, we pursue the wretched creature who the day before was our idol; we tear away from her the golden veils of our poetry, which tomorrow we will again throw on the shoulders of an unknown who at once becomes the idol with the aureole; and that's just what all of us are like, monstrous egoists, furthermore, who love love for love's sake—you understand don't you?—We drink this divine liqueur out of the first vase we find."

"What matters the glass, if one can be gay?"

"What you have just said is as true as that two and two make four," Rudolph told the poet.

"Yes," responded the latter, "it is both true and sad, as half truths are.—Good-night."

Two days later, Mademoiselle Mimi learned that Rudolph had a new mistress. She only inquired about one thing: to know whether he kissed her hands as often as he had hers.

"As often," Marcel said. "Furthermore, he kisses each hair one after the other and they must stay together until he has finished."

"Ah," Mimi replied, as she shoved her hands through her own hair, "it is very fortunate that he didn't think of doing so much to me for we would have stayed together all our lives. Do you believe that it is really true that he loves me no longer, —do you?"

"Pooh! . . And you, do you still love him?"

"I, why I never did love him."

"Yes, Mimi, yes, you did love him, in those hours when women's hearts change places. You did love him, and don't deny it, for it is your justification."

"Ah, bah!" said Mimi. "He loves another now."

"That's true," said Marcel, "But later your memory will be for him like those flowers which one puts, while still quite fresh and fragrant, between the leaves of a book. A long time after, one comes across them dead, discoloured and withered, but still preserving forever a certain vague suggestion of their first sweetness."

One evening as she hummed in a low voice near him, Monsieur the Viscount Paul said to Mimi:

"What is that you are singing, my dear?"

"The funeral song of our love which my lover Rudolph has recently composed." And she began to sing:

> I haven't a cent, my dear, and they say
> 　In just such cases, forget—
> And you'll forget me in the time-old way
> 　My Mimi, with no regret?
> You see we have had, my dear—that's true—
> 　Of nights and days, the sweetest.
> They didn't last long, but what could we do?
> 　The loveliest joys are the fleetest.

ROMEO AND JULIET

DRESSED as an illustration in his magazine, the *Scarf of Iris,* gloved, polished, shaven, waved, mustaches curled, stick in hand, monocle in eye, beaming, vital, altogether smart, as anyone could have seen, our friend Rudolph, who one November evening, standing on the street, was waiting for a carriage to take him home. Rudolph awaiting a carriage? What thunderbolt was this that had suddenly come into his private life?

At the same hour when the poet, so transformed, was twirling his moustaches, chewing between his teeth an huge lily and attracting the glances of the lovely ladies, one of his friends was also passing by the same way. It was the philosopher, Gus-

tave Colline. Rudolph saw him coming and recognized him very quickly; and of those who have ever seen him once, who could not recognize him? Colline as usual was laden with a dozen or more books. He was clothed in that timeless nut-coloured great coat whose endurance led one to believe that it had been built by the Romans. His head was covered by that famous hat with the wide rim and a crown of beaver, under which swarmed a host of hyperphysical dreams, the hat, which had been surnamed the Manbrin helmet of modern philosophy. Gustave Colline was walking slowly, and muttering very low the preface to a work which had been on the press for three months—in his imagination. As he approached the place where Rudolph had stopped, Colline for a moment thought he knew him, but the sumptuousness displayed by the poet threw the philosopher into doubt and uncertainty.—Rudolph with gloves on, with a stick,—illusion. Utopia, what an aberration—Rudolph curled, he who has less hair than l'Occasion! Where has my mind gone? Moreover, at this time my unfortunate friend is now mourning and is composing sad poems over the disappearance of the youthful Mademoiselle Mimi, who has left him in the lurch, as I have heard say. Indeed, I miss her, myself, her youth; she lent a great distinction to her manner of making coffee, which is the beverage of serious minds. But I wish to think that Rudolph will console himself, and that he will soon find a new coffee maker. And Colline was so pleased with his pitiful pun that he would happily have cried to himself had not the solemn voice of philosophy awakened within him and energetically put to flight this debauch of wit.

Now, as he had stopped near Rudolph, Colline was forced to submit to the evidence before him; it was certainly Rudolph, marcelled, gloved, with a stick; it was impossible, but it was true.

"Oh, oh, dear," said Colline. "I am not deceived, it is surely you. I am sure of it."

"And I too," responded Rudolph.

Colline now began to study his friend, assuming the expression used by Lebrun, artist for the king, to show surprise. But suddenly he noticed two bizarre objects which Rudolph held! First, a cord ladder; second, a cage in which teetered some kind of bird. At this sight, Colline's face registered a sentiment that Lebrun, artist to the king, has forgotten in his portrayal of the passions.

"Oh well," said Rudolph to his friend, "I see distinctly the curiosity of mind which your transparent expression reveals; I will satisfy you. Only let's leave the public highway,—it engenders a coldness which would freeze both your questions and my answers." And they went into a café.

Colline's eyes never once left the rope ladder or the cage where the little bird, revived by the warm air of the café, began to sing in a tongue unknown to Colline, who was something of a language scholar.

"Well," asked the philosopher, pointing to the ladder, "what might that be?"

"It is a bond between my well-beloved and me." responded

Rudolph, speaking in a voice as sweet as the tone of a mandolin.

"And that?" Colline indicated the bird.

"That," said the poet, and his voice became soft as the song of a zephyr, "that is a clock."

"Answer me without hyperboles, in plain prose, but rightly."

"So I will. Have you read Shakespeare?"

"Have I read him? 'To be or not to be.' He was a great philosopher. Yes, I have read him."

"Do you remember Romeo and Juliet?"

"Yes, I remember!" And Colline began to recite:

> It is not yet near day:
> It was the nightingale, and not the lark,
> That pierced the fearful hollow of thine ear;

"My word, yes, I remember well. But go on."

"What," exclaimed Rudolph pointing to the ladder and the bird, "you don't understand now? Here you have the poem: I am in love, my dear fellow, in love with a woman whose name is Juliet."

"Well, go on," Colline urged him impatiently.

"And as my new idol is named Juliet, I have formed a project to re-enact with her the drama of Shakespeare. First, I no longer call myself Rudolph. I am named Romeo Montague and you will oblige me by not calling me anything else. Moreover, that all the world may know, I have had new visiting cards engraved. Nor is that all. As it isn't carnival time I am going to dress in a velvet doublet and wear a sword."

"To kill Tybalt?" enquired Colline.

"Of course," continued Rudolph. "Finally I shall use this ladder which you see here to enter my mistress's apartment, which actually possesses a balcony."

"But the bird, the bird," obstinately pursued Colline.

"Oh yes, this bird, which is a pigeon, must play the part of the nightingale, to indicate each morning the exact minute when I must be ready to leave the adored arms of my mistress who will embrace me about the neck and tell me in her soft voice exactly as in the balcony scene: 'No, it is not the day; it is the nightingale;' that is to say, it is not yet eleven o'clock, there is mud in the street, do not go away, we are so comfortable here! In order to perfect the re-enacting of the scene I shall try to find a nurse for my well beloved; and I hope that from time to time the almanac will be good enough to provide me with a little moonlight when I will climb to the balcony of my Juliet. What do you think of it, philosopher?"

"It is pretty like everything else," replied Colline, "but could you explain to me too the mystery of this elegant casing which makes you unrecognizable? Have you become rich?"

Rudolph did not respond, but motioned to a waiter and carelessly tossed him a louis, saying "our bill"; then he patted his purse, which began to sing.

"Have you a bell in your pockets which rings like that?"

"Only a few louis."

"Gold louis?" Colline choked in his astonishment. "Explain to me what has happened to you." At this point the two friends separated,—Colline, to go spread the news of Rudolph's opulence and new love affair; Rudolph, to return home.

This had taken place the week following the second rupture of Rudolph's relations with Mademoiselle Mimi. Accompanied by his friend Marcel, the poet, when he had broken with his mistress he felt the need of a change of air and surroundings and left the gloomy furnished hotel whose other clients saw him as well as Marcel, leaving without too many regrets. Both, as we have already said, went to look for lodgings and found two rooms in the same house and on the same floor. The room chosen by Rudolph was incomparably more comfortable than any he had ever had up to that time. Furnishings which could be rated seriously could be found there. Above all, a couch in red stuff imitation velvet, which did not observe in any way the proverb: Be what you seem. There were also upon the mantel two porcelain vases with flowers, and between them an alabaster clock with horrible ornaments. Rudolph put the vases in a wardrobe; and when the proprietor came to start the clock, which had stopped, the poet begged him to do nothing. "I will let you leave the clock upon the mantel," said he, "only as a work of art. It has stopped at midnight, that is a lovely hour and let it keep it. The day it shows five minutes after midnight I shall leave. A clock," went on Rudolph, who had never been able to submit to the imperial tyranny of the dial, "well, it is an intimate enemy who implacably counts your existence for you hour by hour, minute by minute and says to you at every instant: here is a bit of your life which disappears. Ah, I could not sleep quietly in a room where there is one of these instruments of torture, even near it carefreeness and meditation are impossible. A clock whose hands reach even to your bed and come to annoy you in the morning when you are deep in the soft languor of first awakening! A clock whose voice cries to you, ding, ding, ding. It is the hour for business, leave your lovely dream, slip from the caresses of your visions (and sometimes from those of reality). Put on your hat, your boots, it is cold, it is raining, leave for your job, it is time, ding, ding. It is well enough to have an almanac. Let my clock stay dumb and paralysed. . . ."

And thus communing with himself, he examined his new lodging and left himself disturbed by that secret anxiety which almost always one experiences on entering a new apartment.

"I have noticed," he thought, "the places where we dwell exercise a mysterious influence over our thoughts and consequently over our actions. This room is cold and silent as a tomb. If ever joy sings here, it will be when it is brought in from the outside; and it will not stay a long time for shouts of laughter would die without leaving an echo under this low ceiling, cold and white as a snowy sky. Alas, what a life mine will be between these four walls."

However, a few days later, this room which seemed to sad before was transformed by lights and resounded with joyful clamours; Rudolph had a house warming and a quantity of bottles explained the gaiety of these convivial spirits. Hidden in a corner with a young woman who had come by chance and of whom he had taken possession, the poet made songs with her with words and with hands. Toward the end of the celebration he made an engagement with her for the next day. "Well," he said to himself, when he was left alone, "the party was not a failure, and my stay here has not been inaugurated badly at all."

The next day at the appointed hour Mademoiselle Juliet appeared. The evening was taken up with explanations. Juliet had learned of the recent break Rudolph had made with that blue-eyed girl whom he loved so much; she learned that after she had left him once Rudolph had taken her back again, and she was fearful of being the victim of a new return of love.

"This is the way, you see," she added with a pretty gesture of mutiny, "I have no intention at all of being made ridiculous. I warn you that I am very strong-minded. Once mistress here," and she indicated by a look the meaning she gave to the word, "I stay and yield my place to none."

Rudolph used all his eloquence to convince her that her fears had no foundation and as the young lady for her part was willing to be convinced, they finished by establishing an actual entente. Only they did not agree when midnight sounded, for Rudolph wished that Juliet would stay and she attempted to go. "No," she said as he insisted. "Why so insistent? We shall always arrive where we are to arrive, unless you stop us on the way. I shall return tomorrow." And so she returned every evening for a week, only to go home when midnight struck.

These dallyings did not annoy Rudolph in the least. In love or even while only flirting, he belonged to the school of travellers who have no great urge to arrive, and, to the straight road leading directly to the end, prefer the hidden by-paths which make the journey longer but add to its picturesqueness. This slight sentimental sally resulted in leading Rudolph farther afield than he wished to go. Undoubtedly it was to bring him to the point when a flirtation, nourished by resistance, began to resemble love, that Mademoiselle Juliet had used this strategy.

At every new visit that she made to Rudolph, Juliet noticed in his talk a note of sincerity more pronounced than before.

When she was a little late, he evinced signs of impatience which delighted the young girl. And he even wrote her letters whose language strengthened her hope that she would soon become his legitimate mistress.

As Marcel, his confidant, once came upon one of these letters of Rudolph, he said to him: "Is this style or do you actually think of what you are saying?"

"Of course, I think what I say," answered Rudolph, "and I am slightly astonished at it, I admit, but that is the truth. A week ago, I was in a melancholy mental state. This loneliness and silence which have so suddenly followed on the heels of the agitations of my former home have upset me horribly; but Juliet came almost at once. I have heard sound in my heart the joyous exuberance of twenty years. I have had before me a fresh face, eyes full of smiles, a mouth full of kisses, and I have very quietly let myself pursue the flirtation which has, perhaps, led me away from love. I love to love."

Meanwhile Rudolph was not slow in perceiving that he was not accomplishing anything toward bringing this small romance to a successful end, and it was then that he had thought of re-enacting the loves of Romeo and Juliet. His future mistress had found the idea amusing and agreed to do her part in the play.

It was the very same evening arranged for the play when he had just bought this silk cord ladder which was to serve him to mount Juliet's balcony that Rudolph met the philosopher, Colline. The bird man to whom he went had no nightingale, so Rudolph substituted a pigeon, which, he was assured, sang every morning at daybreak. When he reached home, the poet reflected that an ascent on a cord ladder was no easy matter, and that it was wise to have a small rehearsal of the balcony scene if he did not wish a fall, or to run the risk of appearing ridiculous and awkward in the sight of her who was expecting him. Rudolph attached his ladder by two hooks firmly held in the ceiling, and spent the two hours which remained at his gymnastics; and after an infinite number of attempts he fared better than ill in mounting about ten steps. "Well, well, that's good," he said to himself, "I am now sure of my business, and, further-more, if I remained helpless on the ground, 'love would give me wings.' "

Burdened with his ladder and pigeon cage he went to Juliet's, who lived near. Her room was located in the back of a small garden and really had a kind of balcony. This room however was on the ground floor and it was the easiest thing in the world to step up to the balcony.

Rudolph was quite dejected when he perceived the local situation which put to flight the poetic project of the ascent.

"That doesn't matter," he said to Juliet, "we can always carry out the balcony scene. Here is a bird which will awaken us tomorrow by its melody and inform us of the exact moment in which we ought to separate from each other, full of despair." And Rudolph hung the cage in a corner of the room.

Next morning at five the pigeon was exactly right, filling the room with a prolonged cooing which would have awakened the two lovers if they had slept.

"Well," said Juliet, "this is the time to go on the balcony and make our despairing farewells; what do you think of it?"

"The pigeon is ahead of time," said Rudolph, "it is November, the sun only comes up at noon."

"That doesn't matter," said Juliet, "I am going to get up."

"Stop,—what for?"

"I have a gnawing in my stomach, and I will not conceal from you that I certainly should like to have a little to eat."

"How extraordinary the harmony which exists in our desires; I too have a horrible hunger," said Rudolph, also getting up and very quickly dressing himself. Juliet had already lit a fire and was looking in the sideboard for what she could find. Rudolph helped her in her search.

"Look," he said, "onions."

"And lard," said Juliet.

"And butter,"

"And bread,"

"Alas, that is all."

Meanwhile, the optimistic and carefree pigeon sang on its perch.

Romeo looked at Juliet, Juliet looked at Romeo; both looked at the pigeon. They said nothing more to each other. The doom of the pigeon clock was sealed; to lodge an appeal for it would only have been lost pains. Hunger is such a cruel councillor. Romeo lit some coal and mixed some lard in the sizzling butter; he had a solemn and serious air. Juliet sadly peeled some onions.

The pigeon kept on singing; it was its swan song. To these lamentations was mingled the song of the butter in the bake dish. Five minutes later the butter still sang; but like the templars the pigeon no longer sang. Romeo and Juliet had cut open and boiled their clock. "It had a pretty voice," Juliet remarked as she sat down at the table. "He was very tender," added Romeo, carving his morning reveille, perfectly browned.

And the two lovers looked at each other and were surprised that each had a tear in his eye.

Base hypocrites,—it was the onions which made them weep.

EPILOGUE TO THE LOVE AFFAIR OF RUDOLPH AND MIMI

D URING the first days of his final break with Mademoiselle Mimi, who had left him, as it will be remembered, to ride in Viscount Paul's carriages, the poet Rudolph had tried to forget by taking another mistress.

She was blonde and it was for her he dressed as Romeo one day when he felt carefree and silly. But this liaison, which on his part was only for spite and on hers only a whim, could not last long. This young girl was after all only a silly person, vocalizing in the solfeggio of trickery, clever enough to note others' intelligence and to make use of it at need, and capable of having pains in her heart only when she had eaten too much. Added to this, an unrestrained pride and dreadful vanity made her prefer that her lover have a broken leg than that she have one less ruffle on her dress or a faded ribbon on her hat. Of questionable beauty, and an ordinary personality, she was naturally endowed with all the bad instincts, but in addition she could be seductive in certain ways and at certain hours. She was not slow to see that Rudolph had taken her only to help him forget the absent one, whom, on the contrary, she made him regret, for his ancient lover had never been so dominant and alive in his affections.

One day Juliet, Rudolph's new mistress, was speaking of her lover, the poet, with a medicine student who was flirting with her. The student replied:

"My dear child, that man uses you as nitrate is used to cauterize wounds, since he merely wishes to cauterize his heart. You are certainly wrong to worry about being faithful to him."

"Ha, ha," the young girl burst out laughing, "do you honestly think that I care?" and the same evening she gave the student proof to the contrary. Thanks to the lack of discretion in one of his officious friends, who could not keep untold news likely to irritate him, Rudolph got wind of the affair and used it as a pretext to break with his mistress.

Then he buried himself in absolute solitude, where all the bats of boredom were not slow in coming to make a nest, and he tried to find solace in work; but it was in vain. Each evening, after he had exuded as many beads of perspiration as he had used drops of ink, he wrote about twenty lines in which an old idea, more worn than the Wandering Jew, and badly clothed in tag ends borrowed from literary ragbags, danced heavily on the tight rope of the paradox. On rereading the lines, Rudolph remained astounded, like a man who sees nettles growing in the garden where he thought he had planted roses. Then he tore out the page where he had just woven those garlands of nonsense and crushed them under his feet in rage.

"Come," he said, pounding his chest above his heart, "the rope is broken. We must be resigned."

And, as for a long time a similar deception had followed all his attempts at work, he was overcome by one of those discouraging slumps which make the most robust pride recoil and dull the most lucid intelligence. Nothing is more terrible in reality than these lonely struggles when an obstinate artist sometimes engages with a rebellious art; nothing is more moving than these outbursts alternating with invocation now beseeching, now commanding, addressed to the disdainful or fugitive Muse. The most violent human anguish, the deepest wounds made in the heart's core do not cause a suffering which compares with that which one experiences in these frequent hours of impatience and doubt, which assail those who follow the perilous calling of the imagination.

These violent crises are followed by painful despondency; Rudolph then stayed for whole hours as if petrified in stupid silence. His elbows rested on his table, his eyes were glued fixedly to the sphere of light which the rays of his lamp cast in the middle of this sheet of paper, "a battlefield," where his spirit was conquered daily and where his pen had been broken in trying to seize the elusive idea. He saw slowly file along, like the figures in a magic lantern with which one amuses the children, fantastic pictures which spread out before him the bird's-eye view of his past. At first they were the hardworking days when each hour of the clock tolled the achievement of some duty, the studious nights passed face to face with the Muse, who came to protect him with her enchantments from his lonely and patient poverty. And he recalled then with envy his proud bliss, which formerly filled him when he had accomplished a task imposed by his will. "Oh, nothing is worth so much as you," he cried, "nothing compares with you, oh voluptuous weariness from labour, which makes one find so pleasant the mattress of *far niente*. Neither the satisfactions of self-respect nor those which fortune gives, nor the feverish raptures stifled under the heavy curtains of mysterious alcoves,—

nothing can compare with or equal that honest and calm pleasure, that legitimate self-satisfaction which work gives to workers as a first salary." And with his eyes constantly set on those visions which continued to trace for him the scenes of past epochs, he mounted again the six flights to every room under the eaves where his adventurous existence had led him, and where his Muse, his only love from that time, faithful and persevering friend, had followed him always, living comfortably with misery, and never interrupting his song of hope. But here in the midst of this regular and tranquil life there appeared to him suddenly the figure of a woman; and the poet's Muse, seeing her enter in that lodging place where she had been until then only queen and mistress, raised herself sadly and left the premises to the newcomer in whom she divined a rival. Rudolph hesitated a minute between the Muse, whose look seemed to say stay, and the stranger whose appealing gesture said come. And how to repel her, this charming creature who came to him armed with all the seductions of a beauty in its dawn? Small mouth with rosy lip, speaking a simple and intrepid language, full of seductive promises; how to refuse his hand to this little white hand with blue veins, which was stretched out toward him full of caresses? How to say go away to these eighteen blooming years whose presence already made the house fragrant with the perfume of youth and gaiety?

And then she sang so well with her soft tenderly affected voice the cavatina of temptation! With her lively and shining eyes she said so well: "I am pleasure," likewise with her lips where nestled a kiss, and at last with her whole person, "I am pleasure, I am happiness," and Rudolph gave himself up to her.

And after all, that young woman, was she not poetry that is living and actual? Did he not owe to her his freshest inspirations? Had she not often aroused the enthusiasms which led him so high in the atmosphere of revery that he lost view of earthly things? If he had suffered greatly because of her, was it not in expiation of all the enormous joys that she had brought him? Wasn't it the ordinary vengeance of human destiny, which forbids absolute happiness as an impiety? If Christian law pardons those who have loved a great deal, it is because they have suffered much too; and earthly love only becomes a passion on condition that it is purified by tears. And even when one is intoxicated by the odor of faded roses, so Rudolph was again intoxicated by living over in his memory that life of other days when each day brought forth a new idyll, a terrible drama, a grotesque comedy. He went over every phase of his strange love for the dear absent, from their honeymoon to the domestic upheavals which had finally caused the rupture; he remembered the repertory of all his former mistress's pretenses, he said again all her puns. He saw her go round him in their small room, humming her song of *Mamie Annette* and taking with the same carefree gaiety good and bad days. And he concluded at last that reason was always wrong in love. Actually, what had he gained by breaking off? At the time when he was living with Mimi, she deceived him, it is true; but if he knew it, it was his fault! After all, and it was because he gave himself infinite pain to learn it, by spending his time collecting proofs, it was he himself who sharpened the daggers which he buried in his heart. Moreover, was not Mimi sufficiently skilful to show him at need that it was he who was deceived? And then, with whom was she unfaithful to him? More often it was with a shawl, a hat, with things, and not with men. That tranquillity, that peace which he had hoped for when he separated from his mistress, had he regained them after her departure? Alas! No. None the less she was there, in the house.

In other times his sorrow could be poured out, he could dispel his injuries by mentioning them; he could show what he suffered, and arouse her pity who had caused the suffering. And now his misery was lonely, his jealousy had become raging; for in other times he could at least, when he was suspicious, keep Mimi from going out, hold her near him in his possession; and now he met her in the street on the arm of her new lover and he had to step aside to let her pass, doubtless happy and on pleasure bent.

This wretched life lasted three or four months. Little by little, calm returned to him. Marcel, who had taken a long trip to forget Musette, returned to Paris and went to live with Rudolph. They consoled each other.

One day, a Sunday, while going through the Luxembourg, Rudolph met Mimi all dressed up. She was going to the ball. She nodded to him, to which he responded with a greeting. This encounter was a great blow to his heart, but the feeling was less painful than ordinarily. He continued to walk in the garden for some time and then went home. When Marcel returned in the evening, he found him at work.

"Oh, say," Marcel remarked as he leaned over his shoulder, "you are working, poetry, eh!"

"Yes," Rudolph answered joyfully. "I think that the little beast isn't quite dead. I have been here since four o'clock, and I have found the verve of former days. I met Mimi."

"Pshaw!" Marcel was agitated. "And where were you?"

"Don't worry," said Rudolph, "we did nothing but greet each other. It hasn't gone any farther than that."

"Absolutely true?" asked Marcel.

"Absolutely. It is over between us, I feel it; but if I can get back to work, I will forgive her."

"If it is as finished as all that," added Marcel, who had just read Rudolph's poetry, "why do you write verses?"

"Alas," the poet responded, "I must take my poetry where I find it."

For a week, he worked at this little poem. When it was finished he read it to Marcel, who said he was pleased with it, and he encouraged Rudolph to use in other ways this vein which had returned to him; for he observed to him, "it wasn't worth the trouble of leaving Mimi if you must always live with her shade. After all," he said smiling, "instead of preaching to others, I would do better to preach to myself for I still have Musette close to my heart. Oh well, mayhap we will always be young people madly infatuated with creatures of the devil."

"Alas," replied Rudolph, "there is no need for us to say to youth: go away."

"That's true," Marcel agreed, "but there are days when I would like to be an honest old man, member of the Institute, with several decorations, and saved from the Musettes of this world. Devil take me if I return to her! And you," the artist smiled, "would you like to be sixty?"

"Today," replied Rudolph, "I would prefer to have sixty francs."

A few days later, Mademoiselle Mimi, having entered a café with the young Viscount Paul, opened a review where were printed the stanzas which Rudolph had written for her.

"Good," she cried at first, smiling, "my lover Rudolph is still saying evil about me in the newspapers." But when she had read the poem she stayed silent and meditative. The Viscount Paul, divining that she was dreaming of Rudolph, tried to distract her mind. "I will buy you some earrings," he told her.

"Ah," said Mimi, "you have money, you do."

"And a hat of Milan straw," the Viscount Paul continued.

"No," said Mimi, "if you wish to please me, buy me that." And she showed him the edition where she had just read Rudolph's poem.

"Ah, that, no," the Viscount was irritated.

"That's all right," Mimi replied coldly. "I will buy it myself, with money that I shall earn myself. In fact, I prefer it not to be yours."

And for two days Mimi returned to her former job as flower maker, where she earned enough to buy the issue. She learned by heart Rudolph's poem, and to enrage Viscount Paul she repeated it every day to her friends. The following are the stanzas:

RUDOLPH'S POEM

Epilogue to the Love Affairs of Rudolph and Mimi.

End of Part 1.

When I was thinking of choosing a mistress
And fate one day caused our paths to cross,
I gave into your hands my heart and my youth
And I said: Do what you will with them.

Alas! your will was cruel, my dear:
In your hands my youth is torn into shreds,
My heart is broken in pieces as if it were glass,
  And my room is the cemetery
  Where the remains are buried
  Of him who so loved you a short while ago.

Now all is finished, finished between us,
I am only a spectre and you but a shade;
And over our dead, deep buried love,
We shall sing, if you wish, a last psalm.

But let's not pitch our tune too high,
For neither of us would have a true voice;
Let's choose a low minor, one without gracenotes;
I shall take the bass, and you the soprano.

Mi, ré, mi, do, ré, la.—Not that tune, my child!
If my heart heard the air that you sang yesterday,
Dead though it is, it would tremble violently
And would be revived by this *De Profundis.*

Do, mi, fa, sol, mi, do.—That one reminds me
Of a waltz in double time which makes me sad;
The fife with his sharp laugh jeered at the 'cello,
Which beneath the bow wept in crystal clear tones.

Sol, do, do, si, si, la.—Nor that tune, I pray you,
Which last year we sang together
With some Germans who were praising their land
In the Meudon woods, one summer night.

Well, let's not sing! Let it go at that, my dear;
And without thinking or remembering more,
Let us throw, smiling, without hate or anger,
Over our dead love, a last souvenir.

We were very happy in your small room
When the rain was singing and the wind sighing;
Seated in an arm-chair near the hearth, in December,
By the light of your eyes I have often dreamed.

The fire crackled; while heating over the coals,
The kettle sang its usual song,
Making an orchestra for the ball of the salamanders
Which were fluttering on the hearth.

Turning the pages of a novel, lazy and chilly,
While you closed your eyes, dead with sleep,
I revived my romantic youth,
My lips on your hands and my heart at your feet.

So, when one entered, the door hardly open,
One smelled the perfume of love and of joy
With which our room was full from morn to eve,
For happiness loved our hospitality.

Then winter left; through the open window,
Spring one morning came to waken us,
And that day we two hastened to play
Among green pastures in the sunlight.

It was Friday of Holy Week,
And, strangely enough, it was a fine day;
From valley to hills, from the woods to the fields,
With slow and joyous step we wandered at length.

Finally exhausted by this wandering,
In a spot which formed a natural couch
From which we could see the countryside,
We reclined and gazed at Heaven's expanse.

Hands clasping hands, shoulder to shoulder,
And without knowing why, as we sat together,
Our mouths opened without saying a word,
And we kissed each other.

Near us the hyacinth and the violet
Blended their perfume, which mounted in the pure air,
And both of us, as we raised our heads,
Saw God, who smiled at us from his azure balcony.

"Love each other," He said; "it is to make softer
The road where you walk that I have unrolled
Under your steps the velvet path of moss;
Kiss each other again,—I shall not look.

"Love, love each other; in the winds which murmur,
In the soft waters, in the woods grown green again,
In the star, in the flower, in the song of the nests,
It is for you that I made nature live again.

"Love, love each other; and if you are happy
With my golden sun, with my new springtime
Which gladdens the earth, instead of a prayer
To thank me,—kiss each other again."

A month after that day, when the roses bloomed
In the little garden which we planted,
When I loved you best, without telling the cause,
Suddenly your love for me departed.

Where did it go? Almost everywhere, I think;
For, making one colour after another triumph,
Your inconstant love floats without preference
From the brown knave of spades to the blond knave of hearts.

There! you are happy now; your fancy
Reigns over a court of gallant youths,
And you cannot walk without having bloom before you
A gallery enamelled with songs of praise.

In the gardens for dancing, when you enter,
A languishing circle is formed around you,
And the rustling of your moiré gown
Makes your admiring throngs swoon away in admiration.

Elegantly shod in a graceful slipper
Which would be too narrow for the foot of Cinderella,
Your foot is so small that it can hardly be seen
When a waltz whirls you to and fro so happily.

Bathed with the oil of laziness,
Your hands, once brown, have since regained
The colour of ivory or of the lily which is caressed
With the silvery rays by which the nights are brightened.

Around your white arm a rare pearl
Holds in its place a bracelet carved by Froment,
And over you an elegant Cashmere shawl
Falls beautifully in a cascade of folds.

Flemish lace and English point,
Gothic lace with its heavy whiteness,
Woven art from an age that is gone,
Perfects the splendour of your rich toilet.

As for me, I loved you better in your springlike linen,
Indian cotton or plain organdy,
In those simple and coquettish costumes with plain white collar,
Your hat without a veil, and grey or black sandals.

For this new elegance which makes you so pretty
Doesn't remind me of my love which has gone,
And you are but more dead and buried
In this silken shroud where your heart does not beat.

When I made this funereal poem,
Which is but a long regret for my past happiness,
I was dressed in black like a typical notary,
Except for the gold spectacles and the pleated scarf.

Crêpe swaddled the handle of my pen,
And bands of mourning framed the paper
Upon which I wrote these lines where
I revive the last memory of my last love.

Now as I come to the end of a poem
Where I throw my heart to the depths of an abyss,
Glee of an undertaker who buries himself,—
You see me beginning to laugh.

But that gaiety is only a mockery:
My pen, while I wrote, trembled in my hand;
And when I smiled, my tears, like warm rain,
Blotted away the words upon the parchment.

It was the twenty-fourth of December, and on that evening the Latin Quarter assumed a special character. From four o'clock in the afternoon, the pawn shops, the old clothes dealers, the second hand book dealers had been thronged by a milling crowd who came and went during the whole evening to take by storm the shops of the butchers, the cooks, and the grocers. The clerks at the counters, even if they had had one hundred arms like Briareus, would not have had enough to serve the customers, who broke away with the provisions. They stood in a line at the bakershop as they did in the days of famine. The wine merchants exhausted the products of three vintages, and a smart statistician would have had difficulty in counting the number of knuckles of ham and of sausages which were sold by the famous Borel of the rue Dauphine. In that evening alone, Father Cretaine, otherwise known as Petit-Pain, exhausted eighteen editions of his butter cakes. All during the night, noisy gaiety was heard in the decorated houses the windows of which were gleaming and the spirit of a country fair filled the Quarter.

They were celebrating the old festival of Christmas Eve.

That evening, about ten o'clock, Marcel and Rudolph were going home in a sad frame of mind. Passing along the rue Dauphine, they noted the great plenty in the shop of a butcher who sold victuals too, and they stopped a moment before his windows, tantalized by the sight of the savoury gastronomical exhibition; the two Bohemians resembled, in their gaze, the person in a Spanish novel who made the hams become thin just by looking at them.

"That is called a turkey hen stuffed with truffles," said Marcel, pointing out a superb bird showing through its pink and transparent skin the tubers from Perigord with which it was stuffed. "I have seen impious souls eat that without first genuflecting before it," added the artist as he cast upon the turkey burning glances capable of roasting it.

"And what do you think of that modest salt-marsh-fed mutton?" added Rudolph. "What a beautiful color it has. You would think it had been recently taken down from that butcher's shop that you see in Jordaens' picture. That mutton is the favourite morsel of the gods, and of Madame Chandelier, my godmother."

"Glance at those fish," Marcel went on, indicating the trout.

 "They are the smartest swimmers of the aquatic breed. Those little animals, which have no airs at all could accumulate some rents by making trials of strength. Just imagine that fish can swim up a full stream as easily as we would accept one or two invitations to supper. Once I was on the point of eating some."

"And over there, those large fruits with the decorated cones, whose foliage resembles a display of savage sabres are called pineapples; they are the russet apples of the tropics."

"It means nothing to me," Marcel replied. "To any kind of fruit I prefer that piece of beef, this ham or that simple ham knuckle in jelly as clear as amber."

"You are right," Rudolph agreed; "ham is a friend of man, when he has some. Meanwhile I wouldn't refuse that pheasant."

"I agree with you. It is the dainty for crowned heads."

And as they continued their way running into jolly processions who were returning to celebrate Momus, Bacchus, Comus and all the Divinities of food ending in 'us,' they asked each other who was the Sir Gamache whose wedding feast was being celebrated with such profusion of viands.

Marcel was the first to remember the date and the holiday.

"Today is the day before Christmas."

"Do you remember what we did last year?" asked Rudolph.

"Yes," Marcel replied, "at the café Momus. It was Barbe-muche who paid. I would never have thought that a woman as delicate as Phemie could hold so much sausage."

"How unfortunate that Momus has refused us admittance," Rudolph lamented.

"Alas," said Marcel, "time goes on but things are not the same."

"Couldn't you do well with a Christmas Eve revel?" Rudolph inquired.

"With whom and with what?" replied the painter.

"Well, with me."

"And the money?"

"Wait a minute," Rudolph said, "I am going into this café where I know people who play for big stakes. I will borrow a few sesterces from one of the favoured of fortune, and I will bring back something with which to wash down a sardine or a pig's foot."

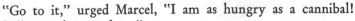

"Go to it," urged Marcel, "I am as hungry as a cannibal! I shall wait for you here."

Rudolph entered the café, where he knew some people. A gentleman who had just won three hundred francs in ten turns of the wheel took real pleasure in lending the poet forty sous which he offered him with the bad grace which gambling fever arouses. At a different time and in any other place but around a green table, he would perhaps have loaned him forty francs.

"Well, what luck?" Marcel asked, when he saw Rudolph reappearing.

"Here are the returns," said the poet as he showed the money.

"A crust and a dram," Marcel decided.

With this modest sum, however, they discovered the opportunity to buy bread, wine, dressed pork, tobacco, candles and some firewood.

They returned to the furnished hotel where they lived, each in a separate room. Since Marcel's room, which served as a studio, was the largest, it was chosen as the banquet room, and the friends together prepared their private feast.

But at that small table where they had sat down, near the fireplace, in which the damp logs of poor driftwood were burning without giving any flames or any heat, had come to sit an unhappy companion, the ghost of a vanished past.

They remained, for at least an hour, silent and thoughtful, both doubtless occupied with the same thought and forcing themselves to hide it.

Marcel was the first to break the silence.

"Look here," he said to Rudolph, "this isn't what we promised each other."

"What do you mean?" asked Rudolph.

"My God, see here," replied Marcel. "You're not going to pretend to me now? You are dreaming about what you ought to forget, and I too, forsooth, I don't deny it."

"Well, what of it?"

"Well, this must be the last time. We'll consign to the devil the memories which make the wine taste bad and make us sad when all the rest of the world is enjoying itself!" Marcel alluded to the gay shouts which emanated from their neighbours' rooms. —"Come on, let's think of something else, let this be the last time."

"That's what we always say, and moreover . . ." Rudolph relapsed into revery.

"And moreover we return to it constantly," Marcel resumed. "It comes down to this, that, instead of searching openly to forget, we do the most useless things which are naught but futile pretexts to remind us. For example, we insist on living in the same place where the beings have tormented us for so long. We are slaves to habit, not to a passion. It is this bondage, which we must escape, where we exhaust ourselves in a ridiculous and shameful slavery. Well, the past is past, we must break the bonds which still tie us to it. The hour has come to go forward without again looking back; we have had our days of fun, of carelessness and of paradox. All that is very fine; a good novel could be made of it; but this comedy of mad love affairs, this wasting of days with the prodigality of people who believe that they have all eternity to throw away, all that must come to an end. Constantly under pains to justify the scorn people have for us, and the scorn we have for ourselves, it isn't possible to go on living for a long time on the edge of society, on the margin of life, almost. For, really, is this a real life that we are leading? And this independence, this freedom of habits of which we boast so vigorously—are there not very moderate advantages from it? True freedom is to be able to do without others and to live on one's self. Do we have that? No! ! The first scoundrel who comes along, whose name we wouldn't bear for five minutes, revenges himself for our ridicule and becomes our master and lord the day when we borrow a hundred sous from him, which he lends us after he forces us to indulge in one hundred écus' worth of pretense of humility. For my part I have had enough. Poetry doesn't exist alone in a disorderly existence, in unforeseen pleasure, in love affairs which last as long as a candle, in more or less peculiar rebellions against prejudices which will always be the rulers of the world; a dynasty is more easily overturned than a custom, even though it is a silly one. To wear a summer coat in December is not enough proof of talent; it is possible to be a real poet or artist and still have warm feet and three meals a day. Whatever you say, or whatever you do, if you wish to get anywhere, you must always take the way of the commonplace. This talk astonishes you perhaps, Rudolph, my friend,—you are about to say that I am breaking my idols; you are about to call me corrupted, but, even so, what I am saying is my real thought. Without my knowledge, a slow and healthy change has come about in me; reason has entered my spirit,—has stolen in, if you like, and perhaps in spite of myself; but it has entered at last, and has proved to me that I was on a wrong path and that it would be at the same time foolish and dangerous to pursue it longer. In fact, what will happen if you and I continue this monotonous and useless vagabondage? We will get to be thirty years old, unknown, isolated, disgusted with everything and with ourselves, full of envy towards those whom we see arriving at any goal whatever it is, and obliged in order to live to resort to the shameful habits of parasites; and don't think that this is an imaginary picture that I draw expressly to overcome you! I don't see the future as black constantly, but I don't see it any longer as rosy; I see it correctly. Until now the life that we have led was imposed upon us; we had the excuse of necessity. Today we would no longer be excused; and if we enter into the ordinary way of living, it will be willingly for the obstacles against which we have had to fight no longer exist."

"Ah indeed!" Rudolph replied, "Where do you wish to go? For what reason and for what good this harangue?"

"You don't understand me perfectly," Marcel answered in the same serious tone. "Just now, like myself, I saw you attacked by memories which made you regret the time that is past; you were thinking of Mimi as I was thinking of Musette, you would have liked to have your mistress at your side as I would. Well, what I am saying is that we must neither one of us think again of those persons. We have not been made or put into the world to sacrifice our lives for these common Manons, and from whom the Knight Desgrieux who is so handsome, so honest and so poetic, only saved himself from being ridiculous by his youth and his illusions which he knew how to preserve. At twenty years of age, he can pursue his mistress to the ends of the earth without ceasing to be interesting; but at twenty-five he would have put Manon out of the house and would have been right. We talk in vain; we are old, you see, my dear fellow; we have lived too much and at too great speed. Our hearts are cracked and only make false sounds; we cannot be in love for three years with a Musette or a Mimi with safety. For me, it is over; and as I wish to divorce myself absolutely from her memory, I am going to throw into the fire certain small things which she left here at various times, which make me think of her whenever I run across them."

And Marcel, who had gotten up, fetched a small box from a drawer in the bureau in which were kept Musette's things— a faded bouquet, a belt, a piece of ribbon, and some letters.

"Come on," he said to the poet, "follow my example, Friend Rudolph."

"Well, so be it," the latter remarked with an effort. "You are right. I too,—I want to get rid of that girl with the pale hands."

And when he had gotten up quickly, he searched for a small package which contained memories of Mimi, almost identical with those of which Marcel was silently making an inventory.

"This happens at the right time," the painter murmured. "These what-nots will serve to lighten the fire which is going out."

"Indeed!" Rudolph added. "It is cold enough here to bring out polar bears."

"Come along," said Marcel. "Let us have a fire duet. There is

Musette's prose which sparkles like fire in the punch. She loved punch a lot, she did. Come along, Friend Rudolph, be careful."

And for a few minutes they took turns throwing into the fire, which burned bright and warm, the remains of their past loves.

"Poor Musette," Marcel whispered very low as he looked at the last thing which was left in his hands,—it was a little faded bunch of wildflowers.

"Poor Musette, she was very pretty; furthermore, she loved me well, isn't that so, little bouquet? Hasn't her heart told you so the day when your flowers were in her belt? Poor little bouquet, you have the air of saying pity to me. Oh well, yes, but on one condition; that is, that you will never speak to me again of her. Never! never!—" And taking advantage of a minute when he thought he was not perceived by Rudolph, he slipped the bouquet in his shirt. "So much the worse, it is stronger than I. I am tricking him," thought the artist;—and, as he cast a hurried glance at Rudolph, he saw the poet, who had arrived at the end of his *auto-da-fé,* and had secretly slipped into his pocket, after having kissed it tenderly, a little boudoir cap which belonged to Mimi.

"There," Marcel muttered, "he is as cowardly as I."

At the same minute when Rudolph was going to his room to go to bed, there were two little raps on Marcel's door.

"Who the devil can be coming at this hour?" the artist asked as he went to open the door.

A cry of astonishment escaped him when he had opened it.

It was Mimi.

As the room was quite dark, at first Rudolph didn't recognize his mistress; and only making out a woman's form, he thought that it was one of the passing fancies of his friend, and discreetly got ready to retire.

"I am not bothering you?" asked Mimi, remaining on the threshold.

At the sound of her voice, Rudolph fell into a chair as if he were unconscious.

"Good-evening," Mimi said as she went up to him and clasped his hand, which he passively let her take.

"What under the sun brings you here," Marcel asked, "at this hour?"

"I am very cold," Mimi replied and shivered, "I saw a light here as I was passing in the street; and although it is very late I came up."

And she continued to shiver. Her voice had certain deep pellucid tones which entered Rudolph's heart like a funeral knell and filled him with an overpowering sorrow. Stealthily he looked at her more carefully. She was no longer Mimi. It was her ghost.

Marcel made her sit in a corner of the chimney.

Mimi smiled as she saw the beautiful flames which danced merrily on the hearth.—"It is very nice," she said as she stretched her poor purple hands out before the heat. "By the way, Monsieur Marcel, you don't know why I came to your room."

"My word, no," the latter responded.

"Well," resumed Mimi, "I came very simply to ask you to get me a room in your house. I have just been put out of my furnished room because I owe two fortnights' rent, and I do not know where to go."

"The devil!" Marcel shook his head. "We aren't in good odour with our landlord, and our recommendation would be dreadful, my poor child."

"Then what's to be done?" asked Mimi. "I don't know where to go."

"Well!" Marcel questioned her. "Then you are no longer a viscountess?"

"Ah, mercy no, not at all."

"But since when?"

"For two months."

"You treated the young viscount badly then?"

"No," she replied stealing a glance at Rudolph, who had placed himself in the darkest corner of the room. "The viscount made a scene because of some verses which were made about me. We quarrelled, and I sent him away; he is a proud miser."

"However, he rigged you out jolly well," said Marcel, "judging from the day I ran into you."

"Well, imagine! He took back everything when I left, and I learned that he had put all my things in a lottery, in a poor restaurant, where he used to take me to dine. He is very rich, that boy, but with all his fortune, he is as stingy as an economical lump of coal, and as mean as a goose. He didn't want me to drink pure wine, and he made me do without meat on Fridays. Would you believe that he wanted me to wear black cotton stockings, with the excuse that they got less dirty than white! You have no idea about him; at last he bored me dreadfully. I can easily say that I have gone through my purgatory with him."

"And does he know your situation now?" Marcel queried.

"I have not seen him again, nor do I wish to see him," Mimi replied. "He makes me seasick when I think of him; I would prefer to die of hunger than to ask him for a single sou."

But Marcel pursued the subject. "Since you left him, you haven't stayed alone?"

"Ah!" Mimi spoke vivaciously, "I assure you I did, Monsieur Marcel. I worked to live, but as the flower maker job didn't go so well, I took another; I pose for artists. If you have any work to give me . . ." she added gaily. As she hadn't taken her eyes off him while she was talking to his friend, she noticed that at this remark Rudolph couldn't refrain from moving. Mimi replied: "Ah! but I pose only for head and hands. I have a lot of work, and two or three persons owe me money which I shall receive in two days, and it is from now until then only that I wish to find some place to room. When I get some money, I shall go back to my lodgings. See here," she said as she glanced at the table, where still remained the preparations for the humble feast which the two friends had barely touched. "You are about to have supper."

"No," said Marcel, "we aren't hungry."

"You are very fortunate," Mimi replied simply.

At this word, Rudolph felt his heart beating dreadfully. He made a sign to Marcel, who understood.

"Now," said the artist, "since you have come, Mimi, you will have to take pot luck. We intended to have a Christmas Eve celebration and then . . . my word, we thought of something else."

"Then I arrive in the nick of time," Mimi said, looking at the table where the food was, with an almost lifeless glance. "I haven't had any dinner, my dear," she whispered to the artist, low enough not to be heard by Rudolph, who was chewing his handkerchief to keep from bursting into tears.

"Now come to the table, Rudolph," Marcel ordered his friend. "The three of us will have supper."

"No," said the poet, staying in the corner.

"It is because you are irritated that I came here, Rudolph?" Mimi asked him sweetly. "Where could I have gone?"

"No, Mimi," Rudolph replied. "Only I am sorry to see you again like this."

"That's my fault, Rudolph, I do not complain; what has happened is past. You mustn't think of it any more than I do. Can't you be my friend now, though you were something more before? It's all the same, isn't it? Then don't look so crossly at me, and come sit at the table with us."

She got up to go take him by the hand, but she was so weak that she could not take a step and fell back on her chair.

"The warmth has made me weak," she explained, "I can't stand up."

"Come along," Marcel said to Rudolph, "come keep us company."

The poet went to the table and began to eat with them. Mimi was very gay.

When the slim meal was over, Marcel said to Mimi: "My dear girl, we can't get you a room in this house."

"Then I must go away," she said, as she tried to get up.

"No, no!" Marcel exclaimed. "I have another way of arranging things; you will stay in my room and I shall room with Rudolph."

"That will bother you a lot," Mimi said, "but it won't last long—two days."

"In this way, it won't bother us at all," Marcel responded. "So it's all arranged—you are here with us, and we'll go to sleep in Rudolph's room. . . . Good-night, Mimi, sleep well."

"Thanks," she held out her hands; one to Marcel and the other to Rudolph, who moved away.

"Do you wish to lock yourself in?" asked Marcel as he went out the door.

"Why?" asked Mimi, all the while looking at Rudolph, "I am not afraid!"

When the two friends were alone in a neighbouring room, which was on the same landing, Marcel said sharply to Rudolph: "Well, what are you going to do now?"

"But," blubbered Rudolph, "I don't know."

"Come, come, don't trifle, go in to Mimi; if you go in there, I warn you that tomorrow you will resume your lives together."

"If Musette had returned, what would you have done?" Rudolph questioned his friend.

"If it were Musette in the next room," Marcel replied, "well, frankly, I think that within a quarter of an hour I should no longer be in this one."

"Well, as for me," Rudolph rejoined, "I shall be more courageous than you. I stay."

"We shall see indeed," said Marcel, who had already gotten into bed. "Are you going to bed?"

"Of course," Rudolph replied.

But, in the middle of the night, Marcel, who had wakened up, perceived that Rudolph had left.

In the morning, he knocked discreetly on the door of the room where Mimi was.

"Come in," she said to him, and when she saw him made a sign for him to talk low in order not to waken Rudolph, who was asleep. He was seated in a chair which he had placed by the bed, and his head was resting on the pillow beside Mimi's.

"That's the way you spent the night?" Marcel was astonished.

"Yes," the young woman replied.

Rudolph waked suddenly, and after kissing Mimi, he held out his hand to Marcel, who appeared most interested.

"I am going to look for some money for luncheon," he told the painter. "You keep Mimi company."

"Well," Marcel asked the young girl when they were alone, "What happened last night?"

"Very sad things," Mimi answered. "Rudolph still loves me."

"I know that well."

"Yes, you wished to take him away from me. I don't blame you, Marcel; you were right. I have hurt this poor fellow."

"And you—do you love him still?" Marcel inquired.

"Oh! do I love him!" she clasped her hands together. "It's that which is killing me. I am much changed, you know, my poor friend, and it took little time to do it."

"Well, since he loves you and you love him and you cannot do without each other, get together again and try to have a good time of it."

"That's impossible."

"Why? Certainly it would be more logical than if you left each other; furthermore never to meet again, you would have to live three thousand miles from each other."

"Before long, I shall be farther than that."

"Why, what do you mean?"

"Don't mention it to Rudolph; it would cause him too much grief. I am going away for ever."

"But where?"

"Stop, my poor Marcel," Mimi was sobbing. "Just look." And raising the coverings of her bed a little, she showed the artist her shoulders, her neck and her arms.

"Ah, for pity's sake!" Marcel was sad. "Poor girl!"

"You see, my friend, I am not deceiving you and I am going to die soon."

"But, how have you become so thin in such a short time?"

"Oh!" replied Mimi, "with the life that I have led for the past two months, it isn't astonishing; every night spent in weeping, every day posing in studios without any fire, poor nourishment, my unhappiness. And then you don't know everything; I wanted to poison myself with Javel water, but some one saved me,—but not for long, you see. With all this, I never was very well; finally, it's all my fault. If I had stayed quietly with Rudolph, I wouldn't be like this now. Poor friend, there is still time for me to fall back in his arms, but it won't be for long. The last dress he will give me will be all white, my poor

Marcel, and I will be buried in it. Oh! if you only knew how
I suffer to know that I am going to die! Rudolph knows that
I am sick; he stayed more than an hour without speaking
yesterday when he saw my arms and my shoulders, which are
so thin; he no longer recognized in me his Mimi, alas! . . .
even my mirror no longer knows me. Oh well, what's the odds!
I was pretty and he loved me a lot. Oh! my God!" she sobbed,
burying her face in Marcel's hands. "My poor friend, I am
going to leave you, and Rudolph too. Oh God! . . ." Sobs
choked her.

"Come, Mimi," said Marcel. "Don't despair, you will get well.
You need a lot of care and rest."

"Ah, no!" Mimi went on, "it's all over, I feel it. I have no
more strength, and when I came here last evening, it took more
than an hour to get up the stairs. If I had found a woman here,
I should have gone out nicely through the window. However,
he has been free since we separated; but, listen, Marcel, I was
pretty sure that he still loved me. It's because of that," she
said, bursting into tears, "it's because of that that I don't want
to die at once. But it's all over, just the same. Oh, the good
God isn't fair if he doesn't give me enough time only to make
Rudolph forget the misery I brought him. He isn't ignorant of
the condition I'm in. I didn't want him to sleep beside me, you
see, for it seems to me that already I have the noises of the
earth about my body. We spent the night crying and occasionally talking. Oh! how sad it is, my friend, to see behind one all
the happiness which was close to one before and wasn't seen!
My chest is burning; and when I move my limbs, it seems as
if they were going to break. Look," she said to Marcel, "hand
me my dress. I want to try the cards to find out if Rudolph will
bring back some money. I should like to have one good luncheon
with you as in other days! It wouldn't hurt me at all; God can't
make me sicker than I am. Look." She pointed out the cards to
Marcel. "I cut a spade. That's the colour of death. And there
is a club," she added more gaily. "Yes, we shall have money."

Marcel didn't know what to say to the insane lucidity of
this girl who had, as she said, the sounds of the tomb about
her.

At the end of an hour, Rudolph returned. He was accompanied by Schaunard and Gustave Colline. The musician was wearing his summer overcoat. He had sold his heavy clothes to lend Rudolph money when he learned Mimi was ill. Colline, for his share, had gone to sell books. He would have consented to sell an arm or a leg more easily than to give up his treasured books. But Schaunard had observed to him that there was no use for his arm or his leg.

Mimi forced herself to resume her gaiety to receive her old friends.

"I am no longer mad," she told them, "and Rudolph has pardoned me. If he will keep me with him I will wear wooden shoes and a kerchief, it's all the same to me. Certainly silk isn't good for my health," she added, with a frightful smile.

Because of Marcel's remarks, Rudolph had sent for one of his friends who had just gotten his medicine degree. He was the same one who had cared for little Francine before. When he came in, they left him alone with Mimi.

Rudolph, warned in advance by Marcel, knew now the danger his mistress was in. When the doctor had seen Mimi, he said to Rudolph: "You can't keep her. Except for a miracle, she is hopeless. She must be sent to a hospital. I shall give you a letter for the 'Pitié'; I know an interne there who will take good care of her. If she lasts until spring, perhaps we can remove her from there; but if she stays here, she will die in a week."

"I will never dare suggest that to her," Rudolph said.

"I told her myself," replied the doctor, "and she consents to it. Tomorrow I shall send you the letter of admission to the 'Pitié'."

"My friend," Mimi said to Rudolph, "the doctor is right; you cannot care for me here. Perhaps I shall be cured at the hospital; you must take me there. Ah, you see, I want so much to live, now that I would be willing to end my days with one hand in the fire and the other in yours. Furthermore, you will come to see me. I won't cause you any further difficulty; I shall be well taken care of, that young man just told me. They give one chicken to eat at the hospital and there is fire burning. While I take care of myself, you will work to earn money, and when I am cured I shall come to live with you. I am very optimistic now. I will become beautiful as ever. I have been sick as this before when I didn't know you; and I was cured. In addition, I wasn't happy then either, and I should have liked to die. Now that I have found you again and we can be happy, I shall be cured again, for I certainly will protect myself from sickness. I'll drink all the unpleasant things they give me, and if death gets me it will be by force. Give me the looking-glass; it seems to me that I have a little colour. Yes!" she said, as she looked at herself in the glass, "my good colour is returning to me so soon; and my hands,—look," she said, "they are always very soft; kiss them once again. It won't be the last time. Leave me, my poor dear," she said, as she clasped Rudolph around the neck and buried her face in his rumpled hair.

Before leaving for the hospital, she wanted her Bohemian friends to spend the evening with her. "Make me laugh," she begged, "gaiety means health to me. It is the viscount's night-cap which has made me sick. He wanted to teach me to spell, imagine! What could I do? And his friends, what a group! A real poultry yard, in which the viscount was the peacock. He marked his linen himself. If he ever marries, I am sure it will be he who bears the children."

Nothing could have been more heartbreaking than this almost posthumous lightheartedness of that wretched child. All the Bohemians made difficult attempts to hide their tears and carry on the conversation in the light tone which the poor girl had started, she for whom destiny was weaving so quickly the material for her last dress.

Next day in the morning Rudolph received the card from the hospital. Mimi could not stand alone; she had to be carried to the carriage. During the ride she suffered excruciatingly from the jolts of the cab. In the midst of this suffering, the last thing which dies in women, vanity, still survived; two or three times she had the carriage stop before the linen draper's shops to look at the window displays.

When she entered the room assigned in her admittance, Mimi felt a great shock to her heart; she had a premonition that it was between these walls, so leprous and devastating, that her life would come to an end. She used all her will power to hide this wretched impression which made her cold as ice.

When she had gone to bed, she kissed Rudolph a last time and said good-bye, begging him to come to see her the following Sunday, which was visiting day. "It smells very bad here," she told him. "Fetch me some flowers,—violets; there must still be some."

"Yes," said Rudolph, "farewell, till Sunday." And he drew

the bed-curtains around her. As she listened to the footsteps of her lover dying away, Mimi was suddenly seized with an almost delirious attack of fever. She quickly opened the curtains, and, leaning half out of the bed, she called in a voice half muffled by tears: "Rudolph, take me away! I want to go away!" The sister responded to her cry and tried to calm her.

"Oh!" said Mimi, "I am going to die here."

Sunday morning, the day when he was to see Mimi, Rudolph remembered that he had promised her violets. In an access of sentiment and love, he walked in bad weather, to search for the

flowers which his friend had asked for in the woods of Aulnay
and of Fontenay, where he had gone so often with her. This
scene, so gay, so happy under the sun of beautiful Junes and
Augusts, he found very desolate and cold. For two hours he
shook the bushes covered with snow, raised the clusters and
heather with a small stick, and succeeded in collecting a few
violets, exactly in a part of a wood which borders on the pool
of Plessis, which was the favourite retreat of both when they
went to the country. While passing through the village of
Chatillon, on his way to Paris, Rudolph met on the church square
a baptismal procession in which he recognized one of his friends,
who had the role of godfather, with an artist from the Opera.

"What the devil are you doing here?" the friend asked, very
surprised to see Rudolph in this country.

The poet told him what had happened to him.

The young man, who had known Mimi, was very saddened
by this story, and, fumbling in his pocket, he took a bag of
bonbons left from the baptismal feast and gave them to Rudolph.

"That poor Mimi, give her these from me and tell her that
I shall come to see her."

"Come quickly, if you wish to arrive in time," Rudolph advised him as they parted.

When Rudolph reached the hospital, Mimi, who could not
move, hugged him with a look.

"Ohhh! there are my flowers," she cried, smiling with satisfaction. Rudolph told her of his walk in that part of the country
which had been the Paradise of their love.

"Darling flowers," caressed the poor girl as she kissed the
violets. The bonbons made her very happy too. "So I am not
completely forgotten! You are good, all you young men! Ah!
how much I love all your friends," she said to Rudolph.

This meeting was almost gay. Schaunard and Colline had
joined them. The nurses had to put them out, as they stayed
over the visiting hours.

"Farewell," said Mimi. "Thursday, without fail and come
early."

The next evening when he returned home, Rudolph received
a letter from a medical student, an interne at the hospital whom

he had asked to take care of his sick girl. The letter contained only these few words:

"My friend, I have very bad news for you: Number eight is dead. This morning when I passed the room her bed was empty."

Rudolph sank down on a chair and did not shed a tear. When Marcel came in later, he found his friend in the same stupefied position; at once the poet showed him the letter.

"Poor girl!" said Marcel.

"It is strange," remarked Rudolph, "I feel nothing there. Did my love die when I found out that Mimi was going to die?"

"Who knows!" murmured the artist.

Mimi's death caused great mourning in the Bohemian group.

A week later Rudolph met in the street the interne who had told him of his mistress' death.

"Ah! my dear Rudolph," the latter said, running up to the poet, "forgive the wrong I did you through my stupidity."

"What do you mean?" Rudolph was astonished.

"What," replied the interne, "you don't know. Haven't you seen her?"

"Who?" cried Rudolph.

"Her, Mimi."

"What?" The poet became very pale.

"I was deceived. When I wrote you that frightful news, I was the victim of an error, and this is the reason for it. I had stayed away from the hospital for two days. When I returned and when making my rounds I found your lady's bed empty. I asked the nurse where the sick girl was; she replied that she had died during the night. This is what happened. During my absence Mimi had been changed from that bed and that room. In number eight, which she had left, they had put another woman who died the same day. So this explains the error which I made. The day after the day when I wrote you, I came across Mimi in an adjacent room. Your absence had put her in a bad way; she gave me a letter for you. I carried it to your lodgings at once."

"Ah! my God!" Rudolph gasped, "since I thought that Mimi

had died I have not returned to my room. I slept here and there with my friends. Mimi is alive! Oh God! What must she think of my absence? Poor girl! poor girl! How is she? When did you see her?"

"On the morning of the day before yesterday. She seemed neither better nor worse; she was very upset and thought you were sick."

"Go with me at once to the 'Pitié'," asked Rudolph. "Let me see her."

"Wait for me a moment," the interne said, when they came to the door of the hospital. "I must ask the director's permission for you to enter."

Rudolph waited a quarter of an hour in the entrance hall. When the interne came back, he took his hand and only said: "My friend, suppose that the letter I wrote you a week ago was true."

"What!" said Rudolph leaning against a post, "Mimi . . ."

"This morning at four o'clock."

"Take me to the morgue. Let me see her."

"She is no longer there," the interne replied. And pointing to a large van which stood in the courtyard in front of a wing of the building, above the door of which could be read: 'Morgue,' he added: "She is in there."

They were just in time to see the carriage in which they carried to the common burying ground the unclaimed bodies.

"Adieu," Rudolph said to the interne.

"Do you wish me to accompany you?" the latter suggested.

"No," Rudolph replied as he went away. "I must be alone."

ONE IS ONLY YOUNG ONCE

A YEAR after Mimi's death, Rudolph and Marcel, who had not left each other, celebrated their entrance into the professional world with a party. Marcel, who had finally gotten into the Salon, had shown there two pictures, one of which had been bought by a rich Englishman, who had formerly been Musette's lover. From the results of this sale and from that of an order from the government, Marcel had partly liquidated the debts of his past. He had furnished himself a suitable apartment and had a serious studio. Almost at the same time, Schaunard and Rudolph came before the public eye, which makes for fame and fortune, the one, with a book of songs which were sung at all the concerts, and which started his reputation; the other, with a book which had the critics' attention for a month. As for Barbemuche, he had given up Bohemia a long time before. Gustave Colline had inherited something and had made an advantageous marriage; he gave parties with music and cakes.

One evening Rudolph, while he was sitting in his own armchair, with his feet on his own rug, saw Marcel come in, completely terrified,

"You do not know what has just happened to me?" he asked.

"No," answered the poet. "I know that I went to your lodgings, and that you were actually there, and that no one showed any willingness to let me in."

"I heard you, to be sure. Think a bit who was with me."

"How would I know?"

"Musette, who has popped in on me, yesterday evening, just like a docker."

"Musette, you have found Musette," Rudolph's tone was one of regret.

"Don't worry,—hostilities have not been resumed; Musette came to spend her last night in Bohemia with me."

"What!"

"She is getting married."

"Ah, bah!" cried Rudolph. "To whom, my lord?"

"To a postmaster who was her last lover's tutor, an odd soul, so it seems. Musette said to him: 'My dear sir, before finally giving you my hand and going to the registry, I want a week's freedom. I have my business to arrange, and I wish to drink my last glass of champagne, dance my last quadrille and kiss my lover Marcel, who is a gentleman like everyone with whom he appears.' And for a week the dear girl has looked for me. It was just chance that she found me last night just at the moment when I was thinking of her. Ah! my friend, we spent a sad night, finally, and it was no more than that, no more indeed. We had the atmosphere of a poor copy of a masterpiece; I have even written on the subject of this last separation a little lament which I shall weep to you if you will permit," and Marcel began to hum the following stanzas:

MARCEL'S SONG

One is only young once.

Today on seeing a swallow
Old thoughts of spring arose,
And I remembered the lovely one
Who loved me when she chose.
And pensively through all the day
I let my fancy touch
The almanac of that one year
When we two loved so much.

—But no, my youth's not dead,
My thoughts of you are true;
And should you knock at my heart, Musette,
It would open wide to you.
It trembles even at your name,—
Muse of unfaithfulness,—
Come back to break with me again
The bread that joy will bless.

—The furniture of our room,
Old friends of passion true,
Today are wearing a gala air
In hope of seeing you.
Come, you'll remember those, my dear,
Who sorrowed when you fled,
The tumbler out of which you drank
My share,—the little bed.

You'll wear the dress of white
Which long ago you wore,
And we'll go wandering through the woods,
On Sundays as of yore.
Beneath the arbour at night we'll sit
And drink the wine, my love,
In whose clear depths your song may dip
Its wings, then soar above.

Musette, inconstant one,
When the carnival was at rest,
Remembering, one morning flew
Back to her ancient nest;
But in embracing the faithless one,
My heart saw love could die;
Musette, who was no longer she,
Said too I was not I.

Farewell, now go, beloved,
Now with the last love dead;
With the old days of the calendar
Our joyous youth is fled.
We've just been searching the ashes of days
That never more arise
For memories that hold the key
To a lost paradise.

"Well," said Marcel when he had finished, "you are now satisfied; my love for Musette is now dead, since the poem has been made for it," he added cynically, showing the manuscript of his poem.

"Poor friend," pitied Rudolph, "your mind is warring with your heart. Take care that it doesn't kill it."

"That's been done already," the artist responded; "we have finished, my old friend, we are dead and buried. We are only young once. Where are you dining this evening?"

"If you like," said Rudolph, "we will dine for twelve sous in our old restaurant on the rue Dufour, there where the plates are of local pottery and where we are so hungry when we have finished eating."

"My word, no," replied Marcel. "I am perfectly willing to reminisce about the past, but it will be over a bottle of good wine, and seated in a comfortable arm-chair. What are you saying? I have been corrupted. I no longer like anything but what is good."